You Must
Change Your Life

American and European Philosophy

GENERAL EDITORS: CHARLES E. SCOTT AND JOHN J. STUHR
ASSOCIATE EDITOR: SUSAN M. SCHOENBOHM

Devoted to the contemporary development of American and European philosophy in the pragmatic and Continental traditions, AMERICAN AND EUROPEAN PHILOSOPHY gives expression to uniquely American thought that deepens and advances these traditions and that arises from their mutual encounters. The series will focus on new interpretations of philosophers and philosophical movements within these traditions, original contributions to European or American thought, and issues that arise through the mutual influence of American and European philosophers.

EDITORIAL ADVISORY BOARD

MITCHELL ABOULAFIA, University of Colorado • BETTINA BERGO, Worcester Polytechnic Institute • ROBERT BERNASCONI, University of Memphis • JUDITH BUTLER, University of California at Berkeley • EDWARD CASEY, SUNY at Stony Brook • VINCENT COLAPIETRO, The Pennsylvania State University • DAN CONWAY, The Pennsylvania State University • SIMON CRITCHLEY, University of Essex • FRANÇOISE DASTUR, Université de Paris XII • PAUL DAVIES, University of Sussex • MIGUEL DE BEISTEGUI, University of Warwick • GÜNTER FIGAL, Universität Tübingen (Eberhard-Karls-Universität) • RUSSELL GOODMAN, University of New Mexico • DAVID HOY, Cowell College • DOMINIQUE JANICAUD, Université de Nice • MARK JOHNSON, University of Oregon • DAVID FARRELL KRELL, DePaul University • JOHN LACHS, Vanderbilt University • LADELLE MCWHORTER, University of Richmond • KRZYSZTOF MICHALSKI, Boston University • JEAN-LUC NANCY, Université de Strasbourg 11 (Université des Sciences Humaines) • KELLY OLIVER, SUNY at Stony Brook • STEFAN GEORGIEV POPOV, University of Sofia • SANDRA ROSENTHAL, Loyola University • HANS RUIN, Stockholm University • DENNIS SCHMIDT, Villanova University • CHARLENE SEIGFRIED, Purdue University LAEB • SHANNON SULLIVAN, The Pennsylvania State University • JOHN SALLIS, The Pennsylvania State University • RICHARD SHUSTERMAN, Temple University • KENNETH STIKKERS, Southern Illinois University • GIANTERESIO VATTIMO, Università degli Studi di Torino • FRANCO VOLPI, Università degli Studi di Padova • DAVID WOOD, Vanderbilt University

David Farrell Krell, *The Purest of Bastards: Works of Mourning, Art, and Affirmation in the Thought of Jacques Derrida*

Bruce Wilshire, *The Primal Roots of American Philosophy: Pragmatism, Phenomenology, and Native American Thought*

John T. Lysaker

You Must Change Your Life

Poetry, Philosophy,
and the
Birth of Sense

The Pennsylvania State University Press
University Park, Pennsylvania

Library of Congress Cataloging-in-Publication Data

Lysaker, John T.
    You must change your life : poetry, philosophy, and the birth of sense / John T. Lysaker.
    p. cm.— (American and European philosophy)
    Includes bibliographical references and index.
    ISBN 0-271-**03432-7**
    1. Simic, Charles, 1938- —Criticism and interpretation.
    2. Literature, Comparative—American and foreign.
    3. Literature, Comparative—Foreign and American.
    4. Heidegger, Martin, 1889–1976—Aesthetics.
    5. Poetry.
    I. Title. II. Series.

PS3569.I4725Z76 2002
811'.54—dc21   2002009843

Copyright © 2002 The Pennsylvania State University
All rights reserved
Printed in the United States of America
Published by The Pennsylvania State University Press,
University Park, PA 16802-1003

It is the policy of The Pennsylvania State University Press to use acid-free paper for the first printing of all clothbound books. Publications on uncoated stock satisfy the minimum requirements of American National Standard for Information Sciences—Permanence of Paper for Printed Library Materials, ANSI Z39.48–1992.

For
Juan De Pascuale and Royal Rhodes,
with gratitude and continuing devotion.

Contents

Preface and Acknowledgments   ix

Introduction: Engaging the Work of Art   1

1 Heidegger's Ear   17
2 Living Poetry   45
3 The White of All "I's"   78
4 Ink   109
5 Characterizing the Cosmos   135
6 "Then Came History"   157
7 Preserving the Possible   180

Afterword   207

Bibliography   211

Index   219

Preface and Acknowledgments

What follows is an attempt to work philosophically with poetry in a way that respects its manner of presentation. Of course, one could attempt to ferret out conclusions and their supporting premises, approaching the poem as a kind of argument.[1] To do so, however, forgoes a dialogue with the poem in its objectivity and effectively reduces its form of presentation to ornamentation—thus suggesting, if only implicitly, that poetry is *petit bourgeois* ratiocination. Unwilling to begin by translating poems into a so-called properly philosophical idiom, I have thus, in a manner that owes much to Heidegger, tried to fashion a site at which poems and philosophical questions, reflection, and argument might meet and complement one another in response to what (after Jean-Luc Nancy) I have termed the "birth of sense." "Sense" here denotes the principal character with which something exists or occurs, e.g., as a part of a large whole, as the creation of a creator, or as atoms collecting and dispersing in a void according to the whims of efficient causality.

My ambitious title, *You Must Change Your Life*, is drawn from Rilke's poem, "Archaic Torso of Apollo." The point is not to install poetry as the vanguard of self-help. Nor is it to suggest that poetry is a potential font of practical maxims by which we might live. Rather, I will try to convince you that certain poems enable us to experience the birth of sense in such a radical fashion that they transform the sense of all that is—ourselves, others, rocks, lichens, asteroids, orbits. Unfortunately, we lack a proper feel for those kinds of poems or that kind of import. In writing this work, I hope to cultivate that feel, to sharpen the ears we bring to certain poems so that we might see how thoroughly they can change our lives.

---

1. One finds such approaches in rhetoric and argumentation texts—for example (and it is nearly a random one), Nancy Wood's 2001 *Perspectives on Argument*, 387–417.

As a dialogue between philosophy and poetry, this text is designed for an audience beyond but including professionally philosophical circles. Poets as well as philosophers may find something fresh here in my notion of "ur-poetry" as well as its import. To the end of a wider audience, however, I have not sacrificed whatever rigor I thought the matter at hand demanded. Given that so little (if anything) is obvious, it is justifiable both to demand clarity and to berate a clarity that obscures. To my mind, one's obligations begin with one's subject matter, and it is out of that obligation that one should determine what clarity and communicability involve, what relation one's diction and syntax should have to ordinary language, if there is such a thing. I have tried to say things as plainly as possible, and at times this has required me to beat against the currents of ordinary language. If I had only held my nose right, I could have done better. However, I do not think I could have tried harder.

As a project, this book owes many debts. Let me begin by thanking my department at The University of Oregon for providing an atmosphere in which interdisciplinary and nontraditional inquiry can flourish and for granting me the two terms of leave during which the bulk of this book was written. I would also like to thank Oregon's Program in Creative Writing, particularly Garrett Hongo. I enjoyed both an opportunity to share my thoughts with its Kidd Tutorial Program and their more general support of my work. Thanks are also due to the many students who, over the last five years, have worked with me on a number of literary texts, including poems discussed here. For me, at least, the occasions were always rewarding, and the discussions here are indebted to those conversations. The various editors at The Pennsylvania State University Press—Laura Reed-Morrisson, Charles Scott, John Stuhr, and Sandy Thatcher—have been quite helpful, and I am grateful for their support and insight. I am particularly grateful to Laura Reed-Morrisson, whose careful and sympathetic editing has made this an appreciably better book. A reader for the Press also made useful suggestions. Whoever and wherever you are, thank you. My thanks also to Jena Jolissaint, who read the entire manuscript in its penultimate stage and offered some very valuable suggestions. I must thank the University of Oregon Humanities Center as well for its generous help with various fees associated with reprinting poems whose language is integral to my study.

Three other debts run deeper. First, much of what follows engages the work of Charles Simic. I hope I have done his work justice. Since I was introduced to it in 1990 by Rebecca Szekely, it has certainly done right by me. Second, as in everything, I must thank my mother, both for the life she has given me and the care she has shown in sustaining it. Finally, I would like to offer special thanks to my two undergraduate mentors, Juan De Pascuale and Royal Rhodes, both of Kenyon College. Their care and indulgence righted me at a tender age and nourished me throughout my time in Gambier and beyond. Moreover, their support and faith has proven as much a catalyst as a buoy. I humbly dedicate this book to them.

Two preliminary studies set the stage for this book: "Heidegger's Absolute Music: What Are Poets for When the End of Metaphysics Is at Hand" (Lysaker 2000) and "White Dawns, Black Noons, Twilit Days: Charles Simic's Poems Before Poetry" (Lysaker 2001). I want to thank John Sallis of *Research in Phenomenology* and Susan Hahn of *TriQuarterly* for their support of that work. I want to acknowledge, too, that while those essays have been substantially reworked for inclusion in this volume, I have drawn upon them in several chapters. I must also note that "Heidegger's Absolute Music" was first published in *Research in Phenomenology* 30 (2000): 180–210, and that I use portions of it again with the permission of the Humanities Press Inc., Boston, Mass.

Many other sources have permitted me to publish copyrighted work. Charles Simic has been enormously gracious, allowing me to quote from his work at great length. Many thanks to him. Braziller, Faber and Faber, Harcourt, and Knopf also cooperated with this venture. I thank them for their permission and collegiality. Formal acknowledgments follow.

"Reality Is an Activity of the Most August Imagination," by Wallace Stevens, from *The Palm at the End of the Mind* by Wallace Stevens, edited by Holly Stevens. Copyright © 1967, 1969, 1971 by Holly Stevens. Used by permission of Alfred A. Knopf, a division of Random House, Inc.

"To My Wife," from *Collected Poems,* by Philip Larkin. Copyright © 1988, 1989 by the Estate of Philip Larkin. Reprinted by permission of Farrar, Straus and Giroux, LLC, and by permission of Faber and Faber Ltd.

"Poem Without a Title," "Empire of Dreams," "Interlude," and "Butcher Shop," from *Charles Simic: Selected Early Poems,* by Charles Simic. Copyright © 1999 by Charles Simic. Reprinted by permission of George Braziller, Inc.

"My Mother Was . . . ," "I was stolen . . . ," "A Dog with a soul . . . ," "Things were not . . . ," "Comedy of errors . . . ," and "My secret identity is . . . ," from *The World Doesn't End: Prose Poems*, by Charles Simic. Copyright © 1988, 1987 by Charles Simic. Reprinted by permission of Harcourt, Inc.

"Blindman's Bluff," "Emily's Theme," and "The Road in the Clouds," from *Walking the Black Cat*, by Charles Simic. Copyright © 1966 by Charles Simic. Reprinted by permission of Harcourt, Inc.

"Paradise Motel" and "Crazy About Her Shrimp," from *A Wedding in Hell: Poems*, by Charles Simic. Copyright © 1994 by Charles Simic. Reprinted by permission of Harcourt, Inc.

"History," from *Unending Blues: Poems*, by Charles Simic. Copyright © 1986, 1985, 1984, 1983 by Charles Simic. Reprinted by permission of Harcourt, Inc.

"Mother Tongue," from *Jackstraws*, by Charles Simic. Copyright © 1999 by Charles Simic. Reprinted by permission of Harcourt, Inc.

"War," from *Hotel Insomnia*, by Charles Simic. Copyright © 1992 by Charles Simic. Reprinted by permission of Harcourt, Inc.

Introduction: Engaging the Work of Art

> We never knew his startling head,
> wherein the eyes, those apples, ripened. But
> still his torso glows like a candelabra
> in which its gazing, just twisted back,
>
> holds fast and shines. If not, the breast's bow
> could never blind you, nor in the slight swerve
> of the loins could a grin run towards
> that middle which carried life in the making.
>
> If not, this stone would stand deformed and squat
> under the shoulders' clear, sudden fall
> and fail to glisten so like wild beasts' fur;
>
> and fail to burst forth at every brim
> like a star: for there is no point
> that does not see you. You must change your life.
>
> —Rainer Maria Rilke, "Archaic Torso of Apollo"

Without much exaggeration, I can say that most of the reflections gathered here take their leave from this poem that, in 1908, initiated the "other part" of Rilke's *New Poems*.[1] In fact, near the center of this study and at its rim the poem's final two lines vibrate like a tuning fork, keying the leading questions and lines of inquiry: "for there is no point / that does not see you. You must change your life."

The phenomenon that Rilke presents is stark, even precise in the way that intensity has its own focus. And examples abound. At twenty-one, I picked up Allen Ginsberg's *Howl* (1959) one Friday night, knowing I

---

1. The translation is my own, as most of the translations from the German will be. Where they are not, it is because I was unable to improve upon them.

was to have it read by Monday. Opened, *Howl* was just another assignment, a useful way of killing time until the bars began to fill. And because the apartment was empty, except for me, I read aloud.

> I saw the best minds of my generation destroyed by
> madness, starving hysterical naked,
> dragging themselves through the negro streets at dawn
> looking for an angry fix,
> angelheaded hipsters burning for the heavenly
> connection to the starry dynamo in the machin-
> ery of night
>
> (lines 1–7)

Over the top, no doubt, but I was transfixed, drawn in, even turned around. And I kept on, aloud, equally excessive, equally indulgent, and very twenty-one. I read on and into the "Footnote to Howl" that insists upon an impossible redemption within the "incomprehensible prison" of America, the Moloch to whom so many have been sacrificed. And when it was done, when I had set *Howl* down, showered, and finally set out for the night, I moved about the campus of Kenyon College certain that we were destroying ourselves, selves that were once and potentially again holy.

> The world is holy? The soul is holy! The skin is holy!
> The nose is holy! The tongue and cock and hand
> And asshole holy!
> Everything is holy! everybody's holy!
>
> (lines 3–6)

Fierce thoughts. But whatever resistance I might have had to such severe conclusions had been, in reading, rooted out, and I left that night reworked from gaze to gait.

Some years later, I watched—at least initially—Philip Glass perform pieces for solo piano. I began by *watching* because Glass's minimalist compositions do not immediately grab one by the hair and turn one around. But as the evening lengthened, I began to keep his exquisitely slowed time with my fingers, then my hand, later adding my foot to the patterns opening between us. In short, I played along, even humming now and then, quietly. And gradually, without marked transition, these three or four notes sounded along different intervals and set into various combinations enveloped me, then the room, and then all that there was to see, hear, or even think. Awash, I began really to *hear* the notes, hear moments in time slowed into relief, hear physical resonances lengthened until the fluidity of time-consciousness became palpable, until the depth and texture of a single tone became a thicket unto itself. Again, I was transfixed, sounded out, drawn into the work until it found its way into all of my other engagements. And it became clear as the evening drew to a close that I had taken so much for granted, not only with regard to music but also with regard to whatever I assumed was only the simple component of a larger whole. And I knew I had been remiss.

I do not regard these experiences as exceptional. I could recall several others, and have heard others describe similar encounters. In "A Glimpse into the World of Children's Books," Walter Benjamin notes how children are often swept up into the play of a book: "Draped with colors of every hue that he has picked up from reading and observing, the child stands in the center of a masquerade and joins in, while reading—for the words have all come to the masked ball, are joining in the fun and are whirling around together, like tinkling snowflakes" (Benjamin 1996, 435). But not just children. "Some books he glanced through," writes Nadezhda Mandelstam of her husband, Osip, "others he read with real interest (for instance, Joyce and Hemingway), but on a quite different level from all this there was his reading of really formative books with which he entered, as it were, into lasting contact and which left their mark on some part of his life, or the whole of it" (Mandelstam 1970, 227). Some works have an uncanny power to engage us, to draw us into them such that what occurs there, in the work, overdetermines us, surrounds us, and becomes, for the time being, an integral part of each corner of the world.

Note that I do not say that some works work their way into each corner of "my" world. I avoid the personal modifier because it falsifies the phenomenon at hand. When a work engages me like Ginsberg's did, it is not just that my perceptions change. At least on the face of it, I do not perceive perceptions, but phenomena. When I crossed my college campus, *Howl* running through my head, I perceived a "laundry room," "apartment houses," an "old art building," a "bar," a "post office," and so on. And it is those phenomena that appeared changed in the wake of Ginsberg's rhapsodic language. Now, you might want to say: "Be reasonable. Even accounting for the egoism of twenty-one-year-old white males, it is not as if your reading of *Howl* changed the nature of a college laundromat." So it would seem; I have no reason to believe that such a transformation took place or ever takes place. But I am not claiming that poems somehow transform some mental or spiritual outlook that then reconstitutes the world. Rather, I am resisting the presumption (and at this point, only because it is a presumption) that the work of art, whenever it engages us, does so in a manner apprehendable within what amounts to Europe's default account of our being-in-the-world.

Despite over two hundred years of persistent critique (e.g., from Hegel, Marx, Nietzsche, Dewey, and Heidegger), Cartesian dualisms still dominate the ways in which most European traditions understand themselves, and artworks are certainly no exception. Jane Hirschfield writes:

> A mysterious quickening inhabits the depths of a good poem—protean, elusive, alive in its own right. "Creative" and "creature" hold in their shared root a shared autonomy of being, and we feel something stir, shiver, swim its way into the world when a good poem opens its eyes. For the work of poetry is not simply to record perception, but to make by words the possibility of a new perceiving—to open us into the distinctive realms we see when we see the world by poem-light. (Hirschfield 2000, 9)

But does the work of art always or even primarily address itself to a subject surrounded and impinged upon, at times pleasantly, by a world of objects and other subjects? And should the import of that address be measured in terms of changes in how subjects represent that world to themselves? In what follows, I would ask that you look freshly at some of the ways in which works of art address and possibly transform us, and along the way, I hope to make evident much of what we lose when we subordinate the quickening depths of the work of art to subjective tropes such as "perception" or "representation."

Let us turn to the phenomenon at hand. I have proposed, reading Rilke, that a work fixes us, "engages" us. "To engage" suggests several things: to bargain; to pledge; to enter into swordplay or, more generally, some form of combat; to mesh together; to interlock with so as to produce motion. At this point, the more robust senses of the word seem appropriate: mixing it up with an opponent, being caught up in something. I am drawn to this word because certain artworks set us in motion. At the level of affect, it is as if an engine has been engaged, even ignited.

Under the gaze of the work, our various parts are brought together within a coordinated and concentrated event. As John Dewey says, aesthetic experience is experience in its integrity, that is, seemingly seamless, free of the separations (e.g., subject/object, means/ends) that plague our more mundane encounters (Dewey 1987, 278).

But even as our energies are focused when engaged by the work of art, we are simultaneously laid bare in the intensity of the moment. The work of art thus holds within itself much of what the term "engagement" once suggested, a state of entanglement that proves to be a source of embarrassment, even peril. Ed Hirsch confesses: "As a reader, the hold of the poem over me can be almost embarrassing because it is so childlike, because I need it so much to give me access to my own interior depths. It plunges me into the depths . . . and gives me a tremendous sense of another world growing within. . . . I am pried open" (Hirsch 1999, 8–9). While Hirsch's embarrassment may stem from his need for poetic works, one also might blush—and this is the matter that concerns me—in the exposure one feels when so struck. Whereas Henry in John Berryman's *Dream Songs* was "pried open for all the world to see" by loss, by a "departure," here one is pried open by an abundance, by a surfeit surrounding one: "There is no point / that does not see you."

The matter at hand involves more than a kind of pathos, however. Certain works not only set us in motion but redirect us as well. In a *New York Times* review, "Anselm Kiefer: Works on Paper in the Metropolitan Museum of Art," John Russell writes: "'Works on paper' in the context of art can cover the whole gamut of human experience. Rembrandt and Rubens, Watteau and Goya, Ingres and Cézanne—all made works on paper that can change us forever" (Russell 1998). The point, then, is not simply that artworks have the potential to make us tremble. As several authors have attested, amid the thrills and chills of aesthetic engagement something more profound stirs, more profound because it leaves its mark upon us long after the tremors have halted.

I have suggested that transformative experiences with works of art are not uncommon. And yet in another way they are truly "exceptional," a word that comes to us from the Latin *excipere*, "to take out or except." According to the testimonies compiled above, certain works take us out of or *except* us from the ordinary, that is, they dislodge our habits, our customary bearings. Or, to use Hirsch's language, they pry us open, partly by prying us away from the shorelines to which we have grown accustomed.

Questions are pooling around a phenomenon to which many from various corners have borne witness. While I have not kept this project free from autobiographical contexts, I do want to distinguish my concern from a particular psychological question. To my mind, pursuing in psychological terms the matter of art's life-changing power would entail *(a)* identifying certain human emotions and perceptions that occur in relation to works of art; *(b)* correlating them with certain features of various works or kinds of work (e.g., colors, tones, images, formal relations); and *(c)* explaining the machinery of those correlations, that is, how they travel between work and respondent, whether by hook or crook, synapse or syntax. While genuinely interesting, such an approach nevertheless reduces the relation between work and respondent to an effect in need of explanation. Consider the scene that Rilke presents. When I explore the event as a psychological one, the torso spreads into a set of qualities (whose substratum marks an area for further inquiry), some of which will prove relevant to the effect in question—wanting to change one's life.

Again, such lines of inquiry are genuine. As Dewey argues in *Art as Experience*, greater, even empirical attention to the aesthetic potentialities in all spheres of culture might enable us to develop habits, practices, and institutions capable of supporting or perhaps facilitating experiences richer than contemporary life usually affords, even for the affluent (Dewey 1987, 346). But that is not the kind of inquiry I would conduct here, and for a variety of reasons. First, if we explore the work in terms of its effects on viewers or readers, we presume that subjects responding to works can appreciate the ways in which works address them. But suppose a work addresses me in a way that problematizes the presumption that subjective experience is an adequate arena within which to engage that which the work concerns? Would I still be able to measure the claim it makes upon my life if I begin my reflections from the ways in which subjects respond to works? If it is precisely the nature and relevance of subjective response that is at stake in the work, no.

A second reason for eschewing a psychological orientation when inquiring into the phenomenon invoked by Rilke's poem concerns a question of import. An effect to be explained is not a challenge to reflect upon, scrutinize, and finally embrace or reject. Rather, an effect is to be understood in terms of antecedent causes and eventually predicted. But I want to respect the claim of the work of art as a claim upon me and to approach it as an interlocutor. Again, this is not to say that psychologists should not approach works of art. But it is to say that when they do so, they no longer approach the work as one addressed. Thus, alongside my commitment to engage works of art on their own terms, I am also committed to engaging the import of their address within what one could term the participant's perspective, that is, the perspective of one feeling the full brunt of what is at stake in the work of art when taken on its own terms. I want to ask, "How and with regard to what does a statue address me such that I am compelled to change my life?" but not "What aspects of this thing have caused me to feel that I should change my life?" The former question keeps alive the thought that I might have to change my life; the latter suspends the issue in favor of finding correlations between stimuli and responses. Moreover, the latter question steps outside the potential dialogue that opens once we take ourselves as the addressees of artworks, as participants in a conversation about "how best to bear the beams of life," to paraphrase Blake.[2]

At this point, it seems prudent to state forthrightly those questions that will lead and orient my discussions. Both are apparent in the paragraph above. On the one hand, I wish to fathom how works address us when they fix us fiercely and lay claim to our lives, that is, I wish to understand the nature of that address. Second, I desire a concrete sense of the import of that address. If I am to change my life, I want to know those lines along which it should be changed.

One might wonder why I have not posed my questions as "What is conveyed by the work of art?" and "How is that message embodied?" I do not believe that the matter at hand, how the work of art addresses us when it engages us, always involves a message and its medium. Before explaining why, let me clarify the issue. On the one hand, the issue concerns a distinction between form and content. On the side of content, one finds some theme or thematic elements: the work is *about* something. On the side of form, one finds modes of presentation at work, e.g., the sonata, or a set of syntactic operations such as iambic feet, caesurae, enjambments, and so on. The distinction between form and content does not exhaust the issue, however, for it rests upon another conceptual pair,

---

2. Actually, I am paraphrasing Blake as cited by Philip Levine. The passage reads: "We are put on earth a little space, / That we may learn to bear the beams of love." Levine continues: "And so in my poems I memorialize those men and women who struggled to bear that love" (Levine 1981, xi). I would say that in what follows I am trying to memorialize some works that have struggled to bear the beams of *life*, particularly the life of the work of art—but not only that, as we shall see.

one involving form and matter. The latter marks the materials out of which the work is compiled (e.g., paint and canvas, tones and strings and variously shaped wooden boxes, or twisting and leaping bodies), while the former entails the order into which the materials are brought. Now, as far as either distinction is concerned, "form" entails the same phenomenon: the formal possibilities available in the form/content distinction are simply various possibilities for ordering materials. The opposition between medium and message contains, therefore, a threefold distinction involving content, form, and matter.

While there is an intuitive plausibility to characterizing artworks along these three axes, and while it is often useful to do so (for example, in order to draw attention to various aspects of a work), I will avoid employing the trio. Why? First, to break a work down along these lines forces content into limbo if not the work into a dualism. If we distinguish what the work says from how it says it, dividing the work into component parts, we are left wondering where in the address of the work one finds what is said. Now, it is tempting to suggest that content is in fact drawn out of the otherwise indeterminate sensible qualities of the work by an apprehending mind. But this is troublesome. First, it runs roughshod over our actual experience of being engaged by and with an artwork. In the engagement, "content" is not given to us mentally while our senses remain afloat upon a sea of *aisthesis*. I am drawn into the weave of *Howl*—ink, paper, syntax, rhythms, semantics, and images—as a *poem*, not as an ensemble of elements that I explicitly synthesize into something I then term a "poem." To recall Dewey once again, the experience is integrated such that the work as a whole fixes our attention, and our complete attention, involving our minds and bodies, our thoughts and feelings, even our past, present (and occasionally) future.

Second, content is always part and parcel of the formal and material aspects of a work, speaking through them rather than merely being conveyed by them. In Wallace Stevens's "Idea of Order at Key West," a poem, interestingly enough, about order or form in a general sense (that is, the very order of experience and the world), the speaker describes a woman singing, walking along the sea. As the poem progresses, we are led to wonder where her singing ends and the sea begins, for they intertwine before the speaker and his or her companion(s). Regardless of how or whether one thinks the poem resolves this dilemma, the poem often allows the rhymes (formal elements) of "sea" and "she" to play off one another, often in the same line (lines 1, 8, 14, and 38), thus performing in the resonance of quick, short sounds (material elements) the very slippage and slide between singer and sea that the poem poses as a problem and explores. It is this degree of integration in several works that leads me to resist dividing their powerful address into component parts.

One can see this integration in other ways as well. On the side of materiality, I think one is hard-pressed to find raw media or substrata in the work of art. One need not suppose that English is inherently iambic in order to recognize that iambic feet—and the same holds for those forms that make use of them, such as the sonnet—are possible formal elements only insofar as certain material prerequisites are satisfied by a language as well as by the vocal and auditory capabilities of those who recite and receive iambic poems. To this degree, I agree with Robert Pinsky when he claims that "poetry is a vocal, which is to say a bodily art. The medium of poetry is a human body: the column of air inside the chest, shaped into signifying sounds in the larynx and mouth. In this sense, poetry is just as physical or bodily an art as dancing" (Pinsky 1998, 8). Artworks, then, are materially driven in ways that are inseparable from the various forms and formal operations that, as we have seen, run through and participate in what some would regard as thematic concerns or content.

Allow me a final point about the threefold distinction between form, content, and matter. It strikes me that the very idea of form is abstract. One can no doubt find in the sonnet characteristic (but in no way omnipresent) rhythmic patterns and rhyme schemes, and even characteristic variations thereon. But when one is engaged by a work, one does not read a "sonnet." Rather, one reads Petrarch, Donne, Rilke, or Jarman and then, not really, for one reads one or more of their poems (to the degree that the poems are "theirs" in the first place). The point is this: while forms and formal elements are useful ways of cataloging works of art, one should not confuse taxonomic titles for the living address of the work of art, nor should one try to assemble the *work* of art out of an ensemble of such terms. Rather, one must enter the engagement that works afford and risk the embarrassment and peril that haunt the region. And while various analytical terms and concepts may facilitate and even deepen our appreciation for the work of art, particularly when our concerns are philosophical, we must nevertheless always return them to the engagement itself or risk losing what the work presents to habits buried in what appear to be commonsensical, intuitive categories.

Recall my initial questions. First, how do works address us, even *speak* to us? One might even ask, emphasizing the verbal sense of the term, "What is the *work* of art—how does it work to present whatever comes to presence within and through it?" Dewey notes: "It is no linguistic accident that 'building,' 'construction,' 'work,' designate both a process and its finished product. Without the meaning of the verb that of the noun remains blank" (Dewey 1987, 58). In keeping with this, I would claim that the work of art is always at work, and its labor is that which I hope to illuminate. Second, what is disclosed in the labors we call the work of art, and what is its import? If a work says that we must change our lives, we must consider how.

With all this talk of "the work of art," you might be expecting a global study of art. No such luck. First, I am unsure whether there is some mode of address common to all the arts, to poetry, dance, sculpture, and music, say. There might be, but if I were to suggest that there is, the present volume would exhaust itself in defending that claim, and that is not the kind of book I have set out to write. Rather, I want to slow down the phenomenon apparent in Rilke's poem and explore it from the inside, paying particular attention to the nature and import of its address.

In order to work my way inside the phenomenon at hand, I have elected to focus my efforts on the language of poetry, and then on one poet in particular, Charles Simic (b. 1938), although other poets will be considered as well. Why Simic? My reasons are simple but significant. First, for several years now and on repeated readings, his work has struck me with the force to which Rilke's poem attests. And as I hope to remain engaged in the address of the work of art even as I explore its nature and import, it seems clear that I must actually be engaged by whatever works I consider. Second, and this I aim to show in multiple ways, Simic's work has dramatic import for how we understand and live our lives, addressing the nature of human existence, the origins of sense (and thus the nature of things, the world, and even the cosmos), and the weight and significance of history in and for our many human projects, both personal and collective.

A more general reason also draws me toward Simic. Contemporary American poetry deserves more attention from philosophers. Many of the themes that have animated twentieth-century philosophy have also animated twentieth-century American poetry, including Simic's. They range from the nature of language, the subject, and identity to the relations each has with what might be its other (including questions about representation and responsibility), from threats of totalitarianism to commodification. Even while experiencing the specificity of the poetry, therefore, philosophers might find fruitful interlocutors among poems.

The language of "experience" hearkens back to my insistence that I participate in the phenomenon that I propose to analyze, namely, the claim of a work of art upon my life. But "experience" is a tricky word, one that conjures up a representational subject who has an experience, and it may be that one cannot appropriately hear Simic's work if one presumes that it addresses itself to a representational subject. At the outset, then, I would like to employ Martin Heidegger's distinction between *Erlebnis* and *Erfahrung*. The former, as Heidegger argues in his *Contributions to Philosophy*, concerns the presentations of a self-conscious subject, a process whereby an indeterminate world is translated through pre-reflective cognitive labors and re-presented to an apprehending ego who then has an experience—that is, *Erlebnis* (Heidegger 1989, 129–35). *Erlebnis* is not all there is to experience, however. Heidegger also speaks of *Erfahrung*, regarding the latter as something that one undergoes, and to one's depths—to the point that it could very well address, challenge, and transform the very way in which one comports oneself in the world. Heidegger writes, in "The Essence of Language," that "when we talk in this way about experience as 'undergoing,' it specifically means that we do not bring about the experience through ourselves; undergoing here means: endure, suffer, that we take up what befalls or strikes us, receive and engage it insofar as we submit to it" (Heidegger 1985, 149). With regard to Simic's work, it is *Erfahrung* that I have in mind, for only when we read with that kind of vulnerability will the dialogue to which I aspire have any chance of commencing.

Now, you might regard the above distinction as naïve, arguing that one cannot simply submit to an experience, for the very grounds of experience entail our participation. As Theodor Adorno argues, "Nothing would allow itself to be interpreted out of something that would not, simultaneously, be interpreted into it" (Adorno 1974, 11). I agree, somewhat, and thus I would inflect into *Erfahrung* the notion of experience that drives Hegel's *Phenomenology*. There, experience occurs in the gap between the presumptions of a pattern of knowing, say sense-certainty, and what actually manifests itself within that pattern of knowing when it is submitted to a phenomenological analysis. In Hegel's terms, sense-certainty claims to involve the immediate, rich apprehension of the "pure being of the matter." When sense-certainty is scrutinized phenomenologically, however, something quite different appears: universals arise within a mediated, temporally extended relation between an "I" and a "thing." And it is in that difference that experience occurs, according to Hegel. While what follows cannot pretend to be strictly phenomenological in the Hegelian manner, a manner that purports to proceed in a wholly immanent fashion, I will repeatedly draw attention to the ways in which Simic's work runs counter to common philosophical intuitions as well as the semantics and syntax of my own prose, thus allowing us to undergo an experience in the gap that opens if we follow Simic's poetry beyond the habits and predilections of our own language and thought.[3]

A notion of experience as something undergone is not all that I will draw from Heidegger, however. In fact, his own dialogue with the poets will serve as my point of departure into Simic's corpus and thus into the phenomenon invoked by Rilke's poem. More concretely, I will draw out of Heidegger's work with Trakl and Rilke (and Hölderlin, to some degree) a sense for the nature and import of the language of the poem, using that understanding to guide an extended reading of Simic's work. Why Heidegger? Two reasons motivate this choice. First, Simic himself is interested in and takes his work to be in dialogue with Heidegger. As he says in an interview from 1991: "Already Hölderlin asked the question: 'And what are poets good for in a destitute time?' And Heidegger replies: 'In the age of the world's night, the abyss of the world must be experienced by those who reach into the abyss.' I continue to believe that poetry says more about the psychic life of an age than any other art. Poetry is a place where all the fundamental questions are asked about the human condition" (Weigl 1996, 210). On the face of it, then, Heidegger's own dialogue with the poets offers us a possible route into Simic's work.[4]

Second, Heidegger takes the phenomenon poetized by Rilke exceptionally seriously. In fact, he takes it so seriously that for him the matter is not simply my life or yours, but being itself. In his *Contributions to Philosophy,* he writes: "The searcher of being is the poet who, in the

---

3. I think Heidegger wanted to approach poetry in this manner as well. In his first lecture course on Hölderlin, he insists that "the struggle for the poetry within the poem is the struggle against ourselves, insofar as we, in the everydayness of our existence, have been exiled from the poetry" (Heidegger 1980, 22).

4. As far as I know, Kevin Hart is the only one to compare Heidegger and Simic expressly, although Richard Jackson, in an essay on Simic and Mark Strand, brings Simic into dialogue with deconstruction (Hart 1989; Jackson 1980). While both essays are provocative, neither does much work with the theoretical questions underlying their discussions, preferring to note that similar themes move about the texts they cite. My goal is to bring about a more concrete and theoretically charged engagement between Heidegger's thought and Simic's poetry.

ownmost excess of its searching power, 'founds' [*stiftet*] being" (Heidegger 1989, 11). We shall have to come to terms with what this claim actually entails. Now, simply note that if my goal is to gauge the import of the language of the poem, and Simic's in particular, why not begin by considering an import of the widest reach? After all, should it prove appropriate to the matter at hand, it will outstrip any humbler implications we might otherwise locate.

Yet another reason drives me to Heidegger's dialogue with the poets. While several authors have explored Heidegger's readings, none have done so with an explicit eye on their existential significance, although Véronique Fóti has certainly broached the matter in her own way.[5] Instead, scholars have directed their attention to questions concerning interpretation, textuality, or, to speak more generally, poetics. I thus take my reflections to contribute to Heidegger scholarship, although that is not their primary concern. In fact, I am ultimately more interested in what I draw from Heidegger's texts than in what the community of inquiry might come to regard as the spirit or the letter of those texts, if either exists. Nevertheless, I do expect what follows to enrich our understanding of Heidegger the reader.[6]

Given his involvement with National Socialism, perhaps I should be less concerned with my fidelity to Heidegger's texts than with their politics, incipient or otherwise. Like many readers, I think that questions

---

5. Several studies come to mind, from Beda Allemann's 1954 study, *Hölderlin und Heidegger*, to Marc Froment-Meurice's 1996 book, *C'est à dire: Poétique de Heidegger*, translated in 1998 as *That Is to Say: Heidegger's Poetics*. In between, critics such as Paul Bové (1980), Gerald Bruns (1989), Christopher Fynsk (1993), and Andrzej Warminski (1987) have made important contributions to our understanding of Heidegger's work with the poets. In each instance, however, the focus remains on Heidegger *qua* critic, and the matter of poetic founding is left to the side. Véronique Fóti's 1992 study, *Heidegger and the Poets*, is something of an exception to this rule, although even that work (which remains, to my mind, the most interesting treatment of the subject) only addresses the matter obliquely, preferring to focus on the import of poetry from the point of view of Rilke and Hölderlin in order to demonstrate how Heidegger misconstrues them.

6. I am not oblivious to the fact that instrumental readings run afoul of the kind of criticism that Warminski and Fóti have levied against Heidegger's own readings, namely, that he reads to his own ends at the expense of the poets read. I am unmoved by the irony, however, and for two reasons. First, as I argued in a review of Fóti's book, I do not see how one can avoid "interpretations" of this kind (Lysaker 1993). Second, I do not share the ethical intuitions that lead both scholars to regard such strategies as criminal in principle, preferring, as I do, to measure the worth of interpretations beyond the zero-sum game wherein traces of instrumentality are grounds for exclusion. As I see it, the issue concerns how one comports oneself within instrumental practices, not whether one proceeds instrumentally.

concerning Heidegger's politics are germane to any encounter with his texts. And his work on art is no exception. As Fred R. Dallmayr (1986), Annemarie Gethman-Siefert (1989), and many others have noted, in turning to the work of art as a principal site wherein to raise the question of being, Heidegger had his own ends in mind. Throughout the 1930s, he turned to Hölderlin in particular in the hopes of securing a national identity, an identity for the German *Volk*. In fact, he claims: "Whenever art happens—that is, when an inception occurs—a thrust enters into history; history either begins or starts over again. Here history does not mean a succession of occurrences in time, of whatever sort or importance. History is the ecstatic entrance of a people [*Volk*] into its deliverance as an engagement with its endowment" (Heidegger 1977a, 65). For now, note that Heidegger ties the import of the work of art to a *Volk*.[7] I find this troubling in two ways, one bound to arbitrariness, the other to a sinister overdetermination. If the work of art has the power to initiate history, why delimit that figurative power within the confines of a *Volk*? Why suppose that the work will, in each instance, address a *Volk*? Might another figure play the role of addressee, e.g., community *(Gemeinschaft)*, society *(Gesellschaft)*, or state *(Staat)*? In the context of his dialogue with the poets, I find Heidegger's insistent invocation of the figure of the *Volk* thoroughly arbitrary, and I have little interest in infecting my analyses with such assumptions. Second, in the 1930s—in Germany's 1930s—the *Volk* is no incidental trope, but part and parcel of Nazi ideology and propaganda. Any uncritical employment of the term at that time renders one a *de facto* fellow traveler, i.e., one who accepts the political terrain then set by National Socialism and marked by thuggery, terror, and eventually genocide.

Still, I would deny that Heidegger's conversation with the poets exhausts itself in so many variations on the theme of Nazi Germany. As I will demonstrate, one can pursue Heidegger's questions about the work of art without committing oneself to his programmatic designs upon the responses he was willing to entertain. This is not to say that readers of Heidegger should not root out the various ways in which his programmatic commitments, some no doubt tied to totalitarian politics, infect his writings. Certainly they should, and many have. But even if Robert Bernasconi is right and Heidegger's own hopes for poetry are inextrica-

---

7. In the 1934 lectures on Hölderlin, Heidegger goes so far as to suggest that the trope *Vaterland* signifies *das Seyn selbst,* that is, being itself (Heidegger 1980, 121).

bly bound to his nationalism—as if only *German* poets could redirect history—we need not share those hopes as we interrogate Heidegger's esteem and feel for the power of the work of art (Bernasconi 1993, 135–48).

Another disclaimer. Just as my focus upon Simic limits the reach of my study, drawing me away from the work of art per se, so too my decision to work out of Heidegger further confines the range of the ear I will bring to the phenomenon that Rilke's poem forces upon us. I realize this and know that I might have taken other paths and come upon a different understanding of the address and import of the language of the poem. For example, I might have taken my leave from Adorno, exploring the language of the poem in terms of a dialectic of subject and object that allegorically discloses the fate of the social subject. Or I might have begun with Benjamin and followed out the language of the poem until it crystallized into a monad from which an epoch of history could leap forth, defiantly disrupting the history of the victors. Or, reading after Richard Rorty, I might have cast the matter as one of self-creation: strong poetry might change our lives, should our readings prove strong as well. And no doubt there are others, such as Emerson or Dewey, who might have led us down still other avenues. But I have elected to follow Heidegger and thus must forgo such journeys, lacking as I do the skill of Jorge Luis Borges's Ts'ui Pen, former governor of Yunan province, to assemble here a "garden of forking paths." I thus leave to future studies any and all comparisons between the argument developed here and those oriented by the work of others named above.

Let me close by outlining, in the most general terms, what awaits you. The book falls into three implicit parts. In Chapters 1 and 2, through a reading of Heidegger, I will explore the nature and import of a kind of poetic address, one I will regard as "ur-poetic." Written through an author's corpus, and irreducible to any given poem, the "ur-poem" is a poem of poetry that enables the reader to experience the birth of sense in an originary fashion, thus changing his or her life (and more).

Chapters 3, 4, and 5 work through several Simic poems in order to present what I regard as the key moments in his ur-poetry. As we shall see, Simic's work is multifaceted and thus requires a reading willing to juggle several balls at once, some of which might appear to collide with one another. In Chapters 6 and 7, I will attempt to render concrete the implications of Simic's ur-poetry. That is, to recall Rilke, I will try to show what sort of life changes Simic's work expects of us.

1

Heidegger's Ear

> Poetry is nothing other than the elementary coming to word, that is, the becoming uncovered of existence as being-in-the-world. With what is thereby articulated, the world first becomes conspicuous for those who earlier were blind.
>
> —Heidegger, *The Basic Problems of Phenomenology*

> Poetry is founding, the effectual grounding of what endures. The poet is the grounder of being. What we call the real in the everyday is, in the end, unreal.
>
> —Heidegger, *Hölderlin's Hymns "Germania" and "The Rhine"*

> The saying of the poet is a founding not only in the sense of a free giving, but also, and at the same time, in the sense of the firm grounding of human existence.
>
> —Heidegger, *Elucidations of Hölderlin's Poetry*

These are some of Heidegger's starkest claims on behalf of poetry, claims lying at the heart of a dialogue with poetry already underway in the 1927 lecture course entitled "The Basic Problems of Phenomenology" and still percolating in the 1972 remarks on Rimbaud. I want to bring these claims to the phenomenon presented by Rilke's poem: a work of art addresses us, overwhelms us, and compels us to change our lives. This is not to say that in what follows I will do justice to the full range of Heidegger's dialogue with the poets. That would require an extended study. Heidegger's collected works contain multiple engagements with poets and their poetry. Aside from the three lecture courses devoted to Hölderlin and the numerous essays engaging his poems, two essays revolve around Trakl, and another works closely with Stefan George's poem "The Word." There is also a lengthy essay devoted to Rilke, the epistolary exchange with Emil Staiger concerning Mörike's "On A Lamp," and three essays (one quite brief) on Hebel.[1] Heidegger's "conversation with the poets" thus involves a vast field of readings, one I could not hope to cover systematically and still engage a variety of poems. I propose instead to sketch an account of what Heidegger finds at stake in poetry, focusing upon what we too might find in the language of the poem were we to follow the general path his many engagements have worn.

Because I want to think about how the language of the poem addresses us, I will start with how Heidegger reads. Heidegger refuses to employ traditional poetic theory. In fact, he avoids literary theory, preferring to allow the poems he reads to determine for themselves the being of poetry. As John Sallis says: "Effacing itself before the poem, [Heidegger's] poetics would listen and respond to what speaks in the poem, to the speaking of the language in which it is said what poetry is" (Sallis 1990, 169). But what would this entail?

I will begin by considering the 1954 distinction between *Erörterung*, "exposition," and *Erläuterung*, "clarification," taking it as a workable example of how Heidegger reads—and how we, following him, might read as well. "Exposition," Heidegger informs us, at least in its preliminary stages, seeks to locate an *Ort*, the "site" of something. Heidegger calls the *Ort* the "tip of the spear. In it, everything runs together. The *Ort* gathers to itself from what is loftiest and most extreme . . . collects and preserves what has been gathered, although not as an encapsulating shell, but by shining through and illuminating that which has been gathered, thus releasing it, for the first time, to its essence" (Heidegger 1985, 33).[2] According to the passage, the *Ort* is a gathering force. Beginning from extremes (i.e., from the origin, the limits at which a being both begins and ends), an *Ort* collects something within its reach and releases it to its essence. Given that the issue here is poetry, the essence in question lies in poetizing, in how a poem comes to poetize some matter or other. To remark upon the *Ort* of a poem is thus to consider the way in

---

1. Remarks on Rilke also appear in several lecture courses, including "The Basic Problems of Phenomenology," "Parmenides," and "Heraclitus," delivered in 1927, 1942, and 1943–44, respectively.

2. I will not translate the word *Ort*. "Site" does it justice in a literal sense, but it proves to be such an unusual term in Heidegger's text that stressing its foreignness reminds one that something out of the ordinary is under consideration.

which the poem is "collected" and "released" into poetizing, into what it does.

One might wonder why I stress the activity of *poetizing* and not the state of *being* a poem. The reason is decisive. Heidegger resists regarding "essence" *(Wesen)* in terms of *quidditas,* or "whatness"—i.e., essence defined in terms of necessary and sufficient conditions or qualities that constitute an identity and distinguish it from other beings. Rather, he tethers *Wesen* to the verb "to be." Now in German, much as in English, the verb "to be" assumes irregular forms, the infinitive being *sein.* But in its past perfect form, the verb "to be" becomes *gewesen.* This is significant, for it suggests that were the verb "to be" a regular verb, its infinitive form could very well be *wesen,* for regular verbs are conjugated by applying the prefix *ge-* to the infinitive and replacing the infinitive ending with a *t.* Thus, if *wesen* were a verb, its past perfect form would be *gewest,* although it might also prove to be irregular in a less tortured way than *sein,* leading to the infinitive *wesen* and the past perfect *gewesen,* much in the manner of *fressen.* I note this because Heidegger often employs *wesen* as a verb, as in the essay "The Thing": "Der Krug west als Ding," that is, "The jug essentially comes to pass [*west*] as a thing" (Heidegger 1954a, 166).[3] I take this to mean that Heidegger would have us regard *Wesen,* "essence," as the nominative form of a verb and thus think of what it names in terms of an event. If we return to the matter of the poem, I think we can say that according to Heidegger, to be a poem is not to have distinguishing marks—iambic rhythms, say, or formal rhyme schemes. Rather, it is to occur in a characteristic manner.

Despite the construal just offered, certain questions might linger about Heidegger's use of "essence." Allow me, then, to clarify the term via negation. First, in asking us to consider how a being comes to be, Heidegger is not supposing that a being comes to be by way of a stable or enduring ground. In fact, the characteristic manner in which a being occurs may be thoroughly dynamic. Second, and this point follows upon

3. Unlike Kenneth Maly and Parvis Emad, I cannot separate *Wesen* in any of its forms from "essence," let alone claim, as they do, that *Wesen* has the "power to say what is utterly other than essence" (see their introduction to Heidegger 1999, xxvi). No work that sets itself the task of thinking about grounds—that which enables beings—can separate itself from the history of thought concerning that which makes a being what it is, i.e., its essence. This is not to say that *Wesen* is identical to *essentia* or any other understanding of essence, but it is to insist, for reasons concerning the historicity of language and thought, that Heidegger's texts are inseparable from the traditions he struggles to think through—and not only when he explicitly confronts those traditions.

the first, the characteristic or essential manner in which a being occurs need not be ahistorical; its manner of occurrence may be very much historical. Third, to claim that X has a characteristic manner of being is not to preclude, necessarily, that it is the result of social construction. It is to insist, however, that social constructivist theorists owe us an account of the essence of any given social construction as an event. Such theorists must account for the set of events that gives any given being its character, even if that event is one of social construction. Considered most generally, then, Heidegger's *Wesen*, rather than marking a theoretical desire for a stable, ahistorical ground, functions instead as something of a placeholder, one that insistently raises a question: "How did things come to pass such that this being came to be the being it is?"

The *Ort*, then, concerns how a poem comes to be a poem, how it comes to be the event that it is. Let us consider an *Ort* at work. Poems say things in many ways. For example, "I Go Back to May 1937," a confessional poem by Sharon Olds from *The Gold Cell* (1991), concerns a child's desire to return and warn her not-yet-married parents of all that is to come, thereby preventing their marriage. Here are some lines:

> I want to go up to them and say Stop,
> don't do it—she's the wrong woman,
> he's the wrong man, you are going to do things
> you cannot imagine you would ever do,
> you are going to do bad things to children,
> you are going to suffer in ways you never heard of,
> you are going to want to die.
>
> (lines 13–19)

These lines present us with the palpable pain of a child who has grown to see the colossal failure that was her parents' marriage and come to think that it might have been better never to have been born at all. The speaker realizes, however, that she would not prevent the union, for then she would never be. Instead, she accepts the life she has inherited, promising to be its witness: "Do what you are going to do, and I will tell about it" (line 30).

Now, if we were to ask what the poem is *about*, we would inquire into some set of issues that the poem addresses (e.g., the marital failure of one's parents) or expresses (e.g., filial rage). But if we raise the question of the *Ort*, we turn our interest away from what the poem is about and toward the language of the poem and how it works, that is, how it comes to poetize themes like marital and familial failure. We would ask this question: "What gathers (and how) this language into these modes of address, an address we clumsily invoke with the word 'about'?"

One might think that because hers is a confessional poem, some notion of "confession" might mark the *Ort* of Olds's poem. *Qua* confession, one that weaves together lyrical and narrative elements, the poem comes together, addressing us with a voice that bares its soul.[4] Such a response is attractive because it sets the question of the *Ort* into familiar terrain and allows us to regard the *Ort*, at least initially, as an amalgamation of traditional poetic elements, such as epic, narrative, lyric, and drama. Such an impulse would be misguided, however, for it leaves the question of the *Ort* unasked, or, to be more generous, it only postpones the interrogation, for one would still want to know how any epic, lyric, or drama (or combination thereof) comes to poetize what it addresses. One should not equate Heidegger's concerns with those orienting traditional poetics, therefore.

Now, I am not claiming that all traditional poetic concerns are necessarily irrelevant to Heidegger's work on poetry. They are not. In clarifying a poet's corpus, one may employ any number of interpretive strategies (for example, tracking internal rhymes in a poem like "The Idea of Order at Key West"). But I do think that the supposed building blocks of poetizing—and this includes terms such as metaphor, symbol, lyric, narrative, and so on—do not offer much by way of explanation if we introduce them into Heidegger's dialogue with the poets. For example, if one looks for the work of metaphor within the *Ort* of the poem, one would want to know how it is that some matter comes to be metaphorized in the language of the poem—how it is engaged by that language and then translated or carried over by some figure, image, or operation. (Recall that *metapherein* means "to carry over," while "translate" comes from the Latin *transferre*, "to bear across.") A metaphor is a complex event, precisely the kind of event that an inquiry into the *Ort* of the poem is designed to fathom. To appeal to metaphorical transpositions in order to explain the labors that take place in the *Ort* of a poem is thus only to open another inquiry into another *Ort*, this one presumably

---

4. With regard to the category of "confession," I do not think it matters whether one equates the speaker with the author. Either way, the poem has a confessional tone, ripe with intimate disclosures about the speaker's life.

concerning a poem before the poem, one coming to pass in the metaphor itself. As Heidegger writes in his course on Hölderlin's poem "Remembrance":

> now we should only mention that the master key of all "poetics," the doctrine of the "image" in poetry, of "metaphor," does not open a single door in the region of Hölderlin's hymnal-poetry, and in no way brings us into the free. Here it is enough only to bear in mind this one thing: . . . the "matters themselves" [those which are poetized] in every case, and before they come to be so-called symbols, are already poetized. The question remains only out of which essential region and out of which truth of poetizing. (Heidegger 1982a, 40)

If we are to engage the matter of the *Ort* without the explanatory power of traditional poetics, perhaps a poem might help us conceive of what it is that Heidegger seeks. Consider "Reality Is an Activity of the Most August Imagination" from *The Palm at the End of the Mind* by Wallace Stevens (1971).

> Last Friday, in the big light of last Friday night,
> We drove home from Cornwall to Hartford, late.
>
> It was not a night blown at a glassworks in Vienna
> Or Venice, motionless, gathering time and dust.
>
> There was a crush of strength in a grinding going round,
> Under the front of the westward evening star,
>
> The vigor of glory, a glittering in the veins,
> As things emerged and moved and were dissolved,
>
> Either in distance, change or nothingness,
> The visible transformations of summer night,
>
> An argentine abstraction approaching form
> And suddenly denying itself away.

There was an insolid billowing of the solid.
Night's moonlight lake was neither water nor air.

Throughout, the speaker invokes a night and struggles to say what shone there. Neither a glass bowl encapsulating a world such that it gathers time (thus lying beyond it) nor accumulating "dust" (and not becoming dust itself), this is not the "big light" of eternity. Rather, the big light of that night was a force, a pulse one can feel in Stevens's fifth line where each word begins with a crunch (*cr*ush, *str*ength, *gr*inding, going *r*ound), thus effecting a kind of proactive relentlessness, like waves crashing on shores.

Suggestive vocables aside, I invoke the sea because *things* fare poorly here. They recede, become other things, or simply dissipate (line 8). In fact, they only seem to exist as manifestations of the night, not as things in themselves (line 10). And as with the night's power, their fate is palpably present in Stevens's fabulous music. When referring to things, the stress (in line 8) falls upon the close of the words (emer*ged*, mo*ved*, dis-sol*ved*), underscoring the passivity of things as they proceed through the night's "going round," subject as they are to its "crush of strength."

But what of the night itself? Thus far we have seen its foreground and background demarcated by things undergoing its operations. But the night per se? It never shows itself, at least directly. Rather, it remains a silvery abstraction, a gleam, a shining that hovers at the edge of form but never settles into one, instead "denying itself away" (line 12). And yet this is not a gentle gleam, starlight comforting or chilling from afar. Rather, it is as if this "insolid billowing of the solid" is rushing out of things, subjecting them to transformations, and shining amid all that motion, remaining throughout an elusive but vigorous power. Note how radical this elusiveness is. Neither water nor air, and as something ultimately insolid, the night does not present itself within any of matter's characteristic states: liquid, solid, gas. It is thus a silvery abstraction more abstract than even these elemental abstractions (for there is no "liquid," only rain, grapefruit juice, spittle, and so on).

We could continue reading, but I would rather stop and pose a question. What is this poem about? If we say that the poem concerns a night, we are correct. But even so, the referent eludes us. This night is no thing at which we could point and say: not that, the other thing, just to your left. Nor will any elemental concept capture it, as if it were some state of affairs, e.g., gravity, that one is forced to invoke in order to explain those things toward which we often point, e.g., falling leaves or nuts.[5] It seems, then, that the poem is about how the surging presence of a given night cannot be located among things or with the basic concepts that allow us to thematize what moves behind and in things.

Now, one might treat the title as a proposition and equate the movement of the night with the august activity of the imagination. On that basis, the claim would be that the poem is about how the imagination, through its robust activity, can turn a nocturnal scene reflecting off a lake into a whirring dance of lights and shapes. But if we run this route, will the imagination not prove as elusive as the night? In taking the crunch of the night to descend from the imagination, the latter, as it approaches form, also will deny itself away. Now, in this context, I would resist taking form too narrowly and imagining some actual shape (definite *or* cloud-like). In fact, given the elusiveness of the night with regard to the poem's own language, I think we need to take "form" in the broadest sense possible, and that includes poetic forms (say, blank verse) and abstract universals (e.g., "imagination," "night") as well as propositions (such as "reality is an activity of the most august imagination"). It thus cannot be the case that if we suppose that the poem is *about* the "imagination," and that its language moves in such a way that what the propositional title states is shown and augustly embodied, we will gain any clearer sense of that to which this poem seems to refer. The imagination may be at issue here, but its presence in the title and (perhaps) in the poem marks a question whose slipperiness the poem underscores.

Rather than insisting that the poem is about some determinate referent, I would suggest that one can hear questions raising themselves within the language of the poem. How does this poem purport to lay hold of "the big light of last Friday night"? What enables the language of the poem to move past the point where *(a)* things break off and *(b)* elemental concepts fail, but *(c)* to nevertheless catch a glimpse of the invisible in the transformations of the visible, such that *(d)* this poem might be *about* an elusive, perhaps imagined (which is not to say imagi-

---

5. The thought is that while gravity is not an empirical phenomenon (that is, it cannot be observed in its own right, in the form of gravitons, for example), we speak of its presence in order to explain the effects various bodies have upon one another, e.g., Y compels X to orbit it. Strictly speaking, "gravity" is a theoretical posit, recalling Hegel's suggestion in *The Phenomenology of Spirit*'s chapter on "Force and the Understanding" that the so-called laws of nature are actually part and parcel of self-consciousness and not the mechanics of some supposedly external world.

nary) night? One of the things that impresses me so about Stevens's poem is the way in which it presses this question upon us. How does a poem lay hold of an "argentine abstraction approaching form / And suddenly denying itself away"?

I have spent this much time with Stevens's poem because it renders concrete what is at stake in the question of the *Ort*. In fact, I think the question of the *Ort* can be found in the language of Stevens's poem. It is not that Stevens's poem is *about* the *Ort*—as if the *Ort* were some thing, event, or force that the poem, through some poetic medium, represented. How could it be when the *Ort* concerns the "aboutness" relation itself, the very possibility of poetic address, thereby eluding any representation as the condition of its possibility? And yet, I would insist that the *Ort* is found in the language of the poem, marked even as an "argentine abstraction," an abstraction that draws the rest of the poem to itself such that one must read the entire poem in a nocturnal, silvery light.

Allow me to clarify. My point is not only that one is compelled to regard the night's "visible transformations" in a silvery vein but also that everything standing under the canopy of its big light, everything addressed by the poem, falls under the sway of this silvery abstraction. Note the various points of reference marked in the poem. Some are concrete: Cornwall, Hartford, Venus (the evening star), and, via negation, Vienna and Venice. Others are abstract: things, distances (both temporal and spatial), changes, even nothingness. The poem sets the drive, Cornwall, and Venus—as well as the abstract terms—in the night's big light. Line ten ("The visible transformations of summer night"), along with "things," includes "distance," "change," and "nothingness." Each point in the poem is thus bathed in the night's big light, each point one of its visible transformations emerging, moving, dissolving. Even the thrill of being there, of driving along ("a glittering in the veins"), seems cast in a silvery hue.

I think we can push the point one step further. Not only is the poem bathed in a silvery light, but its poetizing also pulses with an insolid billowing of the solid. If we presume that the poem issues from the drive, transforming a drive into a poem, then the imaginative activity of translating experience into poetry would be but one more "transformation of a summer night," that is, it would be a response to and a child of this billowing, argentine abstraction.

Suppose, however, we deny that any such drive took place. Suppose the night is a figure and just a figure, a trope without an external referent, a moment in a poem. We then have a night into which things emerge, move, and dissolve, one that approaches form but denies itself away. But would that not have to include poems as well? If there is no existential referent, no particular night, no particular form, all of the figures (e.g., things, distance, change, nothingness, and form) recoil upon the thing and form at hand: this poem, this poetizing. Either way, the night marks a scene in which the poem itself is invigorated, ground out, in which this poetizing emerges and moves, or, we might even say, is gathered—"although not as an encapsulating shell, but by shining through and illuminating that which has been gathered," to recall Heidegger.

From Stevens's poem, let us return to Rilke's "Archaic Torso of Apollo," and specifically to the torso that twists back into itself, holds fast, and shines. Recall that this torso, in twisting back into itself, draws the entire figure together such that along its contours and to its depths the sculpture radiates like a star. What is it, there at the center (like Stevens's night), that holds the work together, draws it into a kind of luminosity? This is the question of the *Ort*. What brings the poem into its poetizing? What enables its address?

Slippery questions. How are we to pursue them? As I noted, Heidegger opts to take the poem at its word, which is to say, he expects the language of the poem to articulate its own *Ort*. But how? Admittedly, taking the poem at its word suggests something odd. As we shall see, it turns on what is more of a regulative ideal or a promise than a method. In fact, like Heidegger's early sense of phenomenology, it is driven in principle by certain restraints, not presumed accounts of the workings of poetizing.[6] For example, Heidegger is explicit about not wanting to force

6. In Joan Stambaugh's translation of *Being and Time*, we read: "Phenomenology neither demonstrates the object of its researches nor is it a title that describes their content. The word only tells us about the how of the demonstration and treatment of *what* this discipline considers. Science 'of' the phenomena means that it grasps its objects in *such* a way that everything about them to be discussed must be directly indicated and directly demonstrated. The basically tautological expression 'descriptive phenomenology' has the same sense. Here description does not mean a procedure, like that of, say, botanical morphology. The term rather has the sense of a prohibition, insisting that we avoid all non-demonstrative determinations" (Heidegger 1996a, 30–31). This is not to say that Heidegger's readings practice what they preach. In her *Heidegger and the Poets*, Véronique Fóti has identified what she regards as interpretive blunders in Heidegger's dialogue with the poets, e.g., "privileging . . . diachronicity over synchronicity," a shortcoming that issues in a "certain disregard for lexis in favor of the event-like singularity and the etymological historicality of the singularized word." Moreover, she objects to what she regards as a phenomenologically unwarranted, totalizing, and violent projection of the history of being upon texts that resist the closure such a vision entails (Fóti 1992, 36, 111). While ungenerous, she is right to suggest that a kind of violence infects Heidegger's readings.

the language of the poem into preexisting categories, particularly philosophical theses. Preparing to read Hölderlin in 1934, he writes: "The danger exists that we [will] set the poetic work within concepts, that we only [will] comb a poem for the philosophical opinions and tenets of the poet, that we [will] piece together Hölderlin's philosophical system and explain the poetry from such an account" (Heidegger 1980, 5).[7] Nor will he allow us to treat the poem as essentially a product of cultural, historical, or psychological processes.[8] While Heidegger does not justify these refusals, we can.

In an essay on Rilke's "Orpheus. Euridice. Hermes," Joseph Brodsky reads the opening of the poem (where we find Orpheus within a "strange, unfathomed mine of souls") back through Virgil. He suggests that Rilke has marked these souls as "silver veins of silent ore," for his poem is a rereading of Virgil's *Aeneid*—specifically, Aneas's encounter, en route to the underworld, with a golden bough, an image that is drawn (according to Brodsky) from caves lying outside Naples where the Sibyl of Cumae purportedly lived. He also contrasts his reading with those that tether Rilke's poem to a bas-relief depicting the three figures (Brodsky 1995, 376, 380–81). According to Brodsky, one ought to leave behind such personal sources of inspiration and look instead toward the processes of a "cultural metabolism," that is, I presume, to look toward the process of change that underwrites the kind of rereadings Brodsky finds in Rilke.[9]

In pursuing the *Ort* of a poem, Heidegger steers us away from the crucible of cultural influence. Why? Such dramas, even if they arise in the language of the poem, are ultimately matters of some extra-poetic agency—often, though not exclusively, the author's. As Brodsky himself claims: "Unwittingly, or consciously trying to avoid imitating Virgil, Rilke changes the metal and, with it, the color of the scene, aspiring

---

7. See a similar remark in "The Essence of Language" (Heidegger 1985, 156).

8. Such refusals can be found throughout his readings (Heidegger 1985, 37; 1981, 42; 1980, 25–29; 1982a, 5; 1984, 182–83).

9. Readings that trace images and words back to events in Rilke's life are common, particularly with regard to "Archaic Torso of Apollo" (Baron 1975; Friedman 1996, 253; Nalewski 1985, 115). While Brodsky seems to reject such accounts for aesthetic reasons (I think he finds them boring), his gripe also stems from a desire to preserve what Osip Mandelstam termed "world culture," a literature that transcends, in principle, the parochialism of individual situatedness or preference, a commitment no doubt partly grounded in Brodsky's belief that it was the existence of such a literature that enabled his generation of Soviet writers to see past state ideology and prepare themselves and their readers for a post-totalitarian future.

evidently to a somewhat more monochromatic rendition of Persephone's domain" (Brodsky 1995, 380). But for Heidegger's purposes, Brodsky's explanatory tack misguides those who wish to locate the *Ort* of a poem because it presumes that somewhere within the alchemy of social psychology, within the metabolism that occurs whenever influence passes over into inspiration, one will find where and how poems are gathered as poems. Here, though, metabolism does no more than *metapherein* in regard to explaining such a gathering. Instead, it only presumes that event, as must all attempts to reduce the *Ort* to the syntheses of personal and/or social forces.

Another negation. Alongside his refusal to locate the *Ort* through the application of philosophy, historiography, anthropology, or psychology, Heidegger, as noted earlier, seriously doubts that traditional poetics can appreciate all that is to be found in the language of the poem. After noting the rather bland fact that Hölderlin's "The Ister" is a hymn, a song of praise, Heidegger hastens to add (in the McNeill/Davis translation): "Initially, however, it must remain open in what sense and with what legitimacy the poetic works of Hölderlin to which we shall refer may be called 'hymns.' We must first become attentive to this poetry. Once we have become attentive, we can then 'pay attention to,' that is, retain, some things that, at favorable moments, will perhaps let us 'attend to,' that is, have some intimation of what might be said in the word of this poet" (Heidegger 1996b, 1). In other words, as I have suggested earlier, general categories such as "hymn" (or "confession," or even more basically, "narrative" and "lyric") may not prove felicitous with regard to the language of the poem. In fact, Heidegger does not even treat terms such as "hymn" as categories. Instead, they are aids, pointers that, "at favorable moments," might lead us into the language of the poem and what rises therein like a wave.

Heidegger's caution toward poetic categories does not stem from a nominalist sentiment. Instead, his caution arises because, as he states in the 1942 lecture course on Hölderlin's "Remembrance," "every genuine word has its concealed and manifold ranges of vibrations. Essential poetry testifies to this in the first place, such that what it has poetized only maintains itself within and speaks out of the realm of these self and super vibrating ranges." In this context, the "genuine word" is a poetic one that "opens and closes an abundance [named above as "concealed and manifold ranges of vibrations"] that is inexhaustible because it has the character of the inceptual" (Heidegger 1982a, 15, 13). As was the case with the *Ort* (and I take the matter to be the same in Heidegger's reading of "Remembrance"), these ranges are not incidental to the language of the poem, for that language "*only* maintains itself and speaks out of the realm of these *self* and *super* vibrating ranges" (emphases mine). I have stressed "super" because these ranges overdetermine the language of the poem. In fact, Heidegger speaks of the *überdichtende Wort*, the word that poetizes over (as one might overrun) a poet's entire corpus (Heidegger 1982a, 33–34). But note also that these ranges are *self*-vibrating. We now have the reason why one must take the poem at its word when seeking out the *Ort*—the *Ort* is opened in and through the word itself. In other words, that which gathers the language of the poem into its poetizing, enabling it to poetize in its characteristic manner, occurs within the language of the poem. In seeking an *Ort* one must travel through the language of the poem because that language figures itself as it occurs; it is an event of autofiguration.

Now that it is clear why Heidegger opts to take the poem at its word when he seeks the *Ort* of poetizing, a further reason for his eschewal of traditional poetics becomes apparent. Rather than allowing the language of the poem to articulate the character of its being, poetics rewrites those founding gestures in its own terms. And it is not as if those terms have proven neutral with regard to originary matters. For example, Heidegger believes that the language of symbol imports a metaphysics into the *Ort* of poetizing. First, symbolization splits language into that which is symbolized and that which symbolizes, thus forcing a distinction between form and content upon the language of the poem. But such a distinction denies autofiguration at the outset, suggesting instead that the language of the poem is merely the husk of some content. Moreover, it risks a kind of Platonism, one that idealizes content and renders form in terms of sensual arrangements (taking "form" here to designate a general form of presentation, not some particular poetic form, such as the sonnet). Heidegger writes (again in the McNeill/Davis translation): "The sensuous indeed makes something perceivable—the essence—but at the same time it shows this essence only in a restricted and disfigured way. Thought Platonically, the sensuous is only ever a restrictive after-image of what truly is, of the essence of something, wherein its proper truth and its sense consist. . . . The sensuous is the symbolic image and the suprasensuous is the 'primary image'—*paradeigma*" (Heidegger 1996b,

25). Given that Heidegger seeks to find the essence of poetizing in an event of autofiguration, it is clear why he would have to think that essence outside of the language of symbolization.

In *The Principle of Reason,* Heidegger argues that one finds a distinction between the sensible and the supersensible within the idea of metaphor (Heidegger 1991, 70–73). The claim is that metaphors work by "transposing" some supersensible content into the realm of the sensible, where it is more readily understood. And this again reduces language to mere chaff for the intelligible. To treat poetic naming in terms of metaphor is thus to rob it of its figuring power.[10] One could of course argue that the transposition effected by metaphor need not be tethered to a supersensible metaphysics.[11] One might suppose instead that metaphor works by transposing certain everyday locutions into unusual contexts. For example, in his acerbically brilliant "To My Wife," Philip Larkin terms possibility a "peacock-fan." Metaphor would thus arise when a poem takes up a common phrase, e.g., "peacock-fan," and inserts it into a new context—in this case, the lost futures that accompany marriage. So transposed, the metaphor offers us a different slant on things, perhaps illuminating them in a novel way. (Here the image suggests that possible futures dazzle our desire like a peacock's tail dazzles a mate.) If we are exploring an event of autofiguration, however, such a theory fails to advance our cause. As should be evident by now, such a transposition ignores the turn of the word into poetizing, because it leaves the depths of *metapherein* unplumbed. In this context, then, the problem with metaphor is not a tacit, supersensible metaphysics, but an insistent repetition of the problem it purportedly resolves.

In showing that Heidegger's resistance to the language of metaphor vis-à-vis the *Ort* of poetizing is not simply predicated on the belief that metaphors presume an opposition between the sensible and the supersensible, I take myself to have buoyed his position with regard to some of Jacques Derrida's criticisms. In "White Mythology," Derrida argues that any attempt to delimit metaphor within the confines of a simple opposition is bound to fail. As David Wood writes in "Metaphysics and Metaphor": "Much of the point of Derrida's 'White Mythology' is to show

---

10. In a reading of Heidegger's early work with Hölderlin, Arthur Grugan develops this line of thought as well (Grugan 1989, 147–49).
11. I obviously cannot do justice to the field of metaphor theory at this juncture. I will thus limit my discussion to Heidegger's fundamental point concerning metaphor with regard to the *Ort* of poetizing. In this limited context, I think his position is sound.

that the concept of metaphor is constituted not by a single opposition at all [such as Heidegger's—JTL], but by a whole discourse . . . on metaphor" (Wood 1990, 38–39). This is perhaps most evident in the "Ellipsis of the Sun" section of "White Mythology," in which Derrida attempts to show how almost all of Aristotle's philosophical vocabulary is involved in his attempt to define metaphor, e.g., *physis, aletheia, mimesis* (Derrida 1982, 230–45). But if Heidegger's squeamishness with regard to metaphor is not solely predicated on the opposition he employs, then his worries may have more substance than one might have thought.

Now, one might object that the real point concerns the position developed by Derrida in "The *Retrait* of Metaphor." Derrida insists that all attempts to circumscribe the play and place of metaphor inevitably return to and employ metaphors in their very circumscription. He writes: "The drama, for this is a drama, is that even if I decided to no longer speak metaphorically about metaphor, I would not achieve it, it would continue to go on without me in order to make me speak, to ventriloquize me, metaphorize me" (Derrida 1978, 8). But I do not think that Heidegger, at least in the midst of his readings, is so much offering a theory of metaphor as explaining why he elects not to employ the term while reading Hölderlin. One could thus agree with Derrida and nevertheless join Heidegger in his refusal to pursue the event of autofiguration within the metaphorics of metaphor theory.

What, though, of "allegory"? Christopher Fynsk suggests that a theory of "allegory" might help us think through what I have termed autofiguration, the intuition being that certain poems offer allegories of the origin of poetizing (Fynsk 1989). His suggestion is based upon lines from the opening of Heidegger's "Origin of the Work of Art." Heidegger suggests that "the work makes public something other than itself; it reveals something other; it is allegory. In the work of art, something else is brought together with the fabricated thing. In Greek, 'to bring together' is *sumballein*. The work is a symbol" (Heidegger 1977a, 4). I find Fynsk's approach wrongheaded, however, and my reasoning should be evident from Heidegger's tethering of allegory to the language of symbol. Moreover, the passage Fynsk cites is followed by another claim: "Allegory and symbol provide the representational frame in whose channel of vision, for quite some time, the characterizing of the work of art has moved" (Heidegger 1977a, 4). Because Heidegger's explicit effort in "The Origin of the Work of Art" is to unseat this "representational frame," the language of allegory hardly seems appropriate to the matter at hand, and this suspicion is borne out by Heidegger's rejection of the language of allegory in his lecture on Hölderlin's "The Ister." Using an argument we have already considered regarding the language of symbol, Heidegger rejects the language of allegory because of its implicit determination of the poetic word as a mere sign of what is poetized, the sensuous trappings of what is, in some way, suprasensuous (Heidegger 1984, 18).[12]

On my reading, then, when seeking an *Ort*, Heidegger takes the poem at its word, not only because that language testifies to the contours of the *Ort* but also because it draws them. That is, according to Heidegger, the *Ort* comes to be through an event of autofiguration. Now, one has to read for autofiguration on many levels, as can be seen in Heidegger's attempt to locate the *Ort* of Trakl's work through an "exposition" that proceeds by way of a "clarification" of individual poems and lines. The former seeks the *Ort* of a poem or poetic corpus as it is articulated in what I will call an "ur-poem," a poem of poetry that discloses its own *Ort*. Heidegger does not employ the figure of the ur-poem, but he does write of a *Gedicht* (poem) that runs through and guides an author's corpus, his or her *Dichtung* (poetry). Moreover, various terms playing similar roles crop up throughout his other readings: *Grundstimmung*, or "fundamental attunement" (1934); the *dichtende Wort*, or "poetic word" (1942); a *Gedichtete*, or "that which is to be poetized" (1943); and *Grundworte*, or "ground words" (1946). And because each term traces and underwrites in a very real way what Heidegger takes to be the essential site of whatever poetry is in question (respectively, Hölderlin's "Germania," "Remembrance," "The Ister," and the corpuses of Rilke and Trakl), I have decided to gather their various senses and significance under the umbrella term "ur-poem."

I claim that Heidegger *posits and seeks* an ur-poem because it is not as if the ur-poem is one poem among many. Rather, it lies unspoken within the language of the poem itself (or poems themselves—for an ur-poem is not limited to any particular poem) and stands in need of extraction or exposition. As he writes, reading Trakl: "The ur-poem of a poet remains

---

12. I would stress, however, perhaps over and against Heidegger's own emphases, that the issue ultimately concerns less the threat of lurking Platonism than the transpositions that underwrite all of these key poetic terms—symbol, allegory, metaphor, and so on. That transposition occurs in the *Ort* of the poem, and that transposition is at stake in autofiguration. Insofar as one would think autofiguration, therefore, one will have to do so without recourse to these figures; even were one to rethink allegory beyond the bounds of Platonism (which is no doubt what Fynsk has in mind), it would only reopen the problem at hand, not resolve it.

unspoken. Neither the individual poems nor the whole says everything. Nevertheless, every poem speaks out of the whole of this ur-poem, and says the ur-poem every time. From the site of the ur-poem rises the wave which, unfailingly, moves the saying as something poetic" (Heidegger 1985, 33).[13] The ur-poem can thus be *read* only via a "clarification" of the language of the poem. "Because the poet's singular ur-poem always remains within the unspoken, we can situate its *Ort* only in trying to point to it by means of what the individual poems speak. And for that reason each poem will be in need of clarification" (ibid.).

At the heart of this reciprocal reading practice lie the markers that readers set in order to open up the language of the poem. In a lecture course from 1943, Heidegger terms these construals "annotations." According to Heidegger, these annotations are signs set along textual paths that direct one toward an ur-poem, signs such as "hymn." Through annotations, Heidegger thus reads until his feel for an ur-poem and for each particular poem coincide. As he notes while introducing a lecture on Hölderlin, also in 1943:

> Whatever else a clarification can or cannot do, this always applies: in order that what is purely poetized [our ur-poem] may stand within the poem a little more clearly, the clarifying speech, at each turn, must break itself and what it has attempted. For the sake of what is poetized [the ur-poem], the clarification of the poem must proceed in such a way that it makes itself superfluous. The final yet most difficult step of every interpretation consists in this, to disappear with its clarifications before the pure standing of what is poetized [the ur-poem]. . . . [If so,] with repeated reading we'll suppose that we had always understood the poems in this way. (Heidegger 1981, 9)

The clarification, therefore, should dissolve into the exposition of an ur-poem that marks and figures the *Ort* of poetizing itself.

Heidegger reading is thus a complex affair. On the one hand, there is the "exposition," a situating by means of which Heidegger would mark within a poet's own language the site, the *Ort* wherein and whereby the poet's work acquires its characteristic way of being. On the other hand,

---

13. Heidegger also terms the ur-poem "unspoken" in two lecture courses on Hölderlin's poetry (Heidegger 1980, 45; 1982a, 15, 39).

such marking occurs in and through readings of individual poems, lines, and even words, and thus the "exposition" requires a "clarification" of the work as a whole. In this "clarification," the *Ort* is distilled in the form of an ur-poem working unspoken within and throughout the language of the poem or poems. Finally, both efforts are caught in a reciprocal play, a perpetual alignment and realignment of suppositions into assumed figures of the ur-poem until the ur-poem eventually sounds within and through the language of the poem, and vice versa.

I have sketched a portrait of Heidegger the reader because I wanted to locate that for which he reads—ur-poems—and how, most generally, he purports to find them, namely, through ventured constructions that are set into and tested against the language of the poem. Again, as with descriptive phenomenology, there is no "method" here, no procedure that, when rigorously followed, would lead any rational observer to the same conclusions. Thus any consideration of how one looks for ur-poems must pursue a practice beyond "method" in any strict sense, for any method, being a medium of investigation, presumes some sense for what it measures, and that is precisely what one must not presume in the case of ur-poems.

Now we must render the ur-poem more precisely, for it is the ur-poem that I hope to bring to Rilke's torso as the kind of poetic address that might sound us out and compel us to change our lives. Described generically, the ur-poem involves the play of an author's principal figures, the ones that characterize the being—or rather, the coming to be—of the poem. For example, Heidegger finds in the interplay of Hölderlin's poetic figures, e.g., the river, the demigod, nature, divinities, and the flowers of the mouth, a saga recounting how the language of the poem comes to pass. But let us be more concrete and look at Heidegger's reading of Rilke, if only briefly.

Heidegger's most sustained reading of Rilke ("What Are Poets For?") comes upon the relative heels of two lecture courses on Hölderlin (from the winter of 1941–42 and the summer of 1942) as well as some brief remarks on Rilke himself in courses on Parmenides (winter of 1942–43) and Heraclitus (summers of 1943 and 1944). Fully convinced by 1946 of Hölderlin's singular import for European culture, Heidegger turns to Rilke in order to determine whether he is a poet of the same rank—or rather, in order to argue that he most likely is not, insisting that Rilke's poetry remains bound to a metaphysics of subjectivity, much as he did in the lecture course on Heraclitus in which he claimed that Rilke is a poet "in whom the age of completed subjectivity poetizes itself to its end" (Heidegger 1979a, 220).[14] While Fóti (1992), Haar (1993), and many others have objected to Heidegger's reading, claiming that it caricatures and even misses Rilke outright, I shall limit my concerns to *how* he reads, focusing upon the ur-poem that he draws out of Rilke's work.

Heidegger's reading revolves around an "improvisational poem" that Rilke inscribed in a gift copy of *The Notebooks of Malte Laurids Brigge* and later enclosed in a letter sent to his estranged (even abandoned) wife, Clara. But Heidegger also concerns himself with what he terms the "ground words" *(Grundworte)* of Rilke's poetry, words that, we are led to believe, carry the key to Rilke's corpus, words whose interplay make up what I have termed an ur-poem. And in another gesture, Heidegger sifts through letters and other poems, thereby supplementing his discussion when other materials complement and enrich his reading. In fact, he resorts to this gesture so often that one can hardly claim that the essay is primarily a reading of the improvised verses, even though he proceeds as if he were doing just that. Rather, Heidegger's central concern is Rilke's corpus, and thus his interpretive work really concerns the meaning and relation of the ground words, not the sixteen lines or any particular poem for that matter.[15]

In the interplay of Rilke's ground words (which I have italicized), Heidegger finds a meditation upon *nature* thought in terms of life and death in spherical transpositions, one another side of the other. The sphere is also figured, according to Heidegger, as an *open* region wherein mortal nature unfolds as it rushes through a *draft* into a series of ventures, ventures that amount to the lives of particular beings. Not all beings are drawn and ventured in the same way, however. Plants and animals live out their fate without the anxieties that often afflict self-conscious beings.[16] *Angels*, on the other hand, are aware of their passage,

14. In "What Are Poets For?" Heidegger repeats the charge in a different guise, claiming that despite their apparent differences, Rilke's angel is "metaphysically the same" as Nietzsche's Zarathustra (Heidegger 1977a, 312–13).

15. This is evidenced by Heidegger's reliance upon the figures of the angel, Orpheus, and the poet, none of whom are named in the cited lines. Moreover, he presumes certain identities that the lines in question do not authorize, e.g., that the "nature" mentioned in the first line is the same as the "primal ground" invoked in the fourth. Given a more general reading of Rilke, however, the connection is not unwarranted.

16. Given their predominance in his reading and in Rilke's poetry, I am surprised that Heidegger does not regard "animal" as a ground word, particularly because our being (again, on Heidegger's reading) lies between angel and beast. Heidegger does pay more attention to Rilke's animals in his 1942–43 lecture on Parmenides, however (Heidegger 1982b, 225–40).

but in an utterly detached way, relating to other beings as finely polished mirrors relate to those gazing upon them. Only humans are riddled with anxiety, aware of their passing and seeking, relentlessly, to become whole as time passes. One finds the thought in Rilke's *Duino Elegies,* here translated by Stephen Mitchell (Rilke 1982):

> Who has twisted us around like this, so that
> no matter what we do, we are in the posture
> of someone going away? Just as, upon
> the farthest hill, which shows him his whole valley
> one last time, he turns, stops, lingers—,
> so we live here, forever taking leave [*Abschied*].
>
> (Eighth Elegy, lines 71–76)

This search for wholeness most often manifests itself in a *parting (Abschied)* of the open, a parting that seeks to transform other beings into entities that satisfy our desires and purposive projects.[17] Rilke would have us move "beyond all parting," however, and forgo our grasping engagements with the draft of the open and all that hurtles therein. Consider his Sonnet XIII from *Sonnets to Orpheus* (Rilke 1985):

> Be ahead of all parting, as though it already were behind
> you, as winter, even now, passes.
> For among these winters is one so endlessly winter,
> That only in being all the more winter will your heart really
>   last.
>
> (lines 1–4)

In its place he would have us be more angelic, transforming our encounters into a kind of singing that seeks nothing but to have sung. Again, Sonnet XIII (lines 5–8) is to the point:

---

17. This supposed notion of parting leads Heidegger to link Rilke's concern with European cultural decay to a confrontation with technology. While there is something to the connection, one finds few traces of technological humanity in Rilke's poetry. Rather, one most often finds the lover, a figure that Heidegger's reading passes over in silence. To my ear, however, "lover" marks another ground word in Rilke's poetry, one that bears upon the figure of parting *(Abschied).* In fact, if we treat "parting" as a figure of eros, there seems little reason to bind it to consciousness as Heidegger insistently does. But this is another matter.

> Be ever dead in Eurydice—, climb fuller of song,
> climb fuller of praise back into the pure draft.
> Here among the vanishing, in the realm of decline, be.
> Be the sonant cup that shattered even as it rang.

In the interrelation of these figures, Heidegger finds that Rilke's poem—but again, I think he really means Rilke's poetry, for his reading moves well beyond the verses he cites at the essay's outset—"thinks the being of beings" (Heidegger 1977a, 313). In fact, he seems at times to treat ground words as theses concerning being, often comparing them to positions developed by Descartes, Leibniz, Nietzsche, and Pascal. While these identifications, as Fóti suggests, are intrusive, heavy-handed, and underdefended, the idea that being is at issue is not unreasonable, given Rilke's ongoing obsession in poems and letters with the nature of existence, human and otherwise. But how is it at issue? That is my question. In answering it, we will deepen our understanding of ur-poetry.

Elsewhere in "What Are Poets For?" Heidegger insists that being may only be engaged via an encounter with language. "Being traverses, as itself, its own province, what is marked and compassed *(temnéin, tempus)* insofar as being essentially comes to pass [*west*] in the word" (Heidegger 1977a, 310). The supposition is that thinking being is a matter of addressing it as it presents and articulates itself in and as language. One has to presume, therefore, that Rilke's ground words must do the same if, as Heidegger insists, they engage being. Unfortunately, Heidegger does not explicitly reflect upon how Rilke's ground words manage to address being. He does, however, regard Rilke's improvisational lines as an "exercise in poetic self-reflection" (ibid., 277). Moreover, toward the close of the essay, he insists that any poet able to respond to a time of need or distress—i.e., to nihilism—must delve into the essence of poetry. "The mark of these poets consists in the fact that for them the essence of poetry becomes question-worthy, for they are poetically on the track of what, for them, is to be said" (ibid., 319). These two passages suggest that Rilke's ground words not only address (or try to address) being as it presents itself but engage their own poetic nature as well. As we shall see, the efforts are related.

One the one hand, we have poetic figures (e.g., angels, an open, nature, and so on) providing presentations of being. They do so, however, only by engaging being where, to use a Heideggerian idiom, it comes to word. But where is that? Heidegger does not say, and yet, where else would poets be able to locate being as it presents itself in and as language except within their own language? Where else might the language of the poem address being except at the precise point where its own being or essence presents itself as poetry? After all, at this juncture, poems cannot posit theses or assertions that aim to represent being. Those efforts ignore how their own saying is an event of being, attending instead to that which is to be represented or posited, thereby failing to comport themselves in an originary fashion. One has the right, then, to suppose that Rilke's ground words, in concert with one another, engage being precisely through engaging their own being at its point of origin, at its *Ort*, the site wherein it comes to be a poem.

How, though, do the ground words of Rilke's poetry (or Rilke's ur-poem) manage to reach back into their own ground and engage being in their own coming to be? I think that Rilke himself (or the Rilke presented by Heidegger) can help us here.[18] In order to transform our technological partitioning of the open into a kind of praise for things, Rilke turns toward poetry as a mode of comportment. On Heidegger's reading, such a turn requires that one venture the play of language in the venture that is one's life. What this entails is less than clear, however.

Of Rilke's vision for a future humanity, Heidegger states: "the more venturesome cannot be the ones who merely say. The saying of the more venturous must genuinely venture or risk the traditional saying [*die Sage*]. The more venturesome are such only if they are sayers to a greater degree" (Heidegger 1977a, 315).[19] First, one has to ask: "What saying renders them sayers of a greater sort?" In part, they risk their linguistic inheritance in their saying, venturing past it, perhaps using it in new ways, as Rilke does in the cases of the angel and Orpheus. But that is not all: "there is a saying that fits itself into the traditional saying, without, however, reflecting upon language, whereby it would become just another object. This entry into the traditional saying characterizes a saying that follows after [*nachgehen*] something to be said solely in order to say it. That which is to be said should be, then, what, in its essence, belongs

---

18. What follows draws more out of Heidegger's text than one could reasonably claim to find there. It is thus less an interpretation than an elaboration of Heidegger's remarks into a notion that remains consistent with and enriches the general direction of thought we have encountered thus far.

19. The German *die Sage* means a legend, a saying, or even a tradition. I have thus rendered it as "traditional saying" in order to underscore that what is at issue here is a manner of speaking that has been around for some time and thus is present in the world as a "saying."

to the province of language" (ibid., 316). First, in speaking of the "province of language," Heidegger is addressing the point wherein language comes to pass as language. In other words, he is addressing the *Ort* of language, the site wherein the speaking that is language is gathered. And insofar as we are here concerned with poetic language, with poets who venture language in an exceptional fashion (i.e., to a "greater degree" than is customary either among poets or in ordinary language), I think we need to treat the province of language as the *Ort* of the poem, the site wherein poetic language is gathered into poetizing.[20] Second, note again that reflection upon language as if it were an object of theoretical concern is not the path proposed. Rather, the path concerns a saying that enters into an inherited way of speaking, e.g., the angel, and follows after it, so to speak—pursues it as something said, as what we might term in English a "figure of speech," or better still, a "poetic figure," because poetizing is the issue and not language itself.

Perhaps we might appreciate the phenomenon of a poetic figure if we consider an example of poetic repetition, contrasting it with how another text might use similar terms. In "Morro Rock" from his *River of Heaven* (1988), Garrett Hongo writes of that "chunk of continent equal to nothing":

>   the great albacore run of the Sixties,
>   men in fraying mackinaws stained with blood
>   crammed thick as D-Day on the decks
>   of an excursion or half-day boat
>   chugging slowly through light fog
>
>   (lines 19–23)

As a matter of common critical practice, words like "albacore run" and "D-Day," despite their ostensible referents, need to be understood primarily through the roles they play in the poem, e.g., thematically, rhythmically, and so on. If one looks up either word in an encyclopedia, however, the word will stand as mere signifier, a stand-in for some event

---

20. This is not to claim that all language is poetry, but that so far as "What Are Poets For?" is concerned, one arrives at the "province of language" within the language of the poem and then at its *Ort*. For the claim that in a certain sense, language is essentially poetry, see "The Origin of the Work of Art" (Heidegger 1977a, 61–63). That Heidegger is not speaking of poetry as distinct from other modes of writing is clear; he says as much. What he means is less clear, however. Unfortunately, I cannot address the matter here.

that it purportedly represents. In other words, within the poem, the words are more than signs. They are figures and they address us as such, departing, in their repetition, from the roles to which they are bound in ordinary language.

In Rilke's case, at least as read by Heidegger (and others), this move away from ordinary language is intense. As with Hongo's poem, the traditional saying is not merely repeated, the tradition not simply replayed. It is repeated without an eye on anything, that is, it is not said for the sake of anything (for that supposedly remains within the tradition of partitioning the open). Rather, it is repeated simply in order to say it; it becomes in a strict sense "something to be said," and nothing more. Those who prove more venturesome in their saying are thus poets who fit themselves into traditional figures and retune them as figures of poetizing through and through, as pure song, free from desire.[21]

It is in this pure song of the Rilkean sort that the province of language is breached (i.e., that region where the essence of language is disclosed, a region I have thus far, following Heidegger, considered in terms of the *Ort* of the language of the poem). Poetic figures are taken and presented as such, as poetizing, and they are not expected to be anything else, not tools for communication or analysis. Their nature as poetry, as language, is thus highlighted in a gesture toward the province of language.[22] But how? If the poetic figure were sufficient unto itself, we would never catch a glimpse of the province of language. Rather, that site would recede behind the figure appearing as something complete unto itself, much as the essential site of things seems to do. But insofar as the poetic figure appears as the repetition of a traditional saying, the poetic figure appears as something said (again), thus underscoring the event of its saying. And it is this poetic emphasis, one that is not a matter of rhythm but of the

---

21. Véronique Fóti, following de Man, has claimed that Rilke's figures of speech would free themselves entirely from the "referentiality of ordinary language or from what Rilke himself calls 'the languages of man': communication, conceptualization, and poetic symbolization. To dare it with language becomes, for Rilke, to approximate an absolute language no longer subservient to the constraints of comprehension and communication" (Fóti 1992, 37). I have always resisted renderings of Rilke's poetic project that recall, if only implicitly, Mallarmé's poetry without reference, and I still do. Rilke wants to translate everyday life into poetic figures—thus maintaining, at least in a dialectical manner, an essential reference to the world he would transform. Nevertheless, I failed to appreciate the subtlety of Fóti's position in an earlier response to her reading (Lysaker 1993).

22. As such, poetic figures stand in contrast to the piece of equipment whose being, Heidegger claims, at least in his "Origin of the Work of Art," lies in a reliability that enables us simply to use it without attending to its being (Heidegger 1977a, 20–21).

being of poetry, that opens for us the province of language, the site wherein language occurs, and as language, for here the figure is neither a cipher for what is other to language nor a means to some extra-poetic end.[23]

But an exposure of the precinct of language is not all that occurs in the language of those who prove more venturesome. Within their own repetitions of traditional sayings, in offering "something to be said" as a figure of poetizing (and nothing more), Rilke's poetic figures also sing of their own ground, thus sliding into ur-poetry. They reach back, recoil upon the ground of that second saying, carry it into their song, and thereby poetize poetry as well. They are thus not just poetic figures but also figures of poetizing, and in a doubled sense. They are events of poetizing and poetize poetizing. One thus finds a third saying at work in the language of the ur-poem, one in which poetic figures become ur-figures. Initially, one has a traditional saying that is repeated or re-said as a figure of speech or poetry, as an instance of language. The language of the ur-poem does not rest with that repetition, however. Instead, it returns in a third saying (or second repetition) to its own ground and figures it. And in Rilke's case, it is a figuration wrought through ur-figures such as nature, the open, the draft, the sphere of life and death, the angel, and so on.

Let us consider this second repetition with greater care, for it lies at the heart of ur-poetry. Rilke's ground words (e.g., the open, nature, the draft) are examples of traditional sayings repeated as poetic figures in Rilke's poems. That is, they are taken from extra-poetic contexts and presented as poetry. As poetic figures, they do not lie still, however. Rather, they also poetize the grounds of poetry: they not only expose the precinct of language insofar as it arises within the language of the poem, but they also figure it. And in figuring that precinct, they also figure their own saying, that saying that they underscore and throw into relief in being poetic (and not simply traditional) figures.

Note that by setting themselves and their saying within the grounds they figure, they draw that ground into the language of the poem. It is not the case, therefore, that the language of the poem somehow drags

---

23. Here I am replaying an argument from "The Origin of the Work of Art" within "What Are Poets For?" In the former essay, Heidegger argues that the createdness of the work of art exposes its lack of self-sufficiency, thus opening for us an origin whose traces can be found in the work's createdness (Heidegger 1977a, 45). I am taking the fact of repetition within the poetic figure to expose an analogous situation.

either its own *Ort* or the precinct of language from some supposed far side of language into its own saying. And thus it is not the case that the language of the poem represents its own ground. Rather, it says those sites by allowing them to manifest themselves in and through the work of autofiguration.

How, though, are we to think about "manifestation" in this context? One might treat it as a matter of expression. Not that an author's views or feelings are expressed, but that a ground (the *Ort* and the precinct of language) is expressed through its consequent (the language of the poem). I do not think that is how ur-figuration says the grounds of its own saying, however. Why not? In the expression of a ground through a consequent, the site of the conjunction of a ground and its consequents dissolves as far as the language of the poem is concerned, perhaps reopening between that language and a reader. The language of expression thus fails to do justice to the poem's *Ort* in a manner that inverts the failure we hung upon the languages of symbol, metaphor, and allegory. Whereas the latter presume what they should explain, namely, how a language is gathered into its saying, the language of expression buries that event of gathering altogether, likening the language of the poem to the side of a triangle, to a facet of a seamless, integral whole. But that is precisely what cannot be done here, given the event of gathering that is so clearly marked in the repetitions through which the language of the poem works.

If manifestation should not be thought along the lines of expression, how should one think about it? As we shall see more clearly in the next chapter (for there we will have an example on hand), the saying of the precinct of language and the *Ort* of the poem occurs in the interplay of the language of the poem, the interplay through which ur-figures speak.[24] I say this because it is only in the interplay of that language that its relationality and differences are preserved and underscored. And it is only in those relations and the differences they require that, in a dramatic fashion, the site that enables those relations is made manifest. If we were to take the event of autofiguration as a simple naming, we would find ourselves once again supposing that the language of the poem somehow

---

24. I will forgo an example here, because Heidegger believes that Rilke's poetry collapses into a would-be poetry of expression. He writes of Rilke's venturesome poets: "The song does not even first follow. The song is the belonging in the whole of the pure draft. . . . The song itself is 'a wind'" (Heidegger 1977a, 318). The identification with the wind is a strong one: this

represents its *Ort* and the precinct of language. That it cannot do, however, without begging the question and relocating it within some event we would term "representation." But if we look for the matter at hand within the interplay of the ur-figures as they recoil upon their own saying, it then remains part and parcel of that saying, of that recoil, and not as something represented but as something appearing alongside the language of the poem—or, to be more precise, the ur-poem. To use language closer to Heidegger's text, what is said in the ur-poem not only "belongs to the province of language" but also carries and exposes that province within its own autofigurations.

At this point, we should have some sense for what is entailed in an ur-poem, the poem of poetry that Heidegger seeks in the poets with whom he enters into dialogue. Such a poem is unsaid within the ostensible presentations of the language of the poem. Rather, it underwrites such presentations, determining in an event of autofiguration the being of those presentations, the being of their poetizing. And yet, ur-poetry is not other to the language of the poem. Rather, an ur-poem arises in the language of the poem (or in some of its principal figures, its ground words) and precisely as that language recoils upon its own ground. This recoil occurs when certain traditional sayings or figures are repeated as figures of poetizing and then are repeated again, such that the figures in question broach their own ground. On the pages of ur-poetry one thus finds something of a palimpsest, for lurking within certain principal figures, one can find three sayings. Initially, one has a saying that bears a tradi-

---

is a song that has become a thing alongside other things, shining like a star, or blooming like a rose, a "pure contradiction, no one's sleep under so many lids," to paraphrase Rilke's self-authored epitaph. Or, to note the close of Sonnet XIII:

> As to what is used up, as to hollow and muted
> provisions of nature, the unsayable sums,
> add yourself, joyfully, and cancel the count.
>
> (lines 12–14)

According to Heidegger, Rilke's identification with the rose, for example, loses or rather forgets the open clearing of being, which, as we shall see in Chapter 2, always fissures the pure belonging to the draft that Rilke seeks. Moreover, it sets Rilke, Heidegger suggests, within the biologism characteristic of nineteenth-century thought and thus merely replaces the representing subject with the vital, unconscious, natural one. That, at least, is the argument in the Parmenides course (Heidegger 1982b, 235). Whether this charge squares with the suggestion in "What Are Poets For?" that Rilke turns away from representation toward the heart (thus repeating Pascal) and whether either characterization of Rilke is justified remain matters for another study.

tion within itself. It is then repeated such that it is translated into the language of the poem, coming to stand as a poetic figure. That figure, that saying, is then said a third time, except that now it coils back upon its own ground as poetry, thus participating in an event of autofiguration, addressing us as a figure of poetizing.

Now, it is worth stressing that ur-poetry is not a theoretical enterprise, as if the grounds of poetry were the object of a thesis or a proposition. Rather, the ur-poem occurs in the interplay of ur-figures, in their intersections and repetitions, and thus in poetic performances that carry out the autofiguration rather than report upon it. Ur-poetry occurs in the charged chorus of ground words, not in theses borne by fancifully dressed metaphysical propositions.

While ur-poetry is a marvelously complex and reflexive affair, we miss its import altogether if we presume that Heidegger, in pursuing the ur-poem, is hoping to transform literary criticism in a radical way. Recall two passages already cited.

> Poetry is founding, the effectual grounding of what endures. The poet is the grounder of being. What we call the real in the everyday is, in the end, unreal. (Heidegger 1980, 33)

> The saying of the poet is a founding not only in the sense of a free giving, but also, and at the same time, in the sense of the firm grounding of human existence. (Heidegger 1981, 41–42)

I mention these passages because *they* recall what is at stake in regard to ur-poetry: human existence and being itself. Remarkable, almost outlandish, such suggestions seem hopelessly inflated. And yet they are what drive Heidegger's conversation with the poets, and to a large extent I share his enthusiasm. I therefore want to take the notion of the ur-poem and bring it into this more radical, far-reaching context. Only then, with a sense of its import, will we appreciate what Heidegger hears in the language of the poem and what that hearing opens for us who read after him, particularly those of us who hope to make sense of the event that prompted this inquiry: Rilke's truncated torso of Apollo, fixing us, demanding, "you must change your life."

2

Living Poetry

At this point we have some sense for what orients Heidegger's dialogue with the poets: ur-poems, poems *of* poetry, and in two senses: such poems concern poetry (in fact, the grounds of poetry) through events of autofiguration. And precisely because autofiguration is at issue, ur-poems belong to and even issue from the poetry they figure.

I am drawn to the language of ur-poetry because it provides us with one way of characterizing how the language of the poem addresses us: through repetitions of traditional sayings that recast them as poetic figures that recoil upon the grounds of their own saying. I now aim to explore the import of ur-poetry's reflexive repetitions, for in those coils, we will experience the claim that ur-poetry has upon our lives. Let us return to Heidegger, for he attributes to poetry a remarkable import,

import of the kind that Rilke registers when he writes, facing a torso of Apollo: "for there is no point / that does not see you. You must change your life." As we shall see, ur-poetry sounds us out in this way by addressing being itself.

Ur-poetry addresses being? An exceptionally radical thought, and one that concerns, in part, what poems are for, or, more generally, what *poets* are for (to recall the title of Heidegger's 1946 essay on Rilke). Admittedly, the question sounds pretentious, even presumptuous. Should a philosopher tell poets what they or their poems are for? I do not think so. Why? In part, because inspiration does not seem to work that way. As Marina Tsvetayeva writes: "But—whether by command or by plea, by fear or by pity the elements overcome us, there are no reliable approaches—neither Christian, nor civic, nor any other kind. There is no approach to art, for it is a seizing. (While you are still approaching, it has already seized you.)" (Proffer 1976, 182). Poets have enough trouble keeping the muse around. I doubt, therefore, that she will find my pleas (or worse yet, my commands) any more compelling. Also, I doubt that any poet worth his or her salt would listen if philosophers did provide assignments.[1] But then, the question "What are poets for?" does not seek an answer that would provide such a command, at least not when Heidegger asks it, nor when I here repeat it.

When Heidegger asked "What are poets for?" in 1946, he did so amid the nihilism that he found characteristic of metaphysics, a nihilism that he aligned with the spread of modern technology. And he suggested that poetry, Hölderlin's poetry in particular, had the power to turn people *(a)* away from technological rationality (a mode of disclosure founded upon an almost insistent forgetting of its own origin), *(b)* away from the markets that such rationality makes possible, and *(c)* toward the basic character of their being. Over a decade earlier, Heidegger also turned to Hölderlin for direction, claiming that "the fundamental happening of the historical *dasein* of human beings" comes to pass poetically (Heidegger 1980, 36). But "direction" skews the matter. Heidegger did not turn to

---

1. This is not to say that there have not been doctrine-driven or even "state" poems. The history of twentieth-century Russian and Polish poetry offers us many examples, some delivered under extreme duress—e.g., Osip Mandelstam's celebratory Stalin poem or Mayakovsky's late work. And yet, those histories also suggest that a far superior poetry arose in resistance to "party lines": Akhmatova, Brodsky, Herbert, Mandelstam, Milosz, and Szymborska, for example. Generalizing from these instances, it strikes me as ludicrous to suppose that one might compel a generation's true talents to adopt a systematic program.

Hölderlin for adornment or for the lyric presentation of an encrypted philosophical project. In fact, not only was Hölderlin *not* supposed to be subjected to the rulings of philosophy, but he was also to be the measure of this epoch: "We do not want to measure Hölderlin according to our time, but the opposite: we want to bring ourselves and those to come under the measure of the poet" (ibid., 4).

What is sought in the question "What are poets for?" is thus not some prescription that might govern poetry. Rather, whatever authority is at work here rests with poetry, with the measures it provides. Note that I say "poetry" and not "the poets." The point is not to hitch up the poets and give them free rein. Poetizing itself is the issue. In fact, Heidegger denies that any subjectivity dictates what comes to pass in the language of the poem *qua* measure, whether it be that of the poet, the critic, or the philosopher. What he says of Hölderlin (in the McNeill/Davis translation) is instructive in this regard:

> This poet's poetizing does not revolve around the poet's own ego. . . . What has for a long time hindered modern, contemporary human beings, who think in terms of self-consciousness and subjectivity, from hearing this poetry is simply this: The fact that Hölderlin poetizes purely from out of that which, in itself, essentially prevails as that which is to be poetized. When Hölderlin poetizes the essence of the poet, he poetizes relations that do not have their ground in the "subjectivity" of human beings. (Heidegger 1996b, 165)[2]

But what is meant by a "measure" that does not have its ground in subjectivity? And is that what poets are for, to provide a measure? In a way, yes. And yet, the question misleads if we take "providing a measure" to be some task brought to the labors of poetry from beyond its borders, as if one were to say: "enough pleasure for the day, let's have a measure." We would do better to pursue the question phenomenologically, focusing upon the language of the poem. Does anything like a measure arise?

---

2. For a similar claim, see "Language." Concerning Trakl's "Winter Evening," Heidegger writes: "That he [Trakl] is the poet remains unimportant here, as with every other greatly successful poem. Great success stands precisely with the fact that it can well deny the poet's person and name" (Heidegger 1985, 15). The thought recalls Robert Frost's claim that "a poem may be worked over once it is in being, but may not be worried into being. Its most precious quality will remain its having run itself and carried away the poet with it" (Frost 1986, iii).

Perhaps the question will seem less intrusive if I make plain that many poets themselves desire a response to the query "What are poets for?" Consider the closing lines from "Asphodel, That Greeny Flower," by William Carlos Williams (1965).

> My heart rouses
>   thinking to bring you news
>   of something
> that concerns you
>   and concerns many men. Look at
>   what passes for the new.
> You will not find it there but in
>   despised poems.
>   It is difficult
> to get news from poems
>   yet men die miserably every day
>   for lack
> of what is found there.
>   Hear me out
>   for I too am concerned
> and every man
>   who wants to die at peace in his bed
>   besides.

These lines appear again and again in the prose (and poetry) of poets. Invoked by writers as diverse as Dana Gioia, Robert Pinsky, and Adrienne Rich, these lines conjure and press questions.[3] What is of concern to many, particularly the dying? What concerns those addressed by the poem, including "you" and presumably the speaker as well? Whatever it is, the new lacks it, or rather, what passes for the new. The key lies in poetry. But what is found there?

In a way, I have provided one response already: ur-poems are found there.[4] But why might ur-poems be of concern? The interests of poets

---

3. Gioia and Pinsky invoke the lines in accounts of what poetry could or even should be for "America," while Rich names an entire collection of essays on poetry and politics *What Is Found There* (Gioia 1992, 19–20; Pinsky 1988, 86; Rich 1993).

4. This is not to say that Williams has ur-poetry in mind. However, the question raised in "Asphodel" has left the confines of this particular poem and fallen into the hands of a general discourse of and about poetry. I see no problem, therefore, in providing responses that Williams never considered.

like Gioia, Pinsky, and Rich revolve around the ends toward which poems labor. Have ur-poems anything to say to them? Recalling her youth, one uneasy in the pews of T. S. Eliot's verse, Adrienne Rich writes: "I was exceptionally well grounded in formal technique, and I loved the craft. What I was groping for was something larger, a sense of vocation, what it means to live as a poet—not how to write poetry, but wherefore?" (Rich 1993, 196).[5] "Vocation," from the Latin *vocare*, "to call," is a strong word, full of Christian connotations: the divine calls one to a profession, perhaps a religious one, and in every case, to salvation. It is also a strange word, and not just because one would be hard-pressed to argue that present employment opportunities have been prepared for particular individuals by a deity. Under economic conditions governed by exchange value, the very idea of a profession oriented toward ends whose value is not a matter of the going price is equally strange—perhaps even more so because, at least in the United States, Christianity still thrives, Nietzsche's autopsy notwithstanding. On my reading, Rich seeks the second strangeness, that of a profession; she desires an understanding of her craft that includes a sense for what its practice realizes.[6] If a physician contributes to the realization of health, to what end does poetry move?

I think that Heidegger's "What are poets for?" leads us toward that which Rich seeks. (The question is also of import for readers, for cogent responses will offer readers something to read for, or, more precisely, they will offer readers a sense for what is at stake in the language of the poem.) Heidegger even writes of the poet's "vocation"—*Berufung*, from *rufen*, "to call." Reading Hölderlin's "The Ister," he writes of poets as those who have received a calling, claiming that the call arrives as a gift, the gift of a date, a present. That present has its own character, however, for its "now," Heidegger says, "names the time of the calling of those

---

5. Interestingly, Rich found this question in an encounter with Rilke's "Torso." She writes: "*Du musst dein Leben ändern.* No poem had ever said it quite so directly. At twenty-two it called me out of a kind of sleepwalking. I knew, even then, that for me poetry wasn't enough as something to be appreciated, finely fingered: it could be a fierce, destabilizing force, a wave pulling you further out than you thought you wanted to be. *You have to change your life*" (Rich 1993, 191).

6. In a letter to Elizabeth Bishop, Marianne Moore expresses a similar desire as she chastises Yeats for lacking a wherefore: "I would be 'much disappointed in you' if you *could* feel about Yeats as some of his acolytes seem to feel. An 'effect,' an exhaustively great sensibility (with insensibility?) and genius for word-sounds and sentences. But after all, what is this enviable apparatus for? if not to change our mortal psycho-structure" (Bishop 1984, 146).

called, a time of the poet. Such a time is determined from out of that which the poets are called to poetize in their poetry" (Heidegger 1984, 8). This passage is remarkable, albeit in a complex way. First, it suggests that the calling of the poet, the actual presentation of the vocation, is received as a gift (that is, it does not result from the poet's own efforts). Second, the calling arrives in its own time, and that time is in fact the gift—the poet's own time. Poetic time does not arrive already formed, however, as new calendars to replace the old. Rather, poetic time occurs in the poet's own poetizing and in a unique way: "Moreover, in each instance, poetic time is different, following the essential manner of the poetry and the poet. For all essential poetry itself also poetizes *anew* the essence of poetry" (ibid.). In other words, according to Heidegger, poets are called to poetize poetry, to figure in their poetry the time of their own calling to be poets. They are called to write autofigurative ur-poems and that is something for which poets might be.

You might still be suspicious, for I know that a question like "What are poets for?" has a utilitarian ring. You might object, recalling Wilde, and say: "Art is for itself." "No artist has ethical sympathies," Wilde writes. "An ethical sympathy in an artist is an unpardonable mannerism of style. . . . All art is quite useless" (Wilde 1930, 69). One wants to know, of course, what "ethical sympathies" entail, and what state "useless" signifies, but I take the point to be that the work of art should not be subordinated to extra-artistic goals such as moral cultivation. Rather, art concerns beauty, the revelation of beauty through beautiful things: "The artist is the creator of beautiful things. To reveal art and conceal the artist is art's aim" (ibid.). Accept, for the moment, Wilde's claim. I would still insist that what is useless, at least on Wilde's terms, nevertheless answers the query. After all, to be for the sake of beautiful things, even by being an instance thereof, is to move toward an end. To be *for* its own sake is thus to have no less an answer to the question "What are poets for?" than those who prefer to cultivate virtue.

I am defending the following claim. If we ask "What are poets for?" we need not, at least not necessarily, subject the work of art to some kind of utilitarianism. One could ask what consequences follow from the writing and reading of poems, but if we pose the question in this way, we will suppose that our sense of the wherefore of poetry must arise beyond the language of the poem, lying instead in the priorities of a cost-benefit analysis. But we need not behave so. Instead, let us consider what the poetry tells us. If we do, we will not need to subject poetry to some external measure, such as the public good, in order to ask "not how to write poetry, but wherefore?" Rather, we can simply ask: "What is found there?"

Once we see that one can ask "What are poets for?" outside the confines of utilitarianism, I think we have a response to an objection implicit in Tsvetayeva's swirling, brilliant, and occasionally baffling "Art in the Light of Conscience." She writes, as if contradicting Williams: "The doctor and the priest are more needed than the poet because they are at the deathbed, and we are not." She is able to make this claim because she presumes that priests and doctors offer some social service (one that contributes to the common good), whereas poets do not. In fact, she goes so far as to claim: "if you wish to serve God or man [sic], if you have any wish to serve, to work for the good, then join the Salvation Army or something like that—and give up poetry" (Proffer 1976, 183, 184). This is not to say that poetry cannot be useful, but that it must go its own way and thus cannot guarantee any net utility. "Art is the same as nature," she insists. "Don't seek in it other laws than its own" (ibid., 145).

Writing in 1932, in self-chosen exile from the Soviet Union (she left less out of frustration with the Bolsheviks than out of a desire to be with her husband, who had fought with the Whites), Tsvetayeva stubbornly refuses to subordinate art to any external measure. But are we so certain that art's laws—if the essence of art is in fact subject to "laws"—have nothing to say to the dying? What is odd about Tsvetayeva's claim is neither that she denies that poetry contributes to the common good in a manner on par with the efforts of doctors or priests, nor that she would leave art to its own laws, but that she assumes that there is nothing about us that might stand in need of what poetry has to offer, irrespective of net utility. Williams, a doctor himself, must have found in poetry something other than rage for those waning in the dying of the light. No doubt you have surmised that I think ur-poetry may offer such medicine. At this point, however, I am only insisting that one need not subordinate the work of art to external measures in order to suggest that it has some import for human life.

Following Heidegger, I have suggested that one finds within the language of some poetry what I call ur-poems, poems of poetry that provide a measure capable of grounding being and orienting our lives. Let us now explore what such a measure involves, how ur-poetry fashions it, and how it might change a life. The key to Heidegger's notion of a poetic measure lies, I believe, in his discussions of "dwelling." In "Building,

Dwelling, Thinking," Heidegger claims that dwelling involves the fundamental character of human beings: it is "the way in which mortals are upon the earth." "Dwelling," he adds, ". . . is the fundamental relation of being according to which mortals are" (Heidegger 1954a, 142, 155). Allow me to amplify.

At base, dwelling concerns the essence of human existence, that is, the basic manner(s) in which human existence occurs or presences. (Recall that "essence" need neither denote nor connote a stable, ahistorical ground that delimits what a human being is or can be.) Thus one might cast human dwelling in terms of a divine creation such that each facet of human presencing (sleeping, digesting, giving birth, talking on the phone, looking through a microscope, and so on) manifests the efficient and final causality of a creator. Or, following Peirce, at the end of inquiry one might find among every human manner of presencing the articulation of universal laws, i.e., thirds, and thus find in human dwelling the articulation of a cosmological semiotic. Or one might think that human dwelling revolves around how human beings—and those with and among whom we presence—are represented. On this account, humans would dwell among representations. Now, one should note that with regard to the question of dwelling, it does not matter if one understands representation materially or dualistically—that is, as the achievement of a mind or a brain. Nor, for that matter, does it matter if one understands representation in terms of the synapses of a solitary subject or the worldview of a collective subjectivity, say a culture, society, or class. In each case, humans would dwell through and among representations. Representations would define the "fundamental relation of being according to which mortals are."

According to Heidegger, humans presence or dwell among various things (e.g., stones, planets, lungs, neighbors, flowers) whose totality he terms the "world."[7] In other words, human dwelling is a relational affair, bound to other beings with which we share the world. I am, Heidegger would insist, never human in isolation, but always engaged with things,

---

7. I should note that in this chapter I offer a skeletal account of dwelling and forgo a detailed analysis of the contours of dwelling elaborated by Heidegger in the 1950s. I do so because the elaborate account works out of Hölderlin's ur-poetry (note the ground words "earth," "sky," "divinities," and "mortals," all taken from Hölderlin's work). Those discussions thus reflect a particular way of dwelling, not dwelling as it must be. Because my goal is only to clarify the concept of dwelling and not to explore Hölderlin's ur-poetry as read by Heidegger, I have elected to streamline Heidegger's account.

events, and persons. Human dwelling thus concerns manifold worldly relations, not simply the occurrence of an atomistic creature.

At this juncture, a reader of Jürgen Habermas might ask that we refine the concept of dwelling along the lines of categorically distinct relations orienting human being-in-the-world, namely, relations to *(a)* an external world of things, *(b)* an intersubjective world of persons, and *(c)* an inner world of self-relation.[8] While it might be intensely fruitful to regard these relations as distinct—particularly if, as Habermas argues, inquiries into these domains are oriented around different conceptions of validity, i.e., propositional truth, justice, and authenticity—it strikes me as misleading to parse out our being in the world categorically along these lines. Why? These relations are not originary. Rather, in each case, they begin in an event of co-presencing. At base, both parties share a world of presencing such that these relations are possible in the first place. The world of co-presencing underwriting these relations becomes evident when two points are considered. First, consider the relations that underwrite and enable the reconstructive social science that Habermas employs in order to generate the theory of communicative action out of which these characterizations are drawn. One finds self-world relations between theorists and their phenomena that displace the would-be originary status of their views in favor of the relations upon which those posits are parasitic. Second, and without any meta-theoretical considerations, note that we can relate to the same being in more than one way. For example, when training for a race, we can relate to ourselves as subjects in need of discipline and as objects in need of nourishment. Likewise, a dermatologist can relate to a patient as another subject engaged in a doctor-patient relationship as well as an ensemble of skin cells, some of which are afflicted by a virus. One can also reasonably argue about whether cats and dogs, for example, belong only to the world of things or to the intersubjective world as well. Finally, when another human dies, our intersubjective relation with that human evaporates, and we are left relating to a thing, a corpse. From all of these examples I draw the following conclusion. These categorically distinct relations are not originary but

---

8. Such a reader could draw (as I do) upon Habermas's social-theoretical inquiries as he presents them in his *Theory of Communicative Action* (1984, 1987a) and as he brings them to bear upon Heidegger's thought in *The Philosophical Discourse of Modernity* (1987b) and *Postmetaphysical Thinking* (1993). Because Habermas does not consider the question of dwelling in these or other texts, I am constructing an objection on his behalf that addresses the question of dwelling.

are determinations made by humans within preexisting relationships. And because such relations are not originary, they cannot sufficiently account for how we dwell.[9] Instead, one needs to burrow beneath them into the relations they presume, and that is what the concept of dwelling aims to do.

For Heidegger, dwelling concerns the originary character of human presencing, and his claim is that we are relational, i.e., worldly beings. But that is not all. Heidegger would also argue that insofar as we are fundamentally relational beings, our dwelling occurs within a dimension of presencing, a dimension wherein relations are possible in the first place, say between a creator and its creations, a causally bound pair, or a subject and the world that it represents to itself.[10] Now, the dimension is neither a thing nor an ensemble of things, nor is it the world within which we and the things with which we live come to pass in relation to one another. Rather, it is the difference between things, ourselves, and the world, that is, the ensemble of relations that surrounds us—e.g., tables, chairs, an atmosphere, plants, a rainy day. It is the differential dimension in and through which things become, interact, and pass away. In the essay "Language," delivered just one year prior to "Building, Dwelling, Thinking" and "... poetically dwells the human ...," Heidegger writes: "The difference is the dimension insofar as it appraises world and thing, each to their own. Its appraisal first opens the out of and toward one another of world and thing" (Heidegger 1985, 23).

In thinking about the dimension, one must be careful not to bind its differing and relational powers to the synthetic or analytic labors of a subject, pre-reflective or otherwise. Cognition at any level only transpires within and along the corridors of the difference that enables the relations presumed by any act of synthesis or analysis. After all, if I

---

9. One should not think that these brief remarks have taken up all of Habermas's objections to Heidegger, some of which have been around since 1959, such as the argument that the fabled Heideggerian turn is only an attempt to make sense of the failure of National Socialism and Heidegger's own political debacle (Habermas 1983). However, my goal is only to address critically a counter-intuition to the notion of dwelling in order to clarify it further.

10. I prefer the language of a dimension of presencing to that of a horizon of disclosure, if only because in the metaphors of "horizon" and "disclosure," the latter seems always to refer us back, if only implicitly, to an apprehending subject; the dimension of presencing is not merely the open field of perception within which a subject moves about the world but also that arena within which such a field (or even a worldview) might occur. This marks a change from my earlier explorations of the matter in "Heidegger's Absolute Music" (Lysaker 2000). Note also that Heidegger's own use of *Dimension* in the 1950s marks a departure from his earlier distrust of the rhetoric of *Dimensionalität* (Heidegger 1989, 382).

engage a thing, I am in relation to it, and thus presume whatever affords me that relation. This is not simply a matter of self-world relation, however, but of self-relations as well. Insofar as I am able to relate to myself, an event transpires whereby my apprehension is differentiated from that which is apprehended. By the time "I think," then, reflectively or otherwise, "I" am always already transpiring within the folds of a differential dimension, and dwelling is precisely the matter of how I transpire there, in the difference, undergoing relations with myself, other people, and things.

We might consider the dimension of presencing from another angle, one bound to the rhetoric of "being." My claim is that dwelling, bound as it is to a differential dimension of presencing, is intrinsically related to being. Now, one might wonder what it means to undergo a relation with being. No doubt our discussion could remain with this question for the rest of the book. In lieu of that, allow me a brief account of what I take to be some of the essential aspects of that relation. To speak of being is to speak of how beings come to presence, how they come to be the particular beings they are. A relation to being is thus not a matter of ontological traits that one apprehends in something that is already there in the world. Rather, at stake in the question of being is the very event of presencing within (and as) a world, the event whereby beings come to be "there" in the first place, and thus become available to sensation, perception, judgment, and inquiry. "Being" thus concerns the birth of sense (or significance) itself, the way in which a being occurs as the determinate being it is. To undergo a relation with being is thus not to reflect upon some being or its essential traits, even if such traits are termed ontological. Rather, undergoing a relation with being entails presencing as the kind of being one is within a dimension of presencing. In other words, a relation to being is simply a determinate or characteristic relation to the differential dimension of presencing, for it is there that sense first occurs.

Having clarified, I hope, what dwelling entails—a characteristic way of engaging a differentiated dimension of presencing—we are now in position to consider its relation to poetry. In ". . . poetically dwells the human . . . ," Heidegger claims: "Poetizing is the originary allowance-of-dwelling" (Heidegger 1954a, 196). At the heart of dwelling, therefore, Heidegger finds poetizing. Or, to be more precise, that which brings us into relation with the dimension of presencing wherein we dwell itself occurs or comes to pass in poetizing. According to Heidegger, then, poetizing holds the measure for human dwelling. But what could this mean? On Heidegger's view, dwelling is intimately bound to "building," and vice versa. As we have seen, dwelling involves our standing within what Heidegger regards as a dimension of presencing. And yet, he claims in ". . . poetically dwells the human . . ." that we are able to dwell amid and within presencing if and only if the dimension has been "measured" or "surveyed," which is to say, if and only if the dimension is rendered determinate (ibid., 189). But then, there can be no measuring building unless we are already dwelling, unless we are already arising within a dimension of presencing. As he writes in "Building, Dwelling, Thinking," "Only when we are able to dwell can we build" (ibid., 155). The two are equally primordial. Why? Consider the reverse. What would a pure, differential dimension entail? Note first that difference requires relation; some X is different from some Y. Or, X occurs at different times or in different places. Second, such difference must be determinate. "Difference" is not a trait that any one being might have. Rather, through the kind of being it is, and in relation to another presence (which might be itself in a different time and/or place), X is different. Now, one might suppose that we could speak of a dimension without difference and thus conceive of a dimension not already measured or made determinate. But if one removes the differences from the matter at hand the dimension devolves into an utter void. I say "utter" because it could not stand in any relation to any other presence, that is, it could not lie here or there, or exist now or then, for then it would belong to a determinate, differential dimension. It would seem, therefore, that not only would a nondifferential dimension be inarticulable (for in positing it we would bring it into relation with ourselves and thus return it to a determinate, differential dimension), but that it simply would not be. I think we can conclude, therefore, that there is no dimension per se, only a given one, one already measured. But then, and this is no doubt easier to see, neither is there building or measuring apart from some dimension—such a building would have no dimensions.

This interplay between dwelling and building recalls the interplay between *Lichtung* and *Einrichtung* underscored in "The Origin of the Work of Art." In discussing how truth comes to pass in the *work* of art, Heidegger insists that the unconcealment of beings occurs only within a doubled event involving a "clearing of openness" and an "arranging across the open" (Heidegger 1977a, 49). The argument is much the same. Truth, in the sense of unconcealment, comes to pass within an open field that is only open relative to some arrangement, some set of determinate presences. "The openness of this open, that is, truth, can be what it is, namely *this* openness, only if and as long as it arranges itself within its open. Hence there must always be some being in this open in which openness takes its stand and attains its constancy" (ibid., 48).[11]

This interdependence between building and dwelling is crucial for an understanding of poetry's measure and its role in human dwelling, for poetizing is, according to Heidegger, building *par excellence.*

> But dwelling happens only if poetizing takes place and comes to pass, and indeed in the way of . . . the measure-taking for all measuring. This measure-taking is itself the most proper, not a bare gauging with ready-made yardsticks for the preparation of maps. Likewise, poetizing is not building in the sense of raising and fitting buildings. Rather, poetizing, as the most proper appraisal of the dimension of dwelling, is inceptual building. Before anything else, poetizing admits the dwelling of human beings into its essence. Poetizing is the originary allowance-of-dwelling. (Heidegger 1954a, 196)

Poetizing is an arranging of the dimension at its inception, an event of originary figuration. Poetizing is thus originary "measure-taking." It does not simply measure a given dimension or area, say a yard, a state, a planet, a solar system, a universe, and the like, but *poetizes the measure of a differentiated dimension of presencing.* This is not to say that it names things or names a world or that it offers a theory about such things. Rather, it measures out how things come to pass, manifesting a world, and how a world unfolds around and through the things that belong to it, e.g., the way in which an animal belongs to a forest, a table to a chair, or a building to an era.

Now, it is through this "most proper appraisal" that poetizing builds a site for human dwelling. In arranging a dimension, in providing a measure, poetizing outfits a dwelling-place such that we might dwell there. More concretely, poetizing opens and determines for us a way of being in the world among things, a way of inhabiting the dimension that spans the difference between world and thing, the difference that enables beings

---

11. One can find a similar claim in *Contributions to Philosophy:* "The clearing must ground itself into [or across] its open. It needs what holds it in openness, and that is in each instance a being (thing-tool-work)" (Heidegger 1989, 389).

to belong to a world and yet not dissolve into it, mere facets of a larger, integral whole.

At this point, at least two questions press themselves upon us: "What is involved in originarily 'appraising' a dimension? And how does this activity facilitate dwelling?" Let us begin with the former. As noted earlier, one cannot apprehend the dimension as if it were some object alongside other presences. Rather, one must throw it into relief through building, for building presumes it. Appraisal is thus not a rarefied form of poetic intuition. Instead, it must take place alongside building, which in this case involves the production of poetic determinations.

Consider an example. Around ten years ago, after an already distinguished career, A. R. Ammons published *Garbage* (1993), a poem ironically described at its outset as "that great poem / the world's waiting for," one of "those celestial guidance systems" (part 1, lines 3–4, 54). The poem, dense and rich beyond what I shall say, presents us with a figure, a garbage mound, "which is about the pre-socratic idea of the / dispositional axis from stone to wind, wind / to stone," which is to say, it is about the generation of form, matter, and sense, of persons, twigs, and waste, of thumbnails, paper plates, and uranium deposits. It is about what is as it occurs (part 2, lines 46–48).

The conceit works by taking the transmutations that govern the "life" of the mound as the play of an energy that moves through and animates all things as "eternity's glint: it all wraps back round, / into and out of form, palpable and impalpable" (part 2, lines 92–93). Interestingly, this conceit is never reduced to the material or the spiritual, a reduction that would define the mound within figures blandly inherited from the history of metaphysics. Instead, both descriptions appear and play off one another without resolution, leaving us to ask:

> but what about the spirit, does it die
>
> in an instant, being nothing in an instant out of
> matter, or does it hold on to some measure of
>
> time, not just the eternity in which it is not,
> but does death go on being death for a billion
>
> years: this one fact put down is put down
> forever, is it, or for forever, forever to be a

> part of the changes about it, switches in the
> earth's magnetic field, asteroid collisions,
>
> tectonic underplays, to be molten and then not
> molten, again and again: when does a fact end:
>
> (part 5, lines 64–74)

The life of the garbage mound is, therefore, and thus the lives of whatever emerges therein are neither simply spirit nor matter, but both, and in such a way that their opposition is overcome without one becoming the other. Concerning the garbage mound, the poem thus directs us toward the nexus wherein what we might call matter (e.g., elements) is always turning over into what we might call spirit (e.g., form).

Not only does the poem avoid crass dualisms or their simple inversion, but the work of transmutation along the "dispositional axis" that is termed a "spindle of energy" never becomes a thing among the things produced. Rather, *Garbage* announces: "only born die, and if something is / born or new, then that is not it, that is not / the it: the it is the indifference of all the / differences, the *nothingness of all the poised / somethings,* the finest issue of energy *in* which / boulders and dead stars float" (part 3, lines 72–77 [emphases mine]). The nexus of spirit and matter, of elements and forms, is thus no-thing, but an impossibly fine web of energies within which the celestial and the earthly, the human and the animal and even trash float.

Finally, we also find the conceit brilliantly woven into syntactic elements. One almost never finds periods in the poem.[12] Instead, one encounters the colon (:). I take this to say several things. First, forms (e.g., sentences, phrases, syntactic operations such as taking direct objects) unfold continuously within the mound. Their birth and transformation seem never to cease, and thus the full stop of the period would prove out of place. Second, the colon is a graphic instance of the hinge upon which the birth and transformation of forms turns. Its continual presence throughout the poem thus indicates the axis along which the language of the poem travels, one meaning moving on toward and into another, one form brushing up against another. If we take the poem at its word, then, every colon is crackling with the "finest issues of energy" as it holds the

---

12. The sole exception comes at the end of the poem, and it marks, to my mind, a shortcoming. Better to have been more rigorous and left the end open to the transformations that no doubt await it: mold, a reading, mulch, a changed life, and a flame, for instance.

poem together and yet keeps its parts apart, preventing its forms and its meanings from collapsing in on themselves, allowing words, phrases, and sections to have their say and yet belong to the poem. Third, and with great humor, the colon (given that word's polyvalence) marks the chute through which all meaning, syntax, form, and so on must travel. When *Garbage* asks whether it will seem "a poem about garbage" or whether its "abstract, hollow junk" will "seem beautiful / and necessary as just another offering to the / high assimilations" one must answer "yes" to both sides of the question (part 4, lines 16, 17–19).

Using Ammons as an example, let us return to our exploration of the nature of poetic appraisal. In reading Hölderlin's "Germania," Heidegger distinguishes between the beginning *(Beginn)* and an inception *(Anfang)*, tethering the latter to the *Ursprung,* or origination. A beginning marks the actual onset of something: Heidegger offers the example of a change in the weather, which "begins" with an event such as a storm. The inception, however, lies in the atmospheric changes that lead to the storm. Thus a "[b]eginning is that with which something commences, an inception that from which something originates, leaps forth" (Heidegger 1980, 3). The inception thus marks an inceptual gathering of elements that results in a certain event. It is origination, the source from which some event leaps forth.[13] If poetizing is inceptual building, then it must "appraise" the dimension at the scene of its emergence, in its leaping forth. But if the dimension only comes to be alongside of a "surveying," in order to catch the dimension at the scene of its emergence one must catch it as it opens in and alongside its surveyance. Or, to use the language of "The Origin of the Work of Art," the task involves "appraising" the clearing of openness within the arranging "sites filled by present beings" (Heidegger 1977a, 48). But is not poetry responsible for the surveyance? Indeed. Appraising thus involves tracking the gathering of the dimension within the poem's own language.

On the reading being developed here, poetic appraisal takes place when the language of the poem arranges and establishes the dimension or an open by tracking that opening within the poem's own language. As we have already seen, tracking of this nature occurs in ur-poems, the kind of poetizing that figures itself. In the Ammons poem, this occurs in various ways, none of which are or can be propositional. After all, if one

---

13. Heidegger offers the same distinction almost twenty years later in the 1951–52 course published as *Was Heisst Denken?* (Heidegger 1954b, 98). Note also that the *Sprung* of *Ursprung* means, among other things, "leap," and thus one might think of the origination of presencing along the lines of a leap into the determinate dimension of presencing.

ascribes a predicate to a subject (claiming that "X is Y"), one presumes *(a)* the presence of X, *(b)* one's own presence, and *(c)* one's relation to X, focusing instead on the assignment of a predicate and, presuming a sense of responsibility is operative, the veracity of that assignment. In doing so, however, one fails to engage the form of the proposition as a form, and necessarily, for the proposition lacks the reflexivity required for engagements with its origin. What is needed is not a new predicate, therefore, but a way of presenting the event that enables predication, among other things. This failing not only delimits the reach of propositional thinking in relation to originary matters but also makes evident a challenge facing those who would read ur-poetry: one cannot do justice to the figurative coils of ur-poetry within an ensemble of propositions. Rather, one must try to trace and show how the language of the poem tracks its own emergence.

Given the limits of propositional speech, should one conclude that appraisal of the dimension of human dwelling is not a matter of naming, of semantic figures that refer us in some fashion to the grounds of signification? This seems too hasty. As John Sallis has argued, even an articulation of the failure of naming involves a kind of naming, if under erasure (Sallis 1990). Second, does the Ammons poem not direct us toward its source, and with names, e.g., "spindle of energy," "dispositional axis"? These figures are not incidental to the ur-poetic power of *Garbage*, for they (and the history they bear) invoke grounds, their own included. But that is not all there is to the appraisal taking place in *Garbage*. The language of the poem also plays these names off one another, resulting, as we saw with "spirit" and "matter," in the emergence of a question concerning that which neither figure can properly name: their interdependence, the site of their entwinement, and the events that conjunction ushers in, namely, the birth of forms, of meanings, and ultimately of sense itself, of the manner in which beings presence. And that includes the forms, meanings, and sense of the poem itself, a fact evident when the figure of the garbage mound, with its endless transmutations, turns back upon the poem itself, as in the following passages: "there is a mound, / too, in the poet's mind dead language is hauled / off to and burned down on, the energy held and / shaped into new turns and clusters, the mind / strengthened by what it strengthens" (part 2, lines 62–66).[14] And less directly:

---

14. I am purposefully avoiding the distinction between sense and meaning as well as the discussions surrounding it, for the matter at hand is not, as we have seen, bound to propositions.

>   but we are natural: nature, not
>
> we, gave rise to us: we are not, though, though
> natural, divorced from higher, finer configurations:
>
> tissues and holograms of energy circulate in
> us and seek and find representations of themselves
>
> outside us, so that we can participate in
> celebrations high and know reaches of feeling
>
> and sight and thought that penetrate (really
> penetrate) far, far beyond these our wet cells,
>
> right on up past our stories, the planets, moons,
> and other bodies
> . . . .
>   oh yes, in the abiding where
> mind but nothing else abides, the eternal,
>
> until it turns into another pear or sunfish
>   (part 2, lines 74–84, 87–89)

And finally, right at the outset of *Garbage:*

> Creepy little creepers are insinuatingly
> curling up my spine (bringing the message)
>
> . . . .
> the world's waiting for: don't you know you
>
> have an unaccomplished mission unaccomplished;
> someone somewhere may be at this very moment
>
> dying for the lack of what W. C. Williams says
> you could (or somebody could) be giving
>   (part 1, lines 1–2, 4–8)

In fact, it necessarily precedes them. From the standpoint of poetic appraisal, one would have to regard the proposition as one form among the many littering this cosmic heap.

An appraisal of human dwelling is thus a multifaceted affair, involving the intersection of multiple figures ("dispositional axis," ":," "spirit," "matter") that, through their interrelation, direct us toward a scene of emergence, an *Ort*. That is, dances of figures push past themselves to the horizonal rim of their origin, only in order to fall off, taking us with them. And yet, they suspend us there as well, exposed to a world rich in determination yet bound to an open clearing, a differential dimension (neither thing nor world) in which those determinations, ourselves, and the things of the world come to pass. Or, to talk trash:

> dance
> peopling the centers and distances, the faraway
> galactic slurs even, luminescences, plasmas,
> those burns, the same principle: but here on
> the heights, terns and flies avoid the closest
> precincts of flame, the terrifying transformations,
> the disappearances of anything of interest,
> morsel, gobbet, trace of maple syrop, fat
> worm
>
> (part 4, lines 32–40)

We might clarify matters if we recall our discussion of how figures of poetizing expose and figure their own ground. Recall that the process begins with the repetition of traditional sayings; in the case of *Garbage*, say, "dispositional axis." Such repetitions are presented as poetic figures, that is, their occurrence within the language of a poem is underscored. But that is not all, for in a second repetition, the figures draw their own grounds into themselves, become ur-figures or figures of poetizing in a double sense: they not only belong to poetizing but figure it as well. How? According to a self-referential logic—and *Garbage* follows one out explicitly—the ground figures invoke a ground to which they belong, and they allow it to manifest itself in and through their interplay. And this interplay is the key, as we saw with spirit and matter in *Garbage*. Through the grounding relations played out in the language of the poem, the ur-poem exposes and throws into relief the opened dimension of presencing that takes place in but nevertheless enables that figurative play, even at its highest pitch of reflexivity.

My claim, then, is that poetic appraisal of the dimension (which drives poetic building and grounds poetic dwelling) takes place in the language of the ur-poem, in that language's turn into an appraising figuration and preservation of its own *Ort*. Admittedly, this rings strangely, and yet Heidegger has claimed that human beings dwell poetically. Where is the sense in this? Put bluntly, I think that the matter of ur-poetry's relation to human dwelling (and ultimately being itself) hinges on the thought that ur-poetry provides what Heidegger might term a *Sprache des Wesens*, a language of essence that extends beyond the confines of the *Ort* of a poem to an inceptual gathering point for all occurrences. More specifically, ur-poetry provides a language of essence that exposes even as it figures the dimension wherein beings *west*—that is, come to presence as the beings they are—and thereby it measures and arranges our dwelling site.

Allow me to clarify. First, I must again stress that essence is not necessarily a matter of stable, ahistorical grounds that delimit what a being is or can be. Rather, it concerns how a being occurs as the being it is, and that may involve contingency, instability, social construction, and so on. A language of essence is thus a language that articulates how these events transpire, whether they involve historical evolutions or events of social construction. And yet, the word "essence" is so burdened by its history of stable, enduring grounds, that from here on I will speak instead of a language of originary occurrence in order to underscore the possibilities open to such a language. Second, and more to the point of ur-poetic appraisal, consider Heidegger's remark from ". . . poetically dwells the human . . .": "From where do humans, as a whole, make the claim of having arrived at the essence of some matter? Humans can make such a claim only from where they have received it. Humans receive such a claim from the exhortation of language. But of course, only when and so long as they respect and abide by the most proper essence of language" (Heidegger 1954a, 183–84). The claim is that we receive our access to the essence of some matter through the exhortation of language, and if and only if we respect or abide by the way in which language comes to presence, i.e., if we respect or abide by its originary occurrence. One can thus imagine the following process. If we attend to the originary occurrence of language, we will be able to hear the exhortation of language properly, whereby we will be granted access to some matter in its originary occurrence.

Let us develop this thought. How does the exhortation of language provide us with access to some matter in its originary occurrence? First, the point is not that some word or concept secretly taps into and represents the essence of X. "Language beckons us, at first, and then again at the end, toward the essence of a matter. This never means that language, in any old word meaning, immediately and conclusively furnishes us with the transparent essence of the matter, as with an object ready for use" (ibid., 184). Second, Heidegger's point should not be confused with the by-now-trite observation that because "essence" is a word, one must come to terms with a "language" of essence in order to reach what purportedly lies on the far side of the sign. Rather, the claim is that in an exhortation, language directs us or bids us into the dimension wherein beings *west*, originarily occur, presence as the beings they are. In this instance, then, language is not representing anything, at least not primarily. Rather, it is beckoning us, drawing our attention to a particular region of presence, even exhorting us.[15] In "Language," Heidegger writes: "The calling of language commits that which it calls to the bidding of the difference.... The difference lets the thinging of the thing rest in the worlding of the world" (Heidegger 1985, 26). Recall that the difference is the dimension wherein we dwell. Now, it is this dimension toward which language directs us when we respect its essence. Or, more precisely, the ex-hortation of language exposes us to the dimension as the site of presencing, and in that way it enables us to engage beings in their originary occurrence.

How, though, do we respect or abide by language in its originary occurrence? Through poetry, Heidegger suggests. "But the responding (accordingly) whereby the human genuinely hears the exhortation of language is the saying that speaks in the element of poetry" (Heidegger 1954a, 184).[16] We find ourselves back within the language of the poem. But this should not be surprising. As we have seen, it is poetry, or rather ur-poetry, that tracks its own language back into the scene wherein it first speaks as poetry. It is that reflexive event of autofiguration, as I suggested in my reading of *Garbage*, that calls us to the dimension wherein we (as well as its own figurations) first arise.

---

15. I use "exhortation" to translate *Zuspruch* because both the German and the English carry connotations of encouragement. Moreover, the English ex-hort stresses what the German only implies: that one is being encouraged "out" of one context and into another, in this case, out of one relation to language into another.

16. In "Language," Heidegger makes a similar point, claiming that in the language of the poem the "speaking" of language is given (Heidegger 1985, 194). While I support this claim, I am not interested in championing the claim that poetry (*qua* a domain of the arts) does this best of all. Perhaps it does, perhaps it does not. At present, I do not know. If I were to defend such a claim, extensive studies would have to be undertaken, and I have neither the time nor the stamina that such inquiries would require.

Let us consider again how ur-poetic autofiguration works, this time focusing upon moments of exhortation. The ur-poem repeats a traditional saying (or any trope or figure) as something said, thus underscoring the fact that it is being said, that saying is occurring. In appearing as something said, poetic figures accentuate their status as language. Ur-poetic disclosures are more severe than this, however, for they invoke and probe the grounds of their own figurative status precisely through their figurative interplays, e.g., drafts running through an open (Rilke), or spindles of energy crackling along the axis of a trash heap of matter becoming spirit (Ammons). Such a figurative return is crucial, for it draws into itself the *Ort* of its own saying, thereby denying us a look beyond the advent of the language of the poem for the poem's own origin. And yet, simultaneously, the ur-poem sets its own figures within that which it invokes and determines, thus exposing within them, as we saw in the case of the colons (:) littering *Garbage,* an open clearing (or axis) underwriting ur-figuration itself. The ur-poem thereby marks both the site wherein it originally occurs as well as the clearing of the open that the occurrence requires. Moreover, it does so within the folds of its own figures, within what it says concerning saying. Now, I say "marks" because, to repeat, this exposition is not a matter of representation but of ex-posure, an ex-posure that ex-horts those who hear it to reach past the folds of figuration into the site, the *Ort,* wherein those figures are gathered and released into poetizing.

As odd as it may sound, I do not believe that the autofigurative forays and expositions of ur-poetry only concern what we would term "poetry." Instead, the ur-poem exposes the scene and event of originary occurrence itself, i.e., the dimension of differentiated presencing. This is not to say that the poem bears an exemplary essence, one from which we might generalize about occurrences in general. Rather, as the being of the poem is ex-posed in the ur-poem, an event of presencing is exposed and marked as such. Of course, much depends upon what is ventured in the language of the poem. Do the traditional sayings that the poem repeats reach far enough into the dimension of presencing such that a ground not confined to the being of the poem is invoked, e.g., an open draft of nature?

We might better appreciate this point through a contrast. In 1951, Philip Larkin wrote "To My Wife," a less-than-complimentary portrait of marriage.

> Choice of you shuts up that peacock-fan
> The future was, in which temptingly spread
> All that elaborative nature can.
> Matchless potential! but unlimited
> Only so long as I elected nothing;
> Simply to choose stopped all ways up but one,
> And sent the tease-birds from the bushes flapping.
> No future now. I and you now, alone.
>
> So for your face I have exchanged all faces,
> For your few properties bargained the brisk
> Baggage, the mask-and-magic-man's regalia.
> Now you become my boredom and my failure,
> Another way of suffering, a risk,
> A heavier-than-air hypostasis.

Here repetitions of inherited terms abound ("wife," "peacock," "potential," "hypostasis"), and the poem casts them in its own way—future alongside peacock-fan, tease-birds and (implicitly) other partners, wife and hypostasis. And in doing so, it suggests something—for example, to marry is to *(a)* forgo other liaisons and *(b)* through a promise to one, render tempting so many others, others who might otherwise fail to be incitements. In its twelfth line, the poem also suggests that one's spouse takes on one's own limits, that one's suffering reemerges in his or her face, thereby adding a kind of literality to lines four and five—potential remains matchless until a path is chosen, and then all the old ghosts find their way back into one's life, hovering, heavier than air, lighter than bodies. The poem thereby recasts the meaning of "wife," thickens it, and asks us to reconsider this corner of our world in light of what it has to say. The poem does not, however, poetize its own repetitions, that is, it does not recoil upon its own ground and the differential dimension wherein its repetitions become possible. It thus neither lays claim to that dimension nor recasts it in any way.

Unlike "To My Wife," *Garbage* seems to engage the differential dimension of presencing. Let me be precise. First, its reach extends to the point at which this or that being emerges (pear, sunfish, star, poem). That is, in *Garbage,* a poem is a possible form, and underscoring this is crucial, for now the matter concerns the determinate presence of a being *qua* determinate presence, and not just this presence named "poem." Second, *Garbage* goes on to poetize the birth of these forms and the energies that surge within them. And third, the very movement and transformation of this life is also poetized, and it is at that point that *Garbage* poetizes the site wherein and whence a being becomes the being it is, i.e., undergoes determination: a site of being elemental or energy, of becoming form (and dying form), of being born, dying (perhaps), of being amid and issuing from transformation.

No doubt, a poem's ur-qualities also depend upon how originary figures are ventured in the language of the poem, or rather, how they are said. Is the venture itself ventured? Does the play of ur-figures push past the limits they mark such that the clearing of the open, an event that has always already transpired by the time ground words turn back into their origin, is exposed in and through the language of the poem? If so, if the venture less consummates than fractures itself, then a language of originary occurrence arises, and this is how language grants us access to the beings in their originary occurrence. Ur-poetry does not name beings, Adam-like, one by one. Rather, through self-figuring and originary exposures as well as the exhortations they become, ur-poetry brings us and pins us to the realm of originary occurrence, or to its rim, to the rim of the differentiated dimension, the region wherein presencing comes to pass. Unlike propositional language, therefore, ur-poetry allows us to engage a matter without ignoring originary occurrence.

A return to *Garbage:*

>   holy, holy,
> holy, the driver [of a garbage truck] cries and flicks his cigarette
>
> in a spiritual swoop that floats and floats before
> it touches ground: here, the driver knows,
>
> where the consummations gather, where the disposal
> flows out of form, where the last translations
>
> cast away their immutable bits and scraps,
> flits of steel, shivers of bottle and tumbler,
>
> here is the gateway to beginning, here the portal
> of renewing change, the birdshit, even, melding

> enrichingly in with debris, a loam for the roots
> of placenta: oh, nature, the man on the edge
>
> of the cardboard-laced cliff exclaims, that there
> could be a straightaway from the toxic past into
>
> the fusion-lit reaches of a coming time!
>
> (part 3, lines 95–109)

It is this "gateway to beginning," or rather, this threshold at the origin that concerns us, this "portal." The ur-poem calls us forth into this portal, sets us there—allows us to undergo presencing, that is, to dwell under its differential canopy. And in dwelling there, we are given access to beings as they come to presence, leaping through the gateway to the beginning, leaping forth in origination.

One should not think that these events of exposure and exhortation are purely formal affairs. In calling us toward the dimension of presencing, in calling us toward originary occurrence, it is not as if a dimension of presencing per se is determined. There is no dimension of presencing per se; only one always already measured, a clearing already arranged such that beings appear within a world. Likewise, there is no being per se, only this or that being occurring. Figuration is thus an inherent aspect of poetic building and dwelling, for the figures are what arrange the openness within which the clearing open of the dimension leaves its trace as what has always already happened.[17]

Heidegger's language is helpful here. In writing of the "calling of language," he employs the verb *heissen*, a word that, on the one hand, means "to bid" or "to summon," to call to and upon someone. But it also means "to name" (as does the English "call"), and both valences are in force here. Through ur-poetry, language figures the ground of its own saying, that is, it calls it by some name or names. But it does so in such a way that its own self-naming, its autofiguration, calls our attention to the clearing of an open dimension in the event of autofiguration itself.

---

17. In a different context, Jean-Luc Nancy writes of "exscription," of a writing that exceeds meaning (or what he terms "inscription"), but only *through* inscription. He writes: "By inscribing significations, we exscribe the presence of what withdraws from all significations, being itself (life, passion, matter . . .). The being of existence is not unpresentable: it presents itself exscribed" (Nancy 1993a, 339). I think something like exscription takes place in ur-poetry, although I ultimately am uncomfortable with the strong opposition Nancy maintains between inscription and exscription.

Figuration and exhortation are thus equally primordial facets of an ur-poetic language of originary occurrence.[18]

Having articulated not only how ur-poetry takes place through a double repetition but also how it "measures" a dimension of presencing—namely, by exposing us to and figuring a realm of originary occurrence—we now can state more forthrightly how such a measure might change our lives. As an ur-poem's ur-figures return the language of the poem to the dimension of presencing that they figure, so too they drag all things, persons, and events to that very same dimension, thus recasting them according to the measure they provide, e.g., that of polyvalent energies running into and between spirit and matter. This recasting is double-edged.

On the one hand, it involves a redetermination, one that refigures the sense of something, the character of its presencing. *Garbage* sets every event of presencing within its drama of energies sliding between spirit and matter, energies leaping from form to form. It thus has the power to alter radically how we understand the various events that make up our lives, including the event of understanding something. If I once held each burst of sense to be the creation of a creator, in the wake of *Garbage* I would now find a seething, authorless potentiality coalescing into forms, and each event of presencing would be a configuration of what was once something else and so will be again. Differences among things would be only variations upon a theme rather than intransigent, and I would be but one variation among others. Moreover, it should eventually dawn upon me that I, my neighbors, the scraps in my mulch pile, and the blocks of asphalt beneath my car's tires share a common ancestry. Try as I might to distinguish myself from my worldly peers, I would have to confess that we have all run through the same birth canal, the gateway where the finest tissues of energy crackle.

Note how different the changes wrought by *Garbage* are from those

---

18. Warminski would have it that exhortation occurs only at the level of syntax, given that one cannot name the birth of presence even with a term like "catechresis," which refers to words that are thoroughly metaphorical, e.g., mountain "face," cabbage "head," or chair "leg" (Warminski 1987, xxx–xxxiii, liii, lx, 70). This position is untenable, however. First, the very distinction between syntax and semantics is a semantic one, and thus the logic of Warminski's claim fails from the outset to escape the binds of semantics, even though he unconvincingly insists that his "syntax" is a non-dialectical other to semantics. Second, Warminski oddly refuses to interrogate the originary occurrence of his own language of "syntax" and "language's material conditions of possibility." Instead, he proceeds as if these were not names, thereby reopening the question these terms were supposed to confront.

effected by Larkin's "To My Wife." The latter might change how we consider marriage, a spouse, or even conjugal desire, but it does not recast how we consider mountains, fish, rusty nails, poems, and coffee cups. Moreover, it does not recast how we understand our own events of understanding. The reach of *Garbage* does, however, because its reach, for all intents and purposes, is infinite, laying claim to whatever, wherever, and whenever sense is born. It thus recasts what we take "insight" to entail, leading one to the same conclusion Denis Johnson presents at the outset of "The Heavens," a poem from *The Veil* (1987).

> From mind to mind
> I am acquainted with the struggles
> of these stars. The very same
> chemistry wages itself minutely
> in my person.
>
> (lines 1–5)

Alongside its redeterminations, ur-poems also effect negations, as is evident in the paragraphs above. In returning sense to its trash heap, *Garbage* displaces those meanings that formerly held sway over the birth of sense, e.g., a doting creator or the labors of the representational subject. As Heidegger writes: "The more solitarily the work stands on its own, . . . the more essentially is the monstrous thrown open and what was long-familiar overthrown. . . . To comply with this displacement means to transform accustomed ties to world and earth and, henceforth, to keep oneself from all well-known ways of acting and assessing, knowing and viewing" (Heidegger 1977a, 54). Just as "To My Wife" might tear the veneer off a conception of marriage that denies what it must forgo in favor of what it enables, *Garbage* displaces dualisms and atomistic conceptions of the individuals who populate the cosmos. It undermines them by disclosing what they omit or even contradict, e.g., matter in spirit, or the life of the stars in the life of the mind.

Engaged by an ur-poem, one's life thus changes in that one comes to see everything quite differently. In a passage that recalls Rilke's "Archaic Torso of Apollo," Charles Simic, introducing the poetry of Aleksandar Ristović, writes: "At times one comes across a poet who strikes one as being absolutely original. There's something genuinely different about him or her, a something that one has never quite encountered in all the poets one has read before. 'I will never look at the world in quite the same way,' one realizes at once, and that's what happens. From that day on, one feels deeply and fatefully changed by the experience of that reading" (Simic 1990c, 113). Now, I am inclined to say that this change in view involves a kind of conversion. If one offsets its religious connotations with its etymology, I think the word speaks to the matter at hand. From the Latin *convertere*, "to turn about or to change in character," the word connotes both turning one's attention to something else—say social as opposed to private matters—as well as acquiring a new character, much as iron does when it is converted into steel. Now, when engaged with an ur-poem, both events are in play. On the one hand, in a mode of negation, one turns away from a certain construal of the birth of sense toward another. On the other hand, the world, one's life, and even one's own turning around is recast according to the ur-poetry in play. One thus becomes a being with a different kind of character, a weigh station for chemical transactions and reactions that belong to everything and nothing, a gateway to the beginning.

In an imagined exchange with Borges, Mark Strand suggests that one might translate poems within one's own language, say Wordsworth into Strand (Strand 1990, 54).[19] Borges agrees in part, but adds: "Wordsworth refuses to be translated. It is you who must be translated, who must become, for however long, the author of *The Prelude*." Reclining in the bath, Strand agrees, but he denies that such a translation could be possible, for "in order to translate one must cease to be" (ibid.). As counterintuitive as it sounds, ur-poetic conversions demand precisely these seemingly impossible translations, translations of our selves into the measure opened and arranged in an ur-poem, translations in which we cease to be *who we once were* and come to be—or rather are converted into—different characters, although not as authors, as I have been trying to show.

Because the matter is ur-poetry, I should stress that this kind of conversion is not oriented toward adopting some new creed or set of positions. Ur-poetry does not work its transformations upon an independent epistemic subject considering the matter from a distance. First, an ur-poetry does not present itself in the form of a creed, and thus engaging

---

19. In a similar vein, Heidegger claims that interpretation effects a translation, even within a language. In the McNeill/Davis translation of the course on Hölderlin's poem "The Ister," we read: "every interpretation, and everything that stands in its service, is a translating. In that case, translating does not only move between two different languages, but there is a translating within one and the same language" (Heidegger 1996b, 62).

one is not akin to converting to a particular outlook, religious or otherwise. Second, in its reach, ur-poetry concerns the very nature of the subject as well as whatever one would apprehend and evaluate. It thus denies us any position outside of itself. Instead, it sweeps us up within the range of its figurations. As Rilke's poem insists, "There is no point / that does not see you."[20]

Permit me another point via negation. In this context, conversion is not a onetime affair, and thus ur-poems do not change our lives *in toto*. Instead, the changes they effect arrive more as tasks than as completed events. Consider Heidegger's language: "To comply with this displacement means to transform accustomed ties to world and earth and, henceforth, to keep oneself from all well-known ways of acting and assessing, knowing and viewing" (Heidegger 1977a, 54). Ur-poems displace and recast our lives, but we must follow them out, submit to the leads they open. In other words, we must run our lives through a poem like *Garbage* in order to know better who we now are, to fathom better the character into which we have been converted. Now, if ur-poetry worked by renaming the cosmos being by being, we might imagine an ur-poetic encyclopedia, one containing every being's proper name. To change our lives, therefore, we only would have to change the names we use for things. But ur-poetry refashions the sense of presencing, and thus it leaves to us the task of translating our "well-known ways" into its less well-known but now all-too-compelling reaches, the task of ceasing to be who we thought we were by becoming who we are.

Although ur-poetic life change involves a task, we must not confuse these tasks with moral or practical imperatives. Ur-poems do not tell us how to act when faced with X; rather, their language of originary occurrence transforms how we face X by rewriting the sense of the whole encounter. *Garbage,* by disclosing my common ancestry with rodents,

---

20. At one point, I thought one might argue that ur-poetry displaces its rivals through a disclosure of truth. However, because ur-poetry so thoroughly envelops the epistemic subject, it seemed misleading to suggest, if only implicitly, that the claim an ur-poem has upon one is akin to a truth claim whose veracity one might entertain and examine. One does not deliberate at this point but complies with what rushes over one. This is not to say, however, that ur-poems have no epistemic import. Although they do not proceed via propositions, they do concern what propositions presume, an open dimension of presencing; one therefore cannot eschew ur-poetry for a proposition-driven relation to being. As to how one might work between ur-poetic life changes and propositional changes in view, that is a matter for another study. For now, I want simply to note that ur-poetic life change is not a change in view accomplished by an epistemic subject.

does not order me to love, honor, and cherish them as well. It recasts my relation with them instead, leaving to other presencings a possible prescription.

What then of the imperative that Rilke employs in his "Archaic Torso of Apollo"? If the ur-poem says, "you must change your life," how should we regard the "must"? Heidegger says, "To comply with this displacement means to transform." And Simic adds, "'I will never look at the world in quite the same way,' one realizes at once, and that's what happens." Engaged, one "complies." Engaged, one never looks at the world in the same way. These experiences do not involve an imperative to convert. Rather, they announce that a conversion has occurred. One is, to recall Simic once more, fatefully changed. To my mind, then, the "must" does not precede the conversion but arrives in its wake, that is, this is a "must" that presents the task to "never look at the world in quite the same way" (or, in Heidegger's language, to "keep oneself from all well-known ways of acting and assessing, knowing and viewing").

With the thought of the nature, import, and life-transforming trajectory of ur-poetry now in tow, we can close this chapter by coming to terms with the remarkable claims Heidegger makes concerning the power of poetry.

> Poetry is founding, the effectual grounding of what endures. The poet is the grounder of being. What we call the real in the everyday is, in the end, unreal. (Heidegger 1980, 33)

> The saying of the poet is a founding not only in the sense of a free giving, but also, and at the same time, in the sense of the firm grounding of human existence. (Heidegger 1981, 41–42)

On the reading offered here, poets ground being through ur-poems. One can speak of a "ground" here insofar as ur-figures both invoke and expose the dimension wherein beings occur, including themselves. This is not to say that ur-poems provide an ideal substratum for being out of which the meaning of being is mined, or that they constitute being, informing what would otherwise be formless matter. Instead, through a language of originary occurrence, ur-poems throw into relief the event of presencing, the event wherein an open dimension is cleared and arranged, an event within which beings and the worlds to which they belong come to pass. In "Hölderlin and the Essence of Poetry," Heidegger writes:

> Poetry is founding through the word and within the word. What is founded so? What endures. But can what endures be founded? Is it not always already what is present at hand? No! Even what endures must be brought to stand against what would tear it away; the simple must be wrested from entanglement, the measure must be set before the measureless. That which carries and reigns through beings as a whole must come into the open. *Being must be thrown open* so that a being may appear. (Heidegger 1981, 41 [emphases mine])

It is ur-poetry that throws open being and keeps it open through recoiling ur-figures that invoke and expose an event they cannot represent. And it is in that sense of exposition that ur-poetry provides a measure for being, a measure by which being might be appraised, within an arrangement of determinations (of presences) as that which has always already arrived and opened a dimension of presencing.

Ur-poetry does not simply concern being, however. In providing a language of originary occurrence, the determinations of an ur-poem overdetermine whatever presences, draw it back to the dimension through and in which it travels. All beings, therefore, are subject to the recoil taking place within the ur-poem. When *Garbage* draws us back to the "gateway to beginning," to the "dispositional axis," and through its own ":," it takes every element, every form, and every transformation back with us. It not only exposes the dimensionality of presencing in and through a measure of its own making, but it poetizes beings and their world as well. And this is why the language of the poem trumps what passes for the real: in our everyday transactions we seem to pass over the differentiated dimension in silence, whereas ur-poetry subjects beings to the recoil that draws its own figurations back toward the dimension wherein presencing occurs.

If ur-poetry overdetermines the character of presencing, it no doubt also overdetermines us. That is, a language of originary occurrence has purchase upon our being just as much as any other. Recall Heidegger's claim that poetry is the "originary allowance-of-dwelling." Poetry enables us to comport ourselves among beings and in relation to being itself without losing sight of the manner in which presencing occurs, without forgetting the dimension whose clearing and arrangement unfolds at the heart of all presencing. Through the recoiling play of its figures (which we have tied to Heidegger's notion of "building"), *Garbage*, for example, throws us and all our engagements into a cosmic dustbin. In other words, where its own figuration goes, there we go as well. Recall a passage from "... poetically dwells the human ...": "poetizing is not building in the sense of raising and fitting buildings. Rather, poetizing, as the most proper appraisal of the dimension of dwelling, is inceptual building. Before anything else, poetizing admits the dwelling of human beings into its essence" (Heidegger 1954a, 196). Again, the point does not revolve around construction, as if ur-poetry "made" us who we are. The constructivist thesis (i.e., that language or culture somehow produces—perhaps through a kind of formal causality—what we take to be the real) presupposes what, at this juncture, it should explain, namely, the co-presencing of *(a)* language or culture; *(b)* language users or cultural agents; and *(c)* whatever is constructed. In short, constructivism fails to think the problem of essence, of *Wesen,* and to come to terms with a language of originary occurrence. In contrast, ur-poems allow us to experience the character of our being by keeping its dimension open while making evident the ways in which that dimension is bound to determinations, to figuration, to presences. Ur-poetry is thus not a matter of the production of identities.[21] Rather, we might say that it enables us to dwell among identities in a certain way, providing a "firm grounding of human existence" by keeping us exposed to our ground, to the differentiated dimension that holds together world and thing (and us) and yet keeps us apart. Or, we could say that ur-poetry enables us to experience our selves at the point of our originary occurrence, selves presencing in an arranged or determinate, differentiated dimension. And then we would have to add

---

21. Gerald Bruns has argued that early texts such as "Hölderlin and the Essence of Poetry" have an "Orphic" drift: they suggest that poetry somehow constitutes the world. Heidegger's later texts, however, are "Hermetic." That is, "they have less to do with poetry as the revelation or establishment of Being than with the way poetry is taken up or appropriated by the withdrawal or reserve of language, its strangeness or otherness as Saying *(Sage),* which will not let itself be put into words" (Bruns 1989, xix). As should be apparent from what I have written thus far, I think that one should not make too much of this distinction between a concern with being and a concern with language, particularly because thinking the founding of being in terms of a language of originary occurrence (which amounts to a language of being) enables one to make some sense of Heidegger's continued attempt to think human dwelling in relation to poetry. This is not to say that Heidegger was ultimately of one mind about such matters, or that Bruns's distinction is simply mistaken, but it *is* to say that one can move between the later and earlier texts with greater ease than Bruns's distinction would suggest.

that it also frees us from the habits—say, those acquired through the repeated use of propositions—that blind us to the drama that underwrites what appears to be there in a simple, uncomplicated fashion.

We began with Rilke, with the phenomenon presented in his "Archaic Torso of Apollo." The work of art transfixes one and demands that one change one's life. In the previous two chapters, I have engaged that phenomenon through Heidegger. My suggestion is that certain works (and I have limited myself to poetry) address us in the form of an ur-poem, a poem of poetry. Such poems not only figure the being of poetry but also expose us to the deepest dimensions of being, which include the deepest dimensions of any possible cosmos, for ur-poems, through a language of originary occurrence, concern and measure presencing itself. Through ur-figures, they take the everyday and return it to the differential dimension of presencing. They thus address us at the point of our being in the world and refigure us, even *trash* us, thus changing our lives.

In accounting for how ur-poetry can change our lives, we have also responded to another question: "Wherefore poetry?" I claimed that one could take up this question without subjecting the language of the poem to a utilitarian calculus, and I take the notion of the ur-poem to have shown that this is possible, for it arises from and within the language of the poem itself. Without seeking consequences, ur-poetry nevertheless provides a measure for being, beings, and human existence, one that remains attuned to its own place within the dimension it exposes. Again, this is not to say "Dear poets, give me some ur-poems." But it is to outline a path down which the language of the poem may indeed travel, should it dare to venture so much and its readers comply.

3

The White of All "I's"

Having explored what an ur-poem is and having witnessed its import, I would now like to consider what I take to be a contemporary instance of ur-poetry. I do not turn to Charles Simic's work in order to "test" or "vindicate" Heidegger's style of interpretation, however. Rather, I turn to Simic because his work recoils in ur-poetic ways and with that degree of import, and I thus think that the idea of an ur-poem can help engage his remarkable poetry. In the end, however, his work will have to speak for itself, for "ur-poem" is no less an interpretive annotation than "hymn," and like all annotations, it must give way to what is found in the language of the poem.

Although it very much is a concept, I want to stress that the idea of the ur-poem is not taxonomic in nature, that is, ur-poetry does not account for or explain all or some region of what we might call "poetry." Rather, a concern with ur-poetry manifests itself in a way of reading, of engaging poems by living with them. *Qua* concept, "ur-poem" directs our attention toward movements within the language of the poem, movements on the part of poetic figures and operations that recoil upon the origin of their own poetizing. In such recoils, a language of originary occurrence may arise (that is, a language that exposes and figures the coming to presence of sense itself). Such a language is of interest because it is *(a)* capable of grounding being through an exposure of the event of presencing, thereby *(b)* overdetermining beings with regard to that event, and *(c)* admitting us into a dwelling site, a site wherein we are able to engage beings in their origins, engage our own originary occurrence, and attend to the birth of sense itself. As I have said, thoughts like these should help us hear and engage the work of Charles Simic. Let us see whether this is so.

Before beginning our engagement with Simic, it bears repeating that Heidegger is no stranger to him. As he explains in an interview from 1978: "I've always felt that inside each of us there is a profound anonymity. Sometimes I think that when you go deep inside, you meet everyone else on a sort of common ground—or you meet nobody. But whatever you meet, it is not yours though you enclose it. We are the container, and this nothingness is what we enclose. This is where Heidegger is very interesting to me" (Simic 1985, 62).

Permit me a second caveat. What follows in Chapters 3 and 4 is an exploration of Simic's work, not a presentation of his greatest ur-poetic hits. If ur-poetry entailed theses or propositions, one might present them and then demonstrate how one culled them from various poems. But ur-poetry is an event in the language of the poem, and thus one needs to track and even participate in it, following out its repetitions and recoils. My readings are thus equal parts journey and exposition. They aim to navigate Simic's poems, not to summarize them. Recently, Simic himself wrote: "Paradoxically, what is most important in a poem, that *something* for which we go back to it again and again, cannot be articulated. The best one can do under the circumstances is to give the reader a hint of what one has experienced reading the poem, but was unable to name. And when that fails, one can quote the poem itself in full, because only poems can trap the 'poetic'—whatever that is" (Simic 2001b, 36). Although Simic is not referring to ur-poetry, his remark nevertheless applies. I cannot transcribe ur-poetry, only hint at it, track and point out its activities—a repetition here, a recoil there, there an exhortation, and here an exposition. Moreover, because life change is at stake, it seems crucial that I re-create for the reader an experience of ur-poetry, something no summary can accomplish. If for a slightly different reason, I will thus follow Simic's own advice and quote poems in full, hoping thereby to give you the full advantage of what is found there and not just a poor meal of assorted annotations, hints, and construals.

Where to begin? Because of its reflexivity, let us begin with Simic's long poem, *White*, an elusive lyric sequence consisting of three parts and totaling 245 lines.[1] The first two parts of *White* (reprinted in Simic 1990b) are comprised of ten segments, each involving five 2-line pairs. The last, entitled "What the White Had to Say," contains two 20-line soliloquies.

White opens in this way.

> Out of poverty
> To begin again:
>
> With the color of the bride
> And that of blindness
>
> (lines 1–4)

The speaker would start anew, and virginally.[2] But having already begun, this is impossible. What seems afoot, therefore, is a desire to return to

---

1. *White* has a complex editorial history. First published in 1972, adorned by Simic's own illustrations and a handful of typographical errors, it was revised and reissued in 1980 sans artwork (Simic 1972, 1980). While the 1980 version was reprinted in *Selected Poems: 1963–1983* (Simic 1990b), yet a third version has recently appeared in *Selected Early Poems* (Simic 1999). Because each version is different to the point of having a character all its own, I think that, despite certain repetitions, each should be regarded as an individual poem and not dissolved into a series of textual variants. Presuming the singularity of each, I have decided to focus upon the second *White*, leaving for future labor a careful comparison of the three.

2. As will become evident, the figure of the white is a gendered figure, one embroiled in a long tradition oriented around inaccessible yet sustaining feminine grounds. *White* is thus open to a reading that explores how it indicates, relies upon, and renders inaccessible the feminine as a source of genesis. I have not pursued that reading, however, and for several reasons. First, the white is not cast in terms of materiality, and thus the poem is not simply repeating a figure of masculine intelligibility and feminine sensibility. Second, and more important, the white is ultimately not marked as other to what she enables, and the poem does not present a mute feminine ground that ceaselessly provides for a masculine world of articulate sense. In fact, I would argue that the poem unsettles as much as it relies upon that classically patriarchal trope. Third—and this is more of a confession than a reason—the literature on the trope of a mute, feminine ground of genesis is so vast that if I were to pursue this theme, it would require a chapter unto itself, and such a chapter would overly distract me from the issue of ur-poetry.

the beginning, to an origin, and to try again with a whiteness (the bride) and a darkness (blindness). The speaker is unsure of how to proceed, however, and thus seeks to

> Touch what I can
> Of the quick,
>
> Speak and then wait,
> As if this light
>
> Will continue to linger
> On the threshold.
>
> (lines 5–10)

Note how empty this beginning is. A desire, a request, but nothing more; only dim light and waiting at a threshold, a point of departure. It would seem that what was once familiar is about to be left behind. As the next couplet proclaims:

> All that is near,
> I no longer give it a name.
>
> (lines 11–12)

Oddly, then, *White* begins by not beginning, by halting.

This paralyzing poverty is peculiar. First, it appears self-imposed, stemming from a refusal to name what is near, most familiar. Second, it is tied to a desire to begin again, freshly, as if existing names had failed or dimmed. Begin what? To write, to poetize—for in the lines that follow, the speaker pursues the white, the page upon which one might write, the scene in which a figure might come into relief, a figure most likely blackened by ink (black being the color of blindness). I take it, therefore, that insofar as the speaker seeks a poem, the poverty apparent here concerns poetizing as well. If this is right, *White* opens by confessing that its poetizing has floundered, that as poetry, it no longer knows how to conduct itself or even what it is. The fact that it continues on for several hundred lines is thus unusual. Are these lines "poetry"? Perhaps they involve something prior to what we would normally call "poetry," something less certain and riskier, for here, what it means to be a poem is profoundly in question.³ *White* thus carries out the task Simic announces in "Composition." "In the beginning, always, a myth of origins of the poetic act. A longing to lower oneself one notch below language, to touch the bottom—that place of 'original action and desire,' to recover our mute existence, to recreate what is unspoken and enduring in words of the poem" (Simic 1985, 110).⁴ In other words, *White* ventures urpoetry. Let us see where its ventures lead.

What remains of Part One is a pilgrimage in pursuit of the white. However, this pursuit is not some psychological journey recorded as a poem. Rather, it is a matter of the writing itself undergoing a journey, of language exploring itself, doubling back upon the words and sentences and punctuation it sets upon a page. I take this to be the case for several reasons. First, the speaker does not recollect a journey that he has taken, a fact that might suggest a jaunt into the mind of creativity. Rather, he journeys himself, as the poem's observance of the present tense indicates.⁵ Now, one could maintain the present tense and report observations of encounters and landscapes, thus leaving (or attempting to leave) the language of the poem in the hope of representing some state of affairs. But several images suggest that this journey never leaves the page. The speaker would begin again with whiteness and blackness, with paper and ink. He also seeks words in *White*, and is drawn toward a vowel (lines 53 and 59). Finally, the first part concludes with

> We haven't gone far . . .
> . . . .

---

3. As Fred Muratori muses in a review of *White: A New Version:* "Why would this particular poem, already published, continue to obsess its author for so long? Perhaps because *White* confronts . . . the creation of poetry itself" (Muratori 1984, 122). The obsession infects readers as well. Simic himself notes: "Poets seek that elusive something called poetry, and so do those who write about them" (Simic 2001b, 36).

4. Although he is not speaking of *White*, I share Richard Howard's appreciation for Simic's "originality": "When we speak of writing as *original*, as I am bound and determined to do in speaking of Charles Simic's writing . . . , we mean that it has to do with something very old, not something very new—it has to do with origins, beginnings, sources" (Simic 1971, xii). And it is my respect for this kind of originality that leaves me distraught when a poet of Kenneth Koch's caliber claims: "Ordinary language is of course where the language of poetry comes from. It has the words, the usages, the sounds that a poem takes up and makes its own. It constitutes, along with thoughts and feelings, what may be called the raw materials of poetry" (Koch 1998, 45). I take it that such tropes—"ordinary language," "thoughts," and "feelings"—mark the points from which poets such as Simic begin to reflect, not where they come to rest.

5. It seems certain that the speaker of *White* is male, for he twice refers to himself as a boy (lines 69 and 105).

> Five ears of my fingertips
> Against the white page
>
> (lines 91, 93–94)

suggesting to me that he had been upon the page all along. There is reason to believe, therefore, that the journey undertaken here transpires within writing itself, that the writing that *White* is is itself the journey.

I consider this initial journey a pilgrimage because it has many of the hallmarks of those travels. First, a pilgrim seeks renewal, inspiration, or healing, as one might at the Wailing Wall, the Dome of the Rock, or the Church of the Holy Sepulcher.[6] And renewal is what the speaker seeks—to begin again. Second, and here the connotation is merely etymological, to be a pilgrim is to move in strange places, "pilgrim" coming from the Latin *peregrium*, "a stranger, one that comes from abroad." In *White*, we also have one who is estranged and seeking; all that is near is now nameless, and a quest is undertaken. Third, a pilgrim is a religious figure. If Christian, the pilgrim will not rely solely on his or her own strength but also on grace, and will pray for guidance and stamina much as the speaker does, praying twice in the first two segments of *White* (lines 7 and 17). Finally, pilgrims are often subject to despair along the way; renewal might not await them at the end of their journey. The speaker has his share of such moments in *White*, e.g., "I went searching. / Is this a deathmarch?" (lines 55–56).

I am underscoring the figure of the pilgrimage for several reasons. First, it remains in force throughout the first part, and thus, particularly given that this quest fails, *White* appears to disrupt the form of "pilgrimage" as a way back toward the origin. Second, the pilgrimage motif underscores the poverty of the speaker: estranged, in need of renewal, searching, requiring help along the way, despairing—"Out of poverty / To begin again" (lines 1–2). This poem is thus not a journey concerning self-possession or self-fashioning. In attempting to begin again, the speaker is humbled, even lost. His search for the origin seems to begin only after the self-confidence of a willful, self-legislating subject has ex-

---

6. In *Sacred Journeys: The Anthropology of Pilgrimage*, Alan Morinis writes: "Pilgrimage is born of desire and belief. The desire is for solution to problems of all kinds that arise within the human situation. The belief is that somewhere beyond the known world there exists a power that can make right the difficulties that appear so insoluble and intractable here and now. All one must do is journey" (Morinis 1992, 1).

pired. We can thus expect the origin of poetizing also to lie beyond the reach of an ego that perceives, represents, reflects, and wills.[7]

Let us rejoin the speaker's journey. A dim threshold, poor light, a prayer, a renunciation of the familiar; from out of this poverty the speaker in *White* seeks

> Enough glow to kneel by and ask
> To be tied to its tail
>
> When it goes marrying
> Its cousins, the stars.
>
> (lines 17–20)

The speaker seeks the stars, hoping to arrive there via "the quick" (line 6) or what remains of their stellar presence, a poor relation—"Now only a chill / Slipping through" (lines 15–16). But how is he to make this journey? Left to its own devices, ink is blind, blackness upon blackness. He thus needs the white to begin again, considers a cloud (lines 21–22) and snow (lines 27–28), and entreats a white-clad nun administering care, a "Sister" who might become a bride with whom he could begin again (lines 43–46):

> Teach me the song
> That makes a man raise
>
> His glass at dusk
> Until a star dances in it.
>
> (lines 47–50)

---

7. If the initial journey that is the first part of *White* takes place within the writing that *White* is, can one still speak of a pilgrimage? I think so. First, the physical journeys with which we associate pilgrimage have metaphorical elements, which is to say, the journey taken is more than a change in location. As Simon Coleman and John Elsner argue, "A physical journey through time and space that is an essential part of pilgrimage can also have metaphorical resonances on many levels. A pilgrimage may be a rite of passage involving transformations of one's inner state and outer status; it may be a quest for a transcendent goal; it may entail the long-desired healing of a physical or spiritual ailment" (Coleman and Elsner 1995, 6). Second, by the Renaissance, "pilgrimage" had become a literary figure in its own right, open to allegorical deployment. In *Pilgrimage and Narrative in the French Renaissance,* Wes Williams writes: "What the apparent confusion of Renaissance writing makes clear is that pilgrimage is—even at its most material—always in part a metaphorical practice; it is consequently open ... to allegorical expansion beyond the literal senses of the journey" (Williams 1998, 17).

What is occurring here? How might we regard the bride and the honeymoon stars? As I have intimated, the bride is the white, and she holds the promise of song, of poetry. Clad in white, muse-like, a giver of song, her dowry includes a poetic word able to conjure the stars, sidereal presences the speaker apparently never reached despite earlier prayers.

But what are these stars? Three times they are invoked, and each time as something sought (lines 20, 50, 180).[8] They are bound to poetizing, for song can purportedly summon them—the speaker thinks that should his ink and the white page meet, the stars will draw near. But *White* never names those stars, never reaches them. We shall have to come to terms with that failure later, but for now, it bears noting that Simic is less reticent elsewhere about that which arrives in the language of the poem. In "Reading Philosophy at Night," he claims: "Both poetry and philosophy, for instance, are concerned with Being. What is a lyric poem, one might say, but the recreation of the experience of Being. In both cases, that need to get it down to its essentials, to say the unsayable and let the truth of Being shine through" (Simic 1990c, 60). And in "Assembly Required," he asserts: "Every poetic image asks why is there something rather than nothing, as it renews our astonishment that things exist" (Simic 1997, 96). Finally, in "Poetry Is the Present," he suggests: "The poets, so we believe, remind the philosophers, again and again, of the world's baffling presence" (Simic 1994a, 55). Note how being appears here: a shine, a baffling presence. Is that not how stars line our sky, their shining baffling us? And are not those of us who are susceptible to wonder often struck so when gazing into the heavens at night? In other words, I take the shimmering stars to be the shimmering of being, of the world in its presencing, of all that is there and not simply nothing, for that is what poetry seeks, according to Simic—to reach into the heavens and sing the baffling presence of the world within a raised glass or word. And it is this future that depends upon the speaker's ability to woo the white, for she opens up the possibility of poetizing, which opens up the possibility of renewing "our astonishment that things exist," of attuning ourselves to being.

But the speaker's pilgrimage results in naught. Segment seven, which reads like a stumbling nursery rhyme, finds him a lost shepherd, strug-

---

8. There may also be an implicit invocation of the stars in segment six of *White*. It begins (as if asking the white): "Who are you? Are you anybody / A moonrock would recognize?" (lines 51–52). This suggests that the speaker believes that were he lunar (a moon rock), and thus closer to the stars, perhaps he might better woo the white.

gling to herd white sheep in the Arctic. Two things seem noteworthy. First, one has the fragments of a poem here, but nothing comes together, just a few rhymes—as if the creep of scattered rhymes brought him only a mock poem. Second, the speaker almost disappears in the overwhelming white of the Arctic, the snow swallowing what he would shepherd, presumably words. This suggests that pure whiteness will not grant a poem. Rather, the white only gives poems if some contrasting presence is there, perhaps the blackness of blind ink. Regardless, nothing comes of this Arctic flurry of words. Segment eight of *White* begins: "Then all's well and white / And no more than white" (lines 71–72).

It is not as if our speaker is alone in his misfortune, however. In segment nine, he meets up with others, presumably fellow pilgrims.

> All bandaged up, waiting
>
> At the spiked, wrought-iron gate
> Of the Great Eye and Ear Infirmary.
>
> (lines 88–90)

What interests me here is less the appearance of other suitors than the infirmary at which they are gathered. Within the failure of the pilgrimage, one also finds the limits of the senses: their inability to apprehend the white is underscored. Moreover, the senses are damaged in their pursuit of the white. Now, this might mean that the white has damaged them. But it has yet to be found, and thus this seems unlikely. Instead, it seems that exile from the white harms the senses, that they fall into disrepair the longer the white is lost to them. It is not surprising that segment ten contains: "Fear lives there too" (line 92).

Segment ten, the final segment of Part One, brings the pilgrimage to an unsuccessful close. Afraid, having seen bandaged eyes and ears, the speaker seeks to touch a white page with the "Five ears of my fingertips" (line 93). Not only does this act unsuccessfully pursue the white through a new sense, touch, but it also suggests that even automatic writing draws a blank at this juncture. "Set down the pen, don't try to write, just let it come," or so the story goes.[9] But nothing comes, and quite literally.

9. About "psychic automatism," André Breton explains: "After you have settled yourself in a place as favorable as possible to the concentration of your mind upon itself, have writing materials brought to you. Put yourself in as passive, or receptive, a state of mind as you can. Forget about your genius, your talents, and the talents of everyone else. Keep reminding yourself that literature is one of the saddest roads that leads to everything. Write quickly, without any preconceived subject, fast enough so that you will not remember what you're writing and

> What do you hear?
> We hear holy nothing
>
> Blindfolding itself.
> It touched you once, twice,
>
> And tore like a stitch
> Out of a new wound.
>
> (lines 95–100)

I hear several thoughts at play here. First, the fingertips hear nothing, a holy nothing. The pilgrimage thus does not lead to a holy site that promises renewal, but to a holy nothing, emptiness and disappointment. True, there is a white page at hand, but it remains mute. What his fingertips do hear is the rustle of a blindfold covering the eyes of the nothing. To my mind, this suggests that the white is not only silent here but that the absence of its voice is being covered over as well. If it were not for memories of the pains her absence had brought two times before, the speaker would thus be doubly removed from his goal. Better to have loved and lost, then, or else this pilgrimage would not simply have failed but would possibly have also lost the white altogether.

Recall that we are tracking the speaker of *White* because in seeking the origins of poetry, the white page upon which poetry can be written, his journey is the journey of ur-poetry, and in that journey ur-poetry may emerge. Thus far, however, it has not. A pilgrimage toward the origins of poetry has concluded (almost literally) empty-handed. As a rhetorical figure, therefore, pilgrimage is not adequate to the labors of ur-poetry. Some other route toward the white must thus be found.

In Part Two, the speaker redirects his search. No longer an itinerant pilgrim, he ascetically turns inward and prepares for the white, should she arrive. The asceticism of *White*'s Part Two is apparent in the first segment, where he interrogates and prepares himself as a sacrificial meal for his beloved, offering to "roast on my heart's dark side" until "the half-moons on my fingernails set," that is, until the death after death

---

be tempted to reread what you have written. The first sentence will come spontaneously, so compelling is the truth that with every passing second there is a sentence unknown to our consciousness which is only crying out to be heard" (Breton 1969, 29–30).

when fingernails cease growing (lines 102 and 108).[10] As with pilgrimage, ascetic journeys are bent on renewal. Through discipline and self-denial, one peels away those aspects of the self that lead one astray from a renewing source.[11] In that way, asceticism (again like pilgrimage) seeks to transcend the everyday. By containing or even ridding itself of corrupting influences, the ascetic prepares for transformation, for connection with a truer source.[12]

The next segment of *White* makes evident, however, that this is far from a labor of self-mastery, underscoring again the poverty of the speaker's situation.

> Well, you can't call me a wrestler
> If my own dead weight has me pinned down.
>
> Well, you can't call me a cook
> If the pot's got me under its cover.
>
> (lines 111–14)[13]

10. Peter Schmidt claims that the speaker is here engaged in an imaginary dialogue with the white (Weigl 1996, 28). I see it otherwise, for the white has been anything but conversationally present until now. Such disputes are difficult to settle, of course, but I take it that across this segment, the speaker of *White* is preparing himself as a sacrificial meal for his bride-to-be, hence the mocking use of "sweetheart" and "loverboy" in his questions (lines 103 and 105).

11. Basil of Caesura, a fourth-century "Church Father" whose work influenced Greek Orthodox monasticism well into the twentieth century, begins his "Ascetical Discourse and Exhortation on the Renunciation of the World and Spiritual Perfection" as follows: "Come to Me, all you that labor and are burdened and I will refresh you, says the Divine Voice, signifying either earthly or heavenly refreshment. In either case, He calls us to Himself, inviting us on the one hand, to cast off the burden of riches by distributing to the poor, and on the other, to make haste to embrace the cross-bearing life of the monks by ridding ourselves through confession and good works of the load of sins contracted by our use of worldly goods" (Wagner 1950, 15). Likewise, Gregory of Nyssa, Basil's brother, writes in "On Perfection": "Subjecting the spirit of the flesh to divine law, let us live peacefully, having been dissolved into the new and peaceful man and having become one from two. . . . Once the civil war in our nature is expelled, then, we also, being at peace within ourselves, become peace, and reveal our having taken on the name of Christ as true and authentic" (Callahan 1967, 103).

12. Pilgrimage also seeks to transcend the everyday, but by leaving it behind in a journey toward another locale, most likely a holy site. Asceticism, however, burrows inward, seeking freedom from dependence upon sites and the like. This is not to say, however, that pilgrimage lacks interiority. Reflecting upon antique Coptic practices, David Frankfurter suggests: "Balancing interior spirituality and exterior rite and icon, individuality and assembly, pilgrimage might seem the perfect idiom for the contemporary faithful" (Frankfurter 1998, 5). Nevertheless, it is fair to say that ascetics, more so than pilgrims, stress inward journeys that sever ties with the outside world. As Basil of Caesura writes in his "Introduction to the Ascetical Life": "Set before yourself a life without house, homeland, or possessions. Be free and at liberty from all worldly cares, lest desire for a wife or anxiety for a child fetter you" (Wagner 1950, 10).

13. Note that the whole point of asceticism is to remove our own dead weight so that we might rise above the errors and pettiness of the everyday.

Nor are the efforts at self-sacrifice entirely successful.

> Nor can you call me a saint,
> If I didn't err, there wouldn't be these smudges.
>
> (lines 119–20)

One should not think, therefore (in supposed contradistinction to pilgrimage), that when an origin is at stake, the answers lie within.

Amid intensifying poverty and disorientation, some insights do seem to flash, however, and this is in keeping with the general drift of asceticism: at points of dissolution and despair, growth occurs. Segment four opens with a discovery: "This is breath, only breath" (line 131). I call this a discovery because thrown back upon a near mantra ("One has to manage as best as one can"), it is as if the speaker hears his voice for the first time: "This is breath, only breath." Breath lies at the base of speech, and it therefore may offer him access to the site where poems come to word.

In the wake of his realization, the speaker is startled by the fragility of this all-important point, what we earlier, following Heidegger, termed the *Ort*, the "tip of the spear" at which breath (or ink) is gathered into poetizing. He says, "A fly weighs twice as much" (line 133). And yet, for all its apparent weightlessness, it is the ground of poetry that is at stake.

As if to mark what has occurred, *White* continues:

> The struck match nods as it passes,
>
> But when I shout,
> Its true name sticks in my throat.
>
> (lines 134–36)

An illumination, a struck match, and the speaker would shout out his discovery. But he cannot. Its name never leaves his throat. Moreover, the "Its" is ambiguous. Does it refer to the match or to something else? It would be odd if the match were at issue—why would the speaker want to know its true name? Breath seems to be the concern. Moreover, the true name of breath would have to stick in his throat: how can one shout out the name of breath without breathing, thus losing what one would name, arriving too late to name the matter at hand?

Having been thrown back upon his breath, having realized that it may hold the key to the site he seeks, and having realized that he cannot simply name it, the speaker attempts to externalize his breath so that it might itself become the white.

> It has to be cold
> So the breath turns white
>
> (lines 137–38)

First, note the renewed asceticism: exposure to the cold. Second, the hope is that this will turn his breath white, and thus he will have a page upon which to write, one drawn solely from his own exhalations, that is, one that does not need a bride but writes entirely from and upon itself. But to no avail.

> And then mother, who's fast enough
> To write his life on it?
>
> (lines 139–40)

White breath "paper" blows away before he can set down the words; he cannot render his breath white and thereby self-sufficiently produce the *Ort*, the site wherein poems are gathered.

A flash of insight, but our speaker is no better off than before. Poems are bound to breath, and yet he cannot name the point at which his breath becomes word. Nor can he externalize breath in such a way that it becomes a white page in itself. As he turns to write, its whiteness has blown away.[14] What else is there to do? The ascetic journey in *White* takes one final turn:

> White—let me step aside
> So that the future may see you,

---

14. I am tempted to render this point in terms of temporality, hearing in the dispersion of white breath the winds of time. And here Breton is vindicated rather than set aside: "Ah! It must indeed be admitted, we're in bad, we're in terrible, shape when it comes to time" (Breton 1969, x). In trying to secure the condition of the possibility of poetizing and simultaneously poetize, the speaker loses the former (a breath now white) when it comes time for the latter (to write upon it). In order to accomplish such a feat, the speaker would have to relate to himself without time passing in the relation. I do not know what kind of being could accomplish this. It might have to be immortal—and in the sense of omnipresent. Interestingly, a confrontation with the infinite is precisely what awaits the speaker in segments six and seven.

> For when this sheet is blown away,
> What else is left
>
> But to set the food on the table,
> To cut oneself a slice of bread?
>
> (lines 145–50)

The white and the poetizing it enables have forsaken the speaker at his altar of self-abnegation, so he pursues abnegation to an extreme, renouncing even his desire for the white. In its stead, he seems to opt for the everyday life that pilgrimages and asceticism necessarily leave behind.

On the surface, this return to the everyday appears to mark the end of an ascetic journey, and in a way it does, for the speaker has elected to end his exile from the common. But the matter is not so simple, for this supposed return is in fact yet another sacrifice, namely, the sacrifice of asceticism itself. The speaker's desire for the white continues unabated, evidenced by the fact that he steps aside for her "[s]o that the future may see you." Segment five thus marks the utmost intensification of an ascetic journey, one in which self-denial (which remains a seeking) turns against itself and becomes a different kind of practice altogether, what one might regard as a kind of *amor fati*, a release of one's desires into an acceptance of what will be. This is to say that at the segment's onset, the speaker is still practicing a kind of asceticism. At its close, however, he no longer sits at a threshold demanding an answer from a silent emptiness. Rather, he enters into the world, having become one being among many.[15]

But perhaps this was what was required all along, for in the wake of his apostasy, fate strikes in segment six (lines 151–60). A "true-blue orphan" encounters an "obscure widow" in the "unknown year" of an "algebraic century" on an "indeterminate street-corner." Note that this world is nearly formless. Earlier, the speaker lost the sunset to forgetfulness and misplaced a mnemonic device. Now the year is unknown, the century full of variables awaiting determination. And space has grown strange. The street-corner is not simply unknown; it is no place in particular. The problem, however, is not just an underdetermined world. He too has been displaced. Orphaned, his lineage is lost, and that includes the lineage of a pilgrimage and asceticism just abandoned, for he is a thorough

---

15. For a discussion of this kind of transformation, what he terms "self-overcoming," see Charles Scott's remarkable reading of *Beyond Good and Evil* in his *Language of Difference* (Scott 1987, 9–52).

orphan, bona fide, true blue. One can see this thoroughness in the poem's move into third-person speech. Having lost in segment five the ego and its desire to begin again, he no longer speaks as a subject, but has dwindled into a figure upon a landscape, a pawn of fate. He thus appears in the voice of objectivity and meets a woman, obscure and widowed, also the result of a familial severance. It would seem, therefore, that the everyday was not recovered in the previous implosion of ascetic striving, but further displaced, for in segment six the world is not only formless but fractured; those who move among it have arrived from broken unions. Earlier, familiar names were withdrawn. Here, the situation is fiercer: indeterminacy, abandoned figures. It is as if after sacrificing asceticism itself, he again becomes a pilgrim, but in an almost literal sense (etymologically speaking): he becomes a stranger moving across a land that is itself strange, less because it is unknown than because it is indistinct.

Somehow, fate pushes through this limbo and the speaker is given

> A tiny sugar cube
>
> In the hand so wizened
> All the lines said: fate.

(lines 158–60)

A wedding ceremony ensues.

> Do you take this line
> Stretching to infinity?
>
> I take this chipped tooth
> On which to cut it in half.
>
> Do you take this circle
> Bounded by a single curved line?
>
> I take this breath
> That it cannot capture.
>
> Then you may kiss the spot
> Where her bridal train last rustled.

(lines 161–70)

There are several things to note. Sugar is white; the widow, "[w]rapped in the colors of widowhood," is black (line 154). One should not mistake, therefore, the widow giving her hand with the white. This is not the bride sought earlier.[16] Rather, the white is given by the widow, or rather, a cube of her sweetness is handed over by the hand of fate, a hand wizened in history and reaching out of the drapery of mourning. Second, the speaker is *receiving* the white cube, thus underscoring again that the white's arrival—and thus the origin of poetry—depends on factors that lie beyond the control of the willful subject, ascetically driven or not. Third, the speaker does not simply accept the vows. Twice he is offered the hand of infinity, what I take to be the infinite lines of fate that converge in the wizened hand of the "obscure widow." The first time he responds with a chipped tooth, cutting in half the fateful line. He later refuses the infinite and perfect loop of the circle (i.e., the wedding ring) in favor of breath, recalling the breath of speech and song uncovered in segment four. What does this suggest? In each instance, I find an affirmation of mortality over and against whatever the infinite would offer. If you recall the spinning Fates of Greek mythology (Clotho, Lachesis, and Atropos), you will also recall that a snip of their lines results in death, and this seems to be what the speaker embraces in place of the infinite line being offered, with its implicit promises of "lineage" and "destiny." Likewise, he elects to remain with the breath that he breathes and that carries whatever song he, as a mortal human being, might sing.

The speaker's clutch upon mortality recalls a problematic encountered earlier. In pure whiteness, poems do not arise. Without the contrast of ink, silence reigns. A difference is required, one that separates white and black and yet holds them together. In infinity, that difference is lost as well, and with it the possibility of poems. Words, poems, and all presences, for that matter, are singular and particular, but neither atomistic nor strictly and originarily solitary. Rather, they are worldly. They come to pass alongside of and amid other words, poems, and presences, e.g., books, bookstores, libraries, trees, printing machines, and so on. They do so, however, only insofar as they span a difference, relate across that difference, remain together yet apart. In the thorough density of an infinite line, that difference disappears, thereby leveling whatever would

---

16. One might suggest that the widow becomes white in remarrying, but those who are brides for a second time (and I presume a Christian ritual is at work here) are not supposed to wear white during the second ceremony.

make a point. In defending mortality, then, the speaker is also defending singularity and the difference it requires. He insists, if indirectly, that poems are particular bursts of presence and require an origin that preserves their particularity.

Despite the irony interrupting his nuptials, the speaker achieves some repose. In a gesture that recalls Wallace Stevens's "The Snow Man," he welcomes winter's white blankets and the way in which winter turns—Persephone in hell, Demeter grieving—our planet into a grave.[17] And the poetic word is granted, albeit in a form appropriate to one who has refused to renounce mortality.

> The snow can fall . . .
> What other perennials would you plant,
>
> . . . .
>
> For those remote, finely honed bees,
> The December stars?
>
> (lines 175–76, 179–80)

In Simic's powerful lines, snow, white crystals falling, become pages, "[t]ossing and turning in the dark" upon which being shines as it presences (line 178). At last, then—or so it would seem—after sacrificing asceticism itself, the speaker receives poetic words, thus abating his poverty. But only for a moment: singular snow poems melt and disappear.

The final two segments of Part Two suggest that the speaker's good fortune is fleeting. Segment nine conveys exhaustion, as if more had been taken than given.

> Had to get through me elsewhere.
> Woe to bone
>
> That stood in their way.
> Woe to each morsel of flesh.
>
> (lines 181–84)

---

17. Recall that it was in virtue of having a "mind of winter," of renunciation, that the listener in Stevens's poem—being "nothing himself"—is able to behold "Nothing that is not there and the nothing that is" (lines 1, 14, 15).

In exchange for melting poems, the speaker (like so many ascetics, even those who would sacrifice asceticism) appears to have sacrificed his body, although here self-denial does not seem to be the destructive force. Rather, something pushes through him on its way elsewhere. The subject of the first line is not given, and one could suppose that it might be "I." After all, asceticism involves the passage of a true self through an untrue self. But the third line employs a plural, "their way," and so we need to look for a plural subject. While no clear-cut resolutions are available, recall the lines of fate in segment six, the lines running along the hand offered by the widow to the speaker. They prompt the ceremony, and they enable the flurry of snow poems that fall in segment eight. I take it, then, that they carry the white sugar cube as well as the speaker, like "White ants / In a white anthill" (lines 185–86).

Perhaps this destruction was inevitable, however. As I noted earlier, pilgrimage and asceticism abandon the everyday, seeking to transcend the self with which it trades. But in doing so, the self is exposed, vulnerable, without the comfort of everyday predictability. And if we remove that comfort, what or who is left? If we interpret the unknown along the lines of the known, with what are the lines of fate received when we move outside known parameters? As segment nine closes, we have no answers—only the speaker at wit's end.

Two grand journeys, then, in pursuit of the origins of poetry: one a pilgrimage, the other ascetic, inward-moving. No grand results. Whereas Part One's final segment began, "We haven't gone far," Part Two's final segment suggests that no distance whatsoever has been traveled: "Solitude—as in the beginning" (line 192). In fact, something has been lost, namely, the prayerful expectation with which the poem began. Here, that expectation has dwindled to what amounts to less than a single, solitary presence. "A zero burped by a bigger zero— / It's an awful licking I got" (lines 193–94). Two journeys, and the speaker finds himself a zero, a null, his breath an empty expulsion. And if one reaches into the pipes from which he was belched, one will find only more emptiness. Hence the incredulity in the question "Does anyone still say a prayer / Before going to bed?" (lines 197–98). And yet some hope remains, for segment ten begins: "This is the last summoning" (line 191). This is not to say that the speaker is sanguine about his chances. He does not sleep, and fear surrounds him—"that dead letter office" (line 195).[18]

18. In poems from *Hotel Insomnia* and *A Wedding in Hell*, insomnia invokes the posture of waiting for a something or someone that may never arrive (Simic 1992b, 1994b). Likewise, "Dead Letter Office" from *Charon's Cosmology* (Simic 1977) depicts a "Dream penitentiary /

If *White* were to come to a close at this point, what would one say about its relation to its *Ort?* Several facets have been poetized. First, the move toward the origin involves a move past everyday habits and meanings. This is not to say that they are entirely left behind: perhaps, perhaps not. Perhaps they hide the key, much as a voice hides breath. But the authority that everyday names carry (their "common sense") has been suspended. Second, the ego loses its right to direct this journey. In fact, self-conscious problem solving is displaced throughout the first two parts of *White* by prayer, in ascetic self-negation, and in the self-effacement of asceticism itself, for example. And self-assertion cannot compensate for what self-consciousness fails to ascertain. When the speaker tries to turn his own breath into the white upon which a poem might come to pass, it evaporates before a word can be written. Third, the senses fail to locate the white; neither sight nor hearing nor touch find her there, ready for writing. Fourth, neither external nor internal journeys locate her. A pilgrimage finds only a holy nothing, and when deep inside, with breath itself, feeling about for the point of a voice's conjuncture with poetizing, breath's true name sticks in the speaker's throat.

What do all of these failures entail? Wherever the origin lies, it will not lie within the inwardness of the self-conscious subject of knowledge or action, that is, within the subject of modernity, the subject professing (or seeking) autonomy. The white always underwrites the efforts of those labors: representing, communicating, willing. Instead, it precedes that subject much as it lies behind the proposition (as we saw in Chap. 2). But this is not to say that the *Ort* occupies some objective point in time and space. Just as it is not "inside" the subject, it is not outside it either, and thus it is not locatable as a spatiotemporal object. It would seem, therefore, that the white is neither subject nor object, although at this point, that realization only clarifies through added obscurity.

As presented thus far, the way of *White* is a *via negativa*, particularly when we recall the other negations apparent along the way, e.g., the impossibility of poetry amid pure whiteness. Without the contrast of black ink, nothing can be written, and the poet in search of words upon that page will stumble about like a shepherd herding white sheep in the Arctic. When the speaker asks, therefore, "Praying, what do I betray / By desiring your purity?" (lines 85–86), I would answer, "Everything." In

---

Without doors or windows," an impregnable repository for lost greetings, wishes, and solicitations (lines 5–6).

pure whiteness, poems will not arise, and the stars will never be sung. Likewise, an infinite ground would overrun poems, fail to open the difference required for there to be particular words and poems. Wherever the *Ort* lies, therefore, it is bound to difference, to events of differentiation that gather words together into poems while keeping them apart.

As we have seen, the two journeys written out in *White* fail. And yet, one should not conclude that *White* thus denies the origin of poetry. Poems presence, they arrive—not as self-sufficient entities, but like snowfall. They are thus sent in some fashion or other, and it is the nature of that sending that *White* and we hope to fathom. Luckily, *White* does not close with Part Two. A third part remains, entitled "WHAT THE WHITE HAD TO SAY."

One might think that Part Three proves the final, desperate summons of Part Two successful. But the white bears curious tidings of her ways and days, and as we shall see, the thought that she would respond to any summons is unthinkable. First, she asserts her radical anteriority to whatever demands might be made upon her, claiming that she has "gone through everyone already" and "thought of you long before you thought of me" (lines 206–7). Moreover, she insists, most radically, "I am nearer to you than your breath" (line 215). In other words, whatever articulations we might employ to name or represent the white, she stands before them, enabling breath, thinking us before we think her. Open your mouth, exhale, let words sound forth—the white is already there. Note how this recoils on the notion of a summons; the breath that calls out has overlooked the fact that what it seeks is always already there.

Though always already there, the white is far from placid.

> Because I am the bullet
> That has baptized each one of your senses,
> Poems are made of our lusty wedding nights,
> The joy of words as they are written.
>
> (lines 225–28)

Speeding like a bullet, the white has already come and gone by the time poems are born, by the time words are written. Moreover, the white is already baptizing by the time one's senses feel the impress of *aisthesis*— the emptiness of a sky, the age of an oak, the mute life of a mannequin, the unnerving independence of a numb finger, whatever prompts the first word or line of a poem. The birth of poems thus testifies to her having already been there, to consummated vows. But this coition eludes our gaze just as the true name of breath precedes our voice.

In "WHAT THE WHITE HAD TO SAY," it becomes apparent that the speaker never catches or renders transparent the grounds of his voice despite the fact that the white appears to addresses him. That bed remains unfathomable. One can only apprehend searing joys of inspiration, the impress of presence.

> Each one of you still keeps a blood-stained handkerchief
> In which to swaddle me, but it stays empty
> And even the wind won't remain in it long.
> Cleverly you've invented name after name for me,
> Mixed the riddles, garbled the proverbs,
> Shook your loaded dice in a tin cup,
> But I do not answer back even to your curses
>
> (lines 208–14)

Note again her insistent anteriority: she is quicker than the wind, which is already too quick for our hankies. How then do we capture her? We cannot: "the most beautiful riddle has no answer" (line 231).

Because of the white's radical anteriority, I think that we need to regard this third section as an event of ventriloquism. The speaker, his final summons made, now speaks *for* the white, drawing stark conclusions in the wake of his two journeys and the *via negativa* opened along the way. On the one hand, I draw this conclusion for logical reasons. Nearer to us than our own breath, the white hovers in the dimension anterior to speech and writing, to utterance and inscription. It thus cannot speak in a human voice; rather, it speaks through it, is exposed by it. Likewise, it cannot be written in ink. Ink remains blind vis-à-vis the white, partially enabling poems that bear the traces of her arrival and departure but do not name her, even if they speak for her.

I have another reason for treating this final section as the speaker's masked performance. What the white has to say has already been said, for the most part, in the preceding parts: in the unspeakable true name of breath, in the white's refusal to be sensed, perceived, or represented, in the poverty of willful subjectivity in relation to originary experience, and so on. In this final part, however, the speaker is coming to terms with what he has undergone. Why the transformation? Rather than writing his way back toward the origin with an eye on and a desire for possession and for poems, he shifts his perspective and looks for the white in the poems he has received, in the flashes of words, phrases, and images with which poems commence, and that includes the poem that *White* is. That is, he allows her to speak through him, through what he has done and undergone. And there, in the language of his own poem of pursuit, he, in a sense, finds her. Let us explore the matter further.

To insist upon the anteriority of the white is not to render it substantial, as if it hovered above poets and things as a transcendental ground or condition of the possibility of meaning or poetry. The white, like the clearing of the open we discussed in Chapters 1 and 2, is located in the everyday.

> One sun shines on us both through a crack in the roof.
> A spoon brings me through the window at dawn.
> A plate shows me off to the four walls
>
> (lines 216–18)

Two thoughts. First, the white must move in the address of things. Pure whiteness, as we saw earlier, buries particular words and poems. Moreover, the white cannot be represented, having always already arrived. If it is to arrive at all it must do so with those presences it enables. Second, because it appears alongside of and in things, the white is not simply a background condition for the appearance of foreground scratches and marks. Rather, it is *of* things as much as it is a matter of some background or spatial realm within which they appear.

> Steadily, patiently I lift your arms.
> I arrange them in the posture of someone drowning,
> And yet the sea in which you are sinking,
> And even this night above it, is myself.
>
> (lines 221–24)

The white is thus ubiquitous, always already there when thing (poem or penguin) or world (e.g., the world of the kitchen—spoon, plate, four walls, window—or a terrestrial world, encompassing morning, night, sun, and so on) comes to presence.

Anterior, searing, ubiquitous, mundane, the white is fated: "Take a letter: From cloud to onion. / Say: There was never any real choice" (lines 235–36). These lines recall the lines of fate carved into the widow's wizened hand, the hand that handed over a white cube of sugar. (Again, note how this realization had been prepared for earlier!) White arrives like fate. There is never any choice. But then, there could not be, for choices come too late within this drama. As we have already seen, the choices of a willful subject are parasitic, relying upon the arrival of presences that the subject cannot compel, forces that include the flash of words, a flash lit up by the white's prior arrival and departure.

To hang the fate of poems upon the gift of precipitation (as we saw in the speaker's snow poems) is to suspend the whole drama in a nether region: "I am the emptiness that tucks you in like a mockingbird's / nest, / The fingernail that scratched on your sleep's blackboard" (lines 232–34). I take it that a fingernail scratching upon sleep's blackboard signifies the gift of a dream, or, given the common association, a poem. But it is a gift wrapped in emptiness, one that turns the prospective poet of origins into a mockingbird, that is, a bird who can sing the song of other birds.

The role played by this emptiness in the language of the poem finalizes the poverty of the speaker. Poems are born of lusty wedding nights, but that bed is suspended in emptiness, an emptiness that cannot be named. Nor, for that matter, will it answer to the demands of those who shout down into it. Here the origin arises, but as the "most beautiful riddle [that] has no answer." Out of the emptiness comes the poetic word, like scratches in the night. Push past those scratches, however, and only emptiness remains. As Simic said in 1972: "Poetry is an orphan of silence. The words never quite equal the experience behind them. We are always at the beginning, eternal apprentices, thrown back again and again into that condition" (Simic 1985, 5). It would seem, then, that earlier, the speaker was right to muse: "A zero burped by a bigger zero—" (line 193).[19]

I have suggested that we need to regard these disclosures of the white's anteriority, ubiquity, fated mundaneness, and now emptiness as yet another effort on the part of the speaker. My first reason was logical: one cannot name the white. Its ubiquitous, empty anteriority eludes the scribbles of inscription. Second, most of what the white does say is forecast in earlier segments, as I have tried to show at various points. We have

19. Other equally vacuous images of the white were thus more appropriate than the speaker had initially realized, e.g., the vowel "O" and the "holy nothing" (lines 59–60, 96). Incidentally, Simic returns to the idea of writing as "A zero burped by / Another zero" in "Figuring" (lines 1–2), found in *Weather Forecast for Utopia* (Simic 1984).

just now chanced upon a third reason in support of my claim. Swaddled in emptiness, receiving poems (and here the familiar "you" is employed, suggesting that the speaker is being addressed), the poet becomes a mockingbird. And this is precisely what I take "What The White Had To Say" to be: the speaker singing the song of the white. I thus do not take these final forty lines as disclosures straight from the horse's mouth, but directives: "look, there is where the white moves, or rather, has moved, has arrived and departed." To announce the mundaneness of the white is thus to direct us, even to exhort us, to look back to the everyday left behind in the two previous journeys, and to find traces of the white. But not just the everyday, for the white is ubiquitous, albeit as something that has always already arrived and departed.

One other reason would seem to support my contention that the final part of *White* involves ventriloquism. We noted earlier that pure whiteness smothers poems. The contrast (albeit a blind one) of ink is required for there to be words, poems, and the like. There is another conclusion to draw here, however; the white needs ink if it is to appear. Pure whiteness is also the color of blindness insofar as one cannot locate a here or a there in a blinding blizzard. And *White* underscores this point in an epigram drawn from Meister Eckhart at the outset of "What The White Had To Say": "For how could anything white be distinct from or divided from whiteness?" It could not be, and thus it needs what is not white, like the language of the poem, to throw it into relief, to exhort us to reach past the blindness of ink into the white emptiness that ubiquitously underwrites the birth of poetry.[20]

As ur-poetry, *White* unveils a stark drama. Poetic words come like scratches in the night, but if one seeks the fingernail dragging down sleep's blackboard, one will only find a riddled emptiness. I take it that this is why the poem closes with the white saying, through its medium, "That milk tooth / You left under the pillow, it's grinning" (lines 244–45). It's grinning because one cannot summon this muse like the tooth fairy; she remains anterior to such antics. I suppose it is also grinning because in the end, the tooth remains "white," and thus the white was already there, grinning in the summons, whispering: "I thought of you long before you thought of [or summoned] me." But these ironies are

---

20. Simic has recently returned to this theme in "The One to Worry About," a poem from *Night Picnic* (Simic 2001c). "I failed miserably at imagining nothing. / Something always came to keep me company" (lines 1–2).

elusive, and thus the mock-white, still coming to terms with what is dawning upon him (or us, for the "you" can also be read to include the reader), worries at the close of the second soliloquy that he has yet to understand her ubiquity, her mundaneness, and above all, her anteriority.

> Street-organ full of blue notes,
> I am the monkey dancing to your grinding—
> And still you are afraid—and so,
> It's as if we had not budged from the beginning.
>
> (lines 239–42)

One cannot summon the poetic word from its ground; it comes when it will, like fate, and refuses to attest to its origin. And yet this is not to render the white otherworldly. Instead, it is there among and alongside every poem, letter, and thing, elusive, riddlesome.[21] In a way, then, one can only ever be at the beginning—at the "gateway to beginning," to recall *Garbage*—a gateway here marked less by transforming forms than by utensils, four walls, and scratches in the night.

For all its self-conscious concern with poetry, I think we do *White* a disservice if we limit the range of its musings to that field of meaning we have come to call "poetry," even given poetry's manifold forms and voices. While *White* no doubt pursues the origin of the poetic word and even poetic inspiration and imagination, it also engages much broader questions concerning the birth of sense per se. I find this to be most poignantly evident in the following lines from "WHAT THE WHITE HAD TO SAY."

> Because I am the bullet
> That has baptized each one of your senses,
> Poems are made of our lusty wedding nights
>
> (lines 225–27)

As I have already suggested, this passage sets the anteriority of the white before the *aisthesis* that initiates the experience of the poet and inspires the poet's work. But we can push further than this and claim that the

---

21. Of the riddle, Simic says (in reference to the work of Vasko Popa): "In the riddle the word truly becomes *mythos*, becomes the place of origins" (Simic 1985, 94).

white is here marked as that which washes over each of the senses—i.e., taste, touch, sight, smell, and hearing—and thus none of them can fathom her. And yet we still have not captured the radical sense lurking in the white's claim upon "each one of your [or even our] senses."

Etymologically, "to baptize" means "to dip," from the Greek *baptizein*. Into what does the white dip "each one of your senses"? Into the "emptiness that tucks you in like a mockingbird's / nest" (lines 323–33). That is, the white baptizes "each one of your senses" into the "profound anonymity" and "nothingness" that Simic senses inside us, what he regards as our "common ground," to recall some lines from the interview with Rick Jackson and Michael Panori (Simic 1985, 62). But note that Simic does not limit this anonymity to the ground of poetic inspiration or language, but marks it as the "common ground" that lurks "inside each of us." One has reason to believe, therefore, that the white lays claim to more than the sense of the poem, although most certainly to the sense of the poem. Second, as a "ground," common or otherwise, this "profound anonymity" lies at our root, and thus it is tethered to the full range of our foliage, that is, to "each one of [our] senses," hearing in "sense" the very figure of sense itself. In other words, I hear in the white's claim to "each one of [our] senses" a claim upon whatever we might suppose to have sense, to be there before us, to be present, to be disclosed as something *that is* rather than nothing: a plate, a poem, our breath. To repeat:

> Steadily, patiently I lift your arms.
> I arrange them in the posture of someone drowning,
> And yet the sea in which you are sinking,
> And even this night above it, is myself.
>
> (lines 221–24)

We drown in the white because she is everywhere, enabling every relation. But this is no different than saying that we are drowning in presences, that the world rushes over us upon the heels of a white bullet quicker than the wind. We could also put the matter this way. Out of *White*, one is led to say that poems are gathered in our exchanges with the world: in the flash of a phrase, the fall of a leaf, the wistfulness of twilight. This is so, however, because the *Ort* of poetry is the very dimension of presencing itself, the dimension in which poems and persimmons, dingoes and doormats all come to pass. An ambiguity in a previously cited line captures this blurring of poem and presence well: "I am the emptiness that tucks you in like a mockingbird's / nest, / The fingernail that scratched on your sleep's blackboard" (lines 232–34). As I noted, the scratches upon sleep's blackboard can be read as dreams and thus as poems. But those scratches may also wake us to day, or, more generally, to the appearing of sense, to the presencing of worlds and things, poems and persons, beings and being. I would insist, therefore, that *White* is not only a poem of poetry but a language of originary occurrence as well.

Earlier, we observed that the speaker never seems to reach the stars he seeks via poetry, stars I equated with the shining of presencing, with being. As we have just seen, however, in exposing the white, the speaker also exposes the shining of being. Thus in "WHAT THE WHITE HAD TO SAY," he does find the stars, albeit in a way he could not have fathomed in Parts One and Two. First, the white appears as the night itself (within which stars shine [line 224]). More important, however, "WHAT THE WHITE HAD TO SAY" redirects the earlier quests, exhorting them to attend to what presences and not simply to the heavens. The white is given as saying, "One sun shines on us both through a crack in the roof," that is, solar light is shining along with and through the mundane worlds she inhabits along with the speaker. There is no need to become a moon rock in order to reach the stars. When are we not already there? This is the conclusion one is driven to here—and driven to most rigorously when one realizes that the white is there before one, on the page, enabling the words one is reading, becoming manifest in a poem that need not reach outside itself in order to present the greatest riddle.

Ur-poetry thus seems to be afoot in *White.* This is not to say, to recall a previous point, that it names beings one by one, that its meaning represents stable, ahistorical essences. Rather, it baptizes beings in its sense of sense, recasting whatever can be said to be there within the ranges it opens. One can thus see how *White* reaches into the "abyss of the world" that Simic seeks, following Heidegger. It reaches beyond what is present and fingers the rim of presencing itself. And this is how *White,* to recall Heidegger himself, "demands a metamorphosis in our manner of thinking and experiencing, one regarding the whole of being" (Heidegger 1984, 205). Rather than effecting transformations at the level of particular things (say, poetry), *White* transforms our sense of sense, thus bearing upon "the whole of being," which includes us, beings, and the birth of sense.

For all the radicality at play in *White,* Simic routinely invokes the philosophy of (un)consciousness in his prose accounts of the origins of poetry, at times sounding Husserlian.[22] Particularly in interviews and essays from the 1970s, he writes as if the origin of the poetic word lay within the poet's psyche, buried beneath the structures and temporality of consciousness. If this were so, then the origin of poetry would not be, as *White* seems to suggest, a radical, fateful silence, but the hidden percolation of human subjectivity. True, unconscious or preconscious eruptions may be mysterious, but they are not truly "orphans of silence." Instead, their silences are mere lacunae within that discourse of the psyche common to surrealism and psychoanalysis.

In his conversation with Jackson and Panori, Simic responds to their questions concerning "the poem's space" by saying,

> I'm one of those who believes that there is something that precedes language. The usual view is that there is some kind of equivalence between thought and language, that if you can't verbalize it you can't think it. I've always felt that there is a *state* that precedes verbalization, a complexity of *experience* that consists of things not yet brought to consciousness, not yet existing as language, but as some sort of inner pressure. Any verbal act includes a selection, a conceptualization, a narrowing down. (Simic 1985, 61 [emphases mine])[23]

Likewise, in "The Partial Explanation," he writes: "This is, indeed, the crucial event. The instant when that slumbering, almost anonymous content becomes audible, when its *privacy* is abolished and it translates itself into language" (Simic 1985, 102 [emphasis mine]). Simic here refers his explanations, partial as they might be, to three fundamental tropes of subjectivity: experience, states, and privacy. And one can understand why. The language of the poem is in some sense written by the poet and

---

22. In "A Clear and Open Place," Simic writes: "The experience of consciousness, however, precedes thinking; thinking derives from it. For Husserl, for example, the living present is the ultimate, universal and absolute form of transcendental experience" (Simic 1985, 109). This is somewhat odd, given that Simic elsewhere claims that part of Heidegger's appeal is precisely his attack on subjectivism (Simic 1990c, 63).

23. This view is not limited to the 1970s, however. In a more recent essay, "Poetry and Experience," he writes: "The experience of being eludes language. We need imagination because the presentness of the present moment cannot be worded except through poetic image. Consciousness is mute" (Simic 1997, 39).

not any old bystander. Likewise, poets have to work on that language, refine it, revise it; it is their affair. Intuitively, then, one can understand why Simic would believe that the language of the poem appears mysteriously within the receptive confines of consciousness.

Despite its intuitive appeal, Heidegger resists locating the origin of poetry within subjective orbits, and here I would follow him. In his 1941–42 course on Hölderlin's "Remembrance," he states: "The poetizing word names that which comes over the poet and transposes him into an affiliation that he has not created but can only follow" (Heidegger 1982a, 7). And in the 1942 course on Hölderlin's "The Ister," he adds, "The poetic is never conceived through the poet, but conversely, the poet is to be conceived only out of the essence of poetry" (Heidegger 1984, 149). Finally, "The Poem," from 1968: "The poet has not invented that which is his poetry's ownmost. It is allotted him. He joins himself to [its] direction and follows [its] call" (Heidegger 1981, 183).

At stake in Heidegger's remarks and Simic's apparent distance from them is the question of the origin of poetry and ultimately of "sense" itself. Heidegger is driven away from subjective tropes because he finds them insufficiently originary. As he argues in an early Marburg lecture from 1925, a phenomenology that focuses upon acts of consciousness (and here it matters not if they are conscious, unconscious, or preconscious) forgoes any interrogation of the being or sense of those cognitive events.[24] Instead, they are taken as primitives, thus foreclosing questions concerning their own coming to be. Second, a poetry that delimits its figurations within such theoretical tropes forgoes all claims to the originary and allows its musing to be circumscribed by the conceptual frame instituted by the adopted theory. Hence the appearance of terms such as "privacy," "experience," "state," and "consciousness" in Simic's prose. Simic's reliance on the tropes of subjectivity counteracts the logic of his belief that "[t]he poem is the place where origins are allowed to think" (Simic 1985, 112). In assuming that something like the human subject lurks at the origin of the poem, Simic precludes his poetry from thinking the origin at all.[25] Instead, his thought, at least in his prose reflections, is forced by its initial assumptions to return again and again to the supposed originariness of the prelinguistic, simple psyche. To be sure, I am

---

24. One can find this critique in the third chapter, sections 10–13, of the "Preliminary Part" of the lecture course entitled *Prolegomena to the History of the Concept of Time* (Heidegger 1979b).

25. Simic seems better off in an aphorism from *Wonderful Words, Silent Truth:* "A metaphysics without a self and without a God! Is that what you want Simic?" (Simic 1990c, 94).

not claiming that a poet's subjectivity is irrelevant to any and all readings of any and all poems. I am claiming, however, that as far as ur-poetry is concerned, the tropes of subjectivity delimit any language of originary occurrence with a subjectivism, and that Simic's poetry strikes me as more radical than some of his prose writings with regard to the origins of poetry.[26]

Painstakingly, we are assembling a feel for Simic's ur-poetry. In exposing us to a riddlesome, empty dimension of presencing that underwrites the theoretical and practical subject, *White* provides us with a startling language of origination. It is thus with good reason that we began with a long reading of *White,* for in exposing the originary moments of sense, its silences punctuate all of his work. To hear a Simic poem is also to hear the white out of which it has emerged and upon which it has been written. In a very real way, then, *White* is part and parcel of every Simic poem, and any attempt to engage his ur-poetry must trace out the journeys it enacts.

White does not exhaust Simic's ur-poetry, however. In "Fried Sausage," he writes:

> This is how I see it. There are three ways of thinking about the world. You can think about the Cosmos (as the Greeks did), you can think about History (as the Hebrews did), and since the late eighteenth century you can think about Nature.... I myself fancy the cosmic angle. The brain-chilling infinities and silences of modern astronomy and Pascalian thought impress me deeply,

---

26. Interestingly, I am asking Simic to do precisely the opposite of what Helen Vendler has requested. She is uncomfortable with his references to the spectral and metaphysical because she views poems as one facet of ordinary human activity. "Poems, like all human fabrications, from straw huts to theology, are made to our measure and by our measure, and are not above or beyond us. We do not need to ascribe more to art than we ascribe to unaided human powers elsewhere" (Weigl 1996, 131). In a certain way, I agree. Poems, like straw huts, emerge out of the scene of human dwelling and thus partake of all that is in force within that dimension. But Vendler takes the dimension of human dwelling to be something that "empirical critics," folks who evidently eschew the metaphysical and spectral, are best suited to explore. With this commitment, I could not agree less, assuming that her empiricism is anything like the empiricism that occasionally recrudesces in philosophical circles. Empiricism routinely appeals to something like "experience" in order to explain matters or settle disputes, e.g., to sensory experience or experience under the controlled conditions of revisionist scientific inquiry. In debates about originary matters, however (i.e., any matter having to do with the nature of X), such appeals are specious. Since Kant, it is precisely the nature of experience that marks the initial point of inquiry. I do not think that Simic needs to be reminded of the limits of empiricism, however. That "experience" itself is part and parcel of the riddle seems quite evident to him.

except that I'm also a child of History. I've seen tanks, piles of corpses, and people strung from lampposts with my own eyes. (Simic 1994a, 20)[27]

This passage suggests, I think, that Simic's ur-poetry is being written by at least two hands, one fingering infinities and silences, the other washing corpses. Before exploring the import of Simic's ur-poetry, we need to read the palm of this other hand.

---

27. Simic finds the "Nature" evoked in much contemporary literature too pastoral, preferring instead to set what we so readily term "Nature" into a more cosmological context: he is drawn to nature's inarticulate stoniness, not its supposed rhapsodic harmonies. In an interview from 1980, he says: "A stone is the uttermost limit; there's nothing beyond stone. . . . Stone is so alien to us, distant from us, any attempt to speak across that distance is interesting" (Simic 1985, 52–53). One should also consult "Stone" and "Stone Inside a Stone" from *Dismantling the Silence,* as well as the fifteenth poem of Part One in *The World Doesn't End* (Simic 1971, 1989). For a quick look at the image of the stone in poems by Robert Bly, Gregory Orr, Mark Strand, and Simic, see David Walker's "Stone Soup" (Walker 1975).

4

Ink

The power of *White*—and thus a pivotal part of the power of Simic's ur-poetry—lies in the silences that occur precisely at the points at which one expects to locate the white, that is, a substantive ground for the poetizing that is to be found there. Even in "What The White Had To Say," one has to make do with the mockingbird song of the speaker, the proclamations that simultaneously fill and point toward a silence. But as we have seen, the matter is not simply poetizing, but a language of originary occurrence that exposes presencing as an event and directs us, even exhorts us, toward the site of human dwelling, engaging presences as well as the differentiated dimension in and through which sense is born. Simic's ur-poetry, as it overpoetizes or even whitewashes our being, beings, and their world, thus riddles what comes to presence, for it underscores its fated emergence out of a silent emptiness (and this "its" refers both to the language of the poem as well as to presencing and what comes to presence).

But recall also that the white requires the smudges of ink and the rasp of the voice in order to appear, albeit as what has always already arrived. As the speaker says on the white's behalf: "Street-organ full of blue notes, / I am the monkey dancing to your grinding—" (lines 239–40). Now, I can think of two reasons for this dependence. First, the clearing of the great white open has always already occurred by the time any sense is present. Therefore, it is never present itself, except as a trace upon what is present. The white needs that upon which it is traced if it is to be present in any fashion, i.e., it requires the notes ground out of ur-poetry's music box. But that is not all, for as we saw in Chapter 2, an open dimension of presencing is "open" only in relation to differentiated, determinate presences. Without them, it collapses into a vacuum of utter nonbeing. As the difference between presences, therefore, the white also must dance to what rings within its silent, empty reaches.

But how should we regard those presences within which the white is traced, those notes to which it does its anterior jig? What appears therein, that is, what do we hear when we listen to the grinding and not just to the emptiness within which it turns? And what does Simic's ur-poetry tell us about these phenomena? Does it offer us any avenues into the black ink with which the speaker of *White* hoped to begin again, if only the white could be wooed?

In taking up the question of the ink at work within the language of the ur-poem, we return to an operation already discussed: ur-poetry's double repetition. Ur-poems begin with the repetition of traditional sayings, turning them into poetic figures. These sayings are then repeated a second time, but now as ur-figures, figures of poetizing that, through their interplay, invoke, cast, and expose the grounds of their own saying (including their own repetitions). But is that all there is to say about these repetitions? Are the echoes of an anterior clearing of an open, differentiated dimension the only music within the ranges that vibrate in sayings three times said?

Take "Poem Without a Title" from Simic's *Dismantling the Silence* (1971); the poem recalls Akhmatova's "Poem Without a Hero."

> I say to the lead
> Why did you let yourself

Be cast into a bullet?
Have you forgotten the alchemists?
Have you given up hope
Of turning into gold?

Nobody answers.
Lead. Bullet. With names
Such as these
The sleep is deep and long.

This is a startling poem. It begins with a recoil, a turn back toward its beginning, addressing the lead of a pencil, that which enables a poem to be written upon white pages.[1] Rather precisely, then, we are confronting the ink poetized in *White* as the necessary complement to the white in the *Ort* of the poem, although here we have a pencil. But where does this confrontation take place? Note that this poem is written in the first person: an "I" addresses the lead. Now, one might think that this "I" is an author addressing his or her pencil, preparing to write. But that cannot be the case, for what we have is something already written. Much like *White*, therefore, "Poem Without a Title" involves a writing turning back on itself—in this case, back upon those specks upon the white that throw it into relief. I thus take the "I" to be the "I" of the poem itself, of its language, an indexical subjectivity to which the various plays and operations of the language of the poem are referred such that they belong to this poem, this speaking.[2]

As we follow the "I," what do we find in these lead specks upon the white? A characterless tool? No. The history lead has led—war, assassi-

---

1. Ben Wooster helpfully pointed out that one could also read "lead" as "to take the lead" or a "dramatic lead." I consider this a complementary semantic ambiguity, for it is the lead of the pencil that leads the pencil to the page. In "Poem Without a Title," we are thus working with the lead venture of ur-poetry, although note that lead only *appears* to be what leads—the point that is the tip of the spear is reserved for the white.

2. Two thoughts. First, do not forget the *Ort*, wherein the "I" of the poem emerges. As we saw, no speaker is quick enough to freeze his or her breath and write upon the white pages that thereby rise to the surface of what before was invisible air. Second, one could construe the "I" of "Poem Without a Title" along the lines of lyric subjectivity, and ask: "Who speaks in the lyric poem?" The question is not inappropriate, but as I suggested in Chapter 1, I do not want to cast ur-poetic elements and operations in terms drawn from traditional poetics, for the translations they effect rob ur-poetry of its originary, figurative power. I thus prefer to regard the "I" as a marker for the whole range of figures and operations that come together in the language of the poem.

nation, domestic tragedy (children accidentally shooting one another), and the mournful heroism of defense—lies in the pencil tip. But it is not as if the language of the poem simply accepts this history. Instead, it challenges it, interrogates it. Pressing questions, the poem tries to awaken promises now dormant. But it fails. "Nobody answers." Instead, lead has become the bullet, and it cannot be reminded of times when its future was less certain, less grim, when it could lie upon an alchemist's table and dream of being gold.

I want to draw several thoughts out of "Poem Without a Title." First, it suggests that the marks that throw the white into relief and draw beings back to their origins (thereby enabling us to dwell there, in that relief) bring with them a host of determinations over which, and this is my second point, the "I" does not wield complete control, as evidenced by the struggle that "Poem Without a Title" is. Third, this poem is telling us that the *Ort* of the poem is, among other things, a site of contestation, a *polemos*. Not that the poem states this, but by enacting a struggle, it exposes us to what transpires within its speaking: the collisions of varying determinations, sometimes within and over the same figure.

Recall that the ink poetized in *White* had the color of blindness. In reading *White*, I intimated that blindness arose in the language of the poem because it covered over the white upon which it lay, much as a word shapes and hides breath. Here, however, another order of blindness is at work. In the initial repetition of the ur-poem, in the traditional saying recast as a figure of poetizing, we are beginning to hear more than the translation of a linguistic inheritance into a poetic figure. One has to ask, therefore, whether more might be at work in the language of the poem than the "I" can fathom, orchestrate, and translate into something to be said. Or, to speak more generally, might the figures ventured in ur-poetry bring a plurality of meanings into the *Ort*? Consider, for example, the semantic ambiguity of "lead" in "Poem Without a Title." In venturing the word, a polysemy enters the venture, overdetermines it, and tugs it down several tributaries. Moreover, this polysemy is a concentration of diachronic lineages that persist in the language of the poem even as it synchronically tunes its figures through relations established in that very same language.

Now, my point is not to suggest that within the language of the poem diachronic forces trump synchronic plays, and I do not think "Poem Without a Title" suggests this either. It does suggest, however, that in the language of the poem, diachronic struggles take place, from the lead of the pencil to leading figures, and thus the being of the poem is part and parcel of that struggle, that is, it is born of that struggle. Moreover, one has to consider that the poem may prove blind to those struggles, just as any subject seems to risk a certain blindness once inquiry, as it must, gives way to action.

For all this talk of blindness, I do not think that blindness is the central fate poetized in "Poem Without a Title," and mostly because the language of the poem is not blind to the fate of lead. But therein lies the rub, or rather, within the rub of the pencil upon the page, the fate of this poem can be heard. Struggle as it might, the "I" cannot turn the lead into gold; it cannot translate the history of the lead into poetry. The poem thus remains "without a title," for it has yet to become a poem fully, or to become a poem and only a poem. It has begun that journey, addressing an element in the hopes of saying it again, of poetizing it, but that element will not be said again in any significantly transformed manner. Rather, its initial determination is too fiercely stamped upon it for the other forces at work in the poem (e.g., the figure of alchemical transformation, the first-person voice, and so on) to take the lead into that region of the poem where determinations flash, new figuration lurks, and a language of originary occurrence might arise.

A failure is thus poetized in "Poem Without a Title." That is, the language of this poem exposes us to a possible limit of ur-poetry. The ur-poem cannot represent the white of its origin; moreover, it might not always be able to redetermine what it has drawn from the well of history. I would thus suggest that "Poem Without a Title" broaches a fate where poetry is almost impossible, unable to twist free of histories that conspire (often within the language of the poem itself) to return it, almost immediately, to the fate it would say again and eventually translate into figures of poetizing.[3]

We are beginning to muck about in the ink of Simic's work, and it is

---

3. Note that Heidegger imagines a similar fate in his epilogue to "The Origin of the Work of Art." There he fears that a continual and intensifying focus upon "experience" in the sense of *Erlebnis* (please recall our discussion in the Introduction) will be the death of art, for it will deny works their disclosive force in favor of the subject's cognitive dispositions or interests (Heidegger 1977a, 67). Here, however, it is not that the prejudices of the audience mishandle the language of the poem, but that within the language of the poem itself, a struggle occurs, a struggle that poetizing might lose. The fate poetized in "Poem Without a Title" is thus closer to Rilke's fate, at least as Heidegger reads him. Arguing that his ground words remain bound to what he considers instances of subjectivist metaphysics (e.g., Descartes, Pascal, and Nietzsche), Heidegger concludes that Rilke's work is ultimately not a matter of ur-poetry.

complicating our conception of that ur-poetry. Consider "Empire of Dreams" from *Classic Ballroom Dances* (Simic 1980a):

> On the first page of my dreambook
> It's always evening
> In an occupied country.
> Hour before the curfew.
> A small provincial city.
> The houses all dark.
> The store-fronts gutted.
>
> I am on a street corner
> Where I shouldn't be.
> Alone and coatless
> I have gone out to look
> For a black dog who answers to my whistle.
> I have a kind of halloween mask
> Which I am afraid to put on.

"Empire of Dreams," like *White* and "Poem Without a Title," is what one could call, aping Derrida, a poem before poetry. It appears to open at a moment before the onset of writing, or rather, it doubles back upon its own inscriptions. Here, however, the speaker encounters something more than an elusive white. Instead of a dimly lit threshold, the speaker finds on the first page of a "dreambook"—the "dream" a classic image of the poem—an occupied country, a pending curfew, and a city in ruins. The curfew suggests that soon the allotted time for dreaming and poetizing will end, that is, forces have come to regulate what a poet might write. That such a fate is not simply the stuff of nightmares should go without saying. Not only are poets killed (e.g., Lorca and Mandelstam) or imprisoned or exiled, but lines of oppression can also be found right on the page, as is evident in the second part of Akhmatova's "Poem Without a Hero," reprinted in the *Complete Poems* (1992).

Stanza ten of Akhmatova's great poem begins with three lines of ellipses followed by: "And the decades file by, / Tortures, exiles and deaths . . . I can't sing / In the midst of this horror." Stanzas eleven and twelve follow, composed only of ellipses that maintain the graphic form of the previous stanzas. How then are we to regard the "can't" of stanza ten, the inability it insists upon? The ellipses signify elisions, for Akhmatova did not believe that she would be permitted to address publicly the atrocities of the Soviet show trials and Stalin's almost cyclical purges. Completed stanzas do exist, however, and thus we know what Akhmatova wanted to and could sing. Stanza eleven, for example, speaks of "How we lived in unconscious fear, / How we raised children for the executioner, / For the prison and for the torture chamber." Such a song had no place in the public text of "Poem Without a Hero," however. Her song had to remain hidden, and her readers had to make do with ellipses, with what addresses us as the punctuated presence of totalitarian rule.

The fate written into "Poem Without a Hero" is severe, but I think that "Empire of Dreams" imagines a fate more sinister than censorship. Its dreambook is open, but before a word is even written, occupation is there. As the short, clipped sentences suggest, these are hushed tones, remarks hurried by fear. Why all this stealth? This open page is a "streetcorner" where the speaker should not be—that is, to open the dreambook is already to brook insubordination. In this empire, even to broach the possibility of poetry is to violate existing rules. Moreover, it is to expose oneself, "alone and coatless" in an evening of occupation. But the speaker has risked these violations and gone out. To write? Not yet. First, the speaker (whose gender is not specified) seeks a "a black dog who answers to my whistle." The image is cryptic but suggestive: on the one hand, the dog may offer protection, as one may be less likely to suffer harm with a quasi-familiar at one's side. On the other hand, the dog, more accustomed to skulking about after hours, may be able to lead the less-adept speaker through mazes of roadblocks and guard posts, enabling him or her to record with greater precision what remains of life in this city. Under occupation, the best muse may not be a nightingale but a streetwise cur. To recall Keats's "Ode to a Nightingale" (see Keats 1990) more explicitly, in order to poetize a scene of occupation, one's language must scuttle through the wreckage and not

>   forget
> What thou amongst the leaves hast never known,
>   The weariness, the fever, and the fret
> Here, where men sit and hear each other groan
>   (lines 21–24)

"Empire of Dreams" closes with an unnerving image. Whistling for a black dog, alone and coatless, curfew time drawing in, the speaker—not yet writing—carries a Halloween mask. Why? To elude detection? To participate in a secret festival of the dead? We cannot be sure. What is more palpable, however, is the speaker's fear. What causes it? The mask. Before a word has even been written, can one don a mask? If so, what will one write? According to Simic, "the poet is driven to tell the truth" (Simic 1994a, 2). Under times of occupation, must the writer risk the distortion of a mask in order to pass through the censors of the day? If so, can the truth be told, whether it concerns "the world's baffling presence" or the slings and arrows of a fate that does more than scratch on sleep's blackboard?

Bathed in twilight, "Empire of Dreams" suggests that, *qua* poem, it is under siege, that more than the labor of poetizing runs through its lines. Instead, decrees are at work, rules, threats, prohibitions; dreams are being colonized by an empire. But perhaps it would be better to say that "Empire of Dreams" suggests that poetizing entails more than what is commonly regarded as the labor of poetizing, that within poetizing itself risks can be and are taken and struggles ensue. I think one can even speak here of the threat of poetic occupation, wherein the language of the poem is, like a hostage, either held to external forces or, to recall the image of the mask, to forces that move the mouth of the "I" that speaks in the language of the poem.

Three thoughts now face us. First, we have found amid the repetitions of the ur-poem histories percolating within traditional sayings. Second, we have seen that the events of repetition essential to ur-poetry take place only with a certain amount of struggle, say the struggle of bringing polysemic figures into the synchronic articulations of the language of the poem, or the struggle of poets to continue writing, if only for themselves, or even the struggle of poets to maintain their voices in the masks they don in order to write in periods of occupation.[4] Third, it appears that such struggles—even the struggles of translation—might fail. The language of the poem might be overwhelmed by the traditions at work in

---

4. I want to stress that the struggle in question here is not the strife between earth and world that Heidegger thematizes in "The Origin of the Work of Art." That strife revolves around the attempt of a worldly figure (say, a temple) to translate that upon which it rests, the earth, into its field of concern, e.g., an opposition between the sacred and the profane. The earth resists such translation in principle, however, and thus only appears within the temple as self-secluding (Heidegger 1977a, 27–36). The struggle that takes place in "Poem Without a Title," however, is what we might term a struggle between world and world, concerning, for example, the relative force of a traditional saying as it enters into relation with the other forces at work in the language of the poem, forces that include other figures, operations, and so on.

the sayings it repeats, or the poem's language might simply be blotted out altogether by a censor's or even an executioner's hand.

A contrast is developing. Whereas *White* bathed presence in an emptiness whistling silently in a mockingbird's song, "Poem Without a Title" and "Empire of Dreams" are anything but silent. Rather, the ink spots they read us through are filled with the scratch and claw of struggles and resistances, and one can hear the march of occupying forces in what only seems to be rhythm. Moreover, the paths that these poems take into the ink seem different from the paths of autofigurative repetition that lead us into the empty ranges of *White*. Rather than repeat figures, translating them first into figures of poetizing and then into ur-figures, "Poem Without a Title" and "Empire of Dreams" confront the figures and operations they inherit, e.g., lead, a dreambook, a first-person address. In other words, they bring a halt to the repetitions required for ur-poetry and expose what speaks within the traditions being repeated.

Let us be more precise about what transpires in these poems. Like *White*, "Poem Without a Title" and "Empire of Dreams" pursue a reflexive course into the grounds of their own poetizing, and in doing so, they expose what is found there and exhort readers to attend to the multiple forces that move about that scene we have termed, following Heidegger, the *Ort* of poetizing. Now, in *White*, exposure occurs in movements that are neither allegorical nor metaphorical nor symbolic. Such concepts fail to apply, because each casts poetizing in terms of the transposition of some extra-poetic element into the language of the poem, an event they presume rather than explore. Moreover, the white is not an extra-poetic element. It is part and parcel of poetizing. One must speak instead of an autofigurative exposure in order to do justice to what *White* poetizes. In "Poem Without a Title" and "Empire of Dreams," however, autofiguration is challenged, and what is transposed in the repetitions of poetizing (i.e., traditional sayings, including the replay of rhetorical operations such as first-person address) is itself the matter at hand. True, traditional sayings are repeated, and as figures of poetizing (e.g., "country," "curfew"), but that initial repetition is denied and recoiled upon. That is, the second repetition of a poem such as *White*, in which poetic figures become ur-figures of poetizing, is refused in favor of a confrontation with what has already occurred.

Now, "Poem Without a Title" and "Empire of Dreams" do not rest content in expressing their situatedness, even though traditional sayings no doubt express the traditions to which they belong. Recoiling upon themselves, these poems do more than serve as a cipher for the grounds from which they take their leave. In fact—and here the contrast to *White* is marked—these poems turn to allegory. They allegorize the transpositions that feed the repetitions of poetizing, including ur-poetry.

Recall "Empire of Dreams." We read it as an allegory of the fate of poetizing, one wherein a scene set prior to the onset of poetizing is recalled and depicted through poetizing. It is as if we were told that the space of poetizing, the dreambook, even on its first page (a page no doubt white), is simultaneously a social space. This is not to say that the poem contains, if only implicitly, a theory of society. Rather, the point is that poetizing finds itself already in a determinate setting not of its own making, one that involves other presences (which is all I mean by "social"). But then, the poem is more concrete than this, for this space is not merely social but also occupied. Alien, hostile forces are afoot and in charge. Furthermore, the occupation is not only physical. It is there before anything is even written, and the speaker to whom the dreambook belongs, the "I" who serves as an index for the work of the poem, holds a mask in his or her hand, a mask that threatens to bring the occupation home in a more thorough fashion.

Before concluding our discussions, we shall have more to say about the threat posed by the mask that appears in "Empire of Dreams." For now, simply note how the poem allegorizes a fate, how it transposes what the language of the poem presumes into the language of poetizing. (This is, after all, the first page of the dreambook, and thus we are supposedly at a point before poetizing commences.) This is a strange allegory, however, for it concerns the roots of its own *allegoresis*, of the determinate, ink-soaked scene wherein allegories commence. As with *White*, therefore, this is an address that calls itself into question, and in doing so, it asks to be read against the grain; it requires that we focus less upon the scene presented than on what it suggests about the scene wherein it (or any such presentation) comes to pass. This is not to say that the tale unfolding in poems like "Empire of Dreams" is a mere shadow play, an elaborate decoration of an injunction. In "The Flute Player in the Pit," Simic writes: "one wishes to say something about the age in which one lives. Every age has its injustices and immense sufferings, and ours is scarcely an exception. There's the history of human vileness to contend with and there are fresh instances of it every day to think about. One can think about it all one wants, but making sense of it is another matter" (Simic 1994a, 2). But this labor of sense making does not exhaust the address of Simic's allegorical directives. Alongside such presentations, an exhortation booms: look further, press into this address, for more is at work here than "I" could ever represent, allegorically or otherwise. In other words, the point of these allegories is not just to represent allegorically what swims in the ink of poetizing but also to slow down and even halt the process of allegorical transposition and poetic repetition in general, such that we might attend to what is found there, to what moves in the traditions of traditional sayings.

Questions are emerging. Have we fractured Simic's ur-poetry, broken it in two, or is there a way in which to bring together these allegories, the autofigurative exposition of *White,* and what they respectively poetize? Before we consider these questions, I want to look at a third allegory concerning the din out of which, even as it is cradled in emptiness, poetizing emerges. Here, from *Jackstraws* (Simic 1999) is "Mother Tongue," a relentless, recoiling allegory of, among other things, its own allegorizing efforts.

> That's the one the butcher
> Wraps in a newspaper
> And throws on the rusty scale
> Before you take it home
>
> Where a black cat will leap
> Off the cold stove
> Licking its whiskers
> At the sound of her name.

Beyond the obvious pun on "tongue," several things merit notice. First, one could read the poem as a response to a query or conversation concerning mother tongues. I imagine the speaker saying, with some degree of authority (for the tone of the poem is not rich in caution, that is, the speaker is not offering a hypothesis), "You want to know what a mother tongue is, well, I'll tell you. That's the . . ." If we read the poem in this way, the "you" named in the poem is generic and could just as easily be "one." Second, the speaker insists that a mother tongue is acquired, not an innate capacity. One goes somewhere to receive it—here, a butcher's shop. Third, the poem presents itself as capable of accounting for the nature of a mother tongue through the tale it offers. Again, there is real confidence in this poem.

Note the tension underlying the reading just given. Poems are written or said in mother tongues; they belong to a language. "Mother Tongue" thus cannot help but set its own poetizing within the allegorical tale it tells about the origin of mother tongues. Given this reflexivity, I think that one can read the "you" of line four as something more than a generic "you," for this "you" includes the speaking that occurs within the language of the poem. Now, I am not suggesting that the former reading is wholly incorrect. I do think that a generic "you" is being addressed. But I think that included in the "you" is the language of the poem as well.

If the "you" of line four does venture into the realm where poetizing and a mother tongue come together, its meaning changes somewhat. Rather than being one of the many possible addressees of the personal pronoun "you," the language of the poem, as something in itself, as something involved in the redetermination of various figures, forms, and operations, is being taken back to a scene through which it once lived. Recall that "Empire of Dreams" and "Poem Without a Title" involved a first-person address, the language of the poem addressing its own situatedness. Here, we confront that "I" in its nascent state receiving a mother tongue from a butcher, wrapped in newspaper. On this reading, then, the 'you' addressed in line four can be only a "you," that is, like a child, it can only be told what is occurring. As the "I" has yet to emerge, there is no first person to apprehend this event explicitly. "Mother Tongue" is therefore less an assertive tale or even a straightforward allegory concerning the nature of mother tongues than an elliptical, recursive depiction of an event germane to the birth of the first person—an event neither perceivable nor recountable in the first person, however.

I am not suggesting that the poem concerns the emergence of human subjectivity per se, as if subjectivity only comes into being within something like a native language. Such a point is not to the point at all, for we still are working with and around the *Ort*, the site wherein poetizing comes to pass, and we are struggling to decipher Simic's two-handed urscript. Here, subjectivity is of the poem, and it concerns the ways in which poetizing acquires a mother tongue, a prerequisite for the power to transpose determinations like "lead" into poetry. And by proceeding without the subject of "Poem Without a Title" and "Empire of Dreams," operating instead with a second-person address to some young, raw "you," "Mother Tongue" opens for us an arena in which that acquisition can be scrutinized. It also takes us to a point familiar from *White:* a point prior to the emergence of theoretical and practical subjects. But what is found there?

As an allegory of the "I" of poems like "Poem Without a Title," "Mother Tongue" suggests that a complex inheritance underwrites poetizing. Of course, there are figures like "lead" and "dreambook" to be drawn from a mother tongue. Second, more formal operations are also acquired, e.g., iambic feet, graphic layouts, or general forms, such as the sonnet. And then there are the plays and juxtapositions that take place through a combination of semantic figures and syntactic operations. Consider, for example, the angel of Rilke's *Duino Elegies.* A figure free from desire, able to reflect beings as they are rather than deform them as humans do through desirous attachments, the angel also appears, if only implicitly, throughout the *Sonnets to Orpheus.* In a letter to Witold Hulewicz, Rilke says of the angel: "The angel of the *Elegies* is that creature in whom the transformation of the visible into the invisible, what we are accomplishing, already appears in its completion" (Rilke 1982, 317). In the *Sonnets,* Orpheus appears as a figure whose labors will redeem us (should we mime them) precisely by helping us become more angelic. His song stands in contrast to the angel; it is what it is only through that contrast.[5] Now, I am not claiming that Rilke received this contrast readymade from his mother tongue, but such a play is only possible through a mother tongue, one that affords the possibility of a contrast between Greek and Christian figures (or between elegies and sonnets, for that matter).

"Mother Tongue" also exposes the fate of a poem whose language lacks the power to speak as an "I." It must, like a child, take directions from another. Those poems that reach behind the emergence of a poetizing "I" must always receive the tale of its (and thus their own) birth secondhand, that is, they must always take another's word for this emergence, unable to rely upon one of their own making. And this means the struggle posed by the mask in "Empire of Dreams" is inescapable. Because one does not choose a "Mother Tongue" but awakens within one, poetizing begins already masked by all that it inherits along with its mother tongue, and it cannot begin otherwise.

At this juncture, I would caution against undue abstraction. The point

---

5. In the very same letter to Hulewicz, Rilke writes: "*Elegies* and *Sonnets* support each other constantly" (Rilke 1985, 162).

we have reached does not simply concern inherited figures, forms, and operations: this is not an allegory of variables. After all, this tongue is being purchased at a butcher's shop that calls to mind the "slaughter-bench" of history upon which Hegelian history unfolds.[6] The suggestion is that a mother tongue is inherited from a site of blood and slaughter, that it comes to be spoken upon fields of contestation and suffering. One can see this by tracing the usage of a word, noting its changes and the contexts to which those changes belong. "Angel," for example, to recall Rilke again, denotes a celestial being, one more akin to "God" in Christian mythology than to humans and one capable of serving as a divine emissary or warrior. But it also denotes one who aids or supports, with money or influence, an artistic venture. And then, particularly striking women also are referred to as angels (although less so now than, say, fifty years ago). If we add to this litany Rilke's use of "angel" in the *Duino Elegies*, we find ourselves back amid the kind of polysemic confluence of meanings that we noted with the figure of "lead," a confluence that accompanies every form, figure, or operation entering into the language of the poem. What we failed to note at that time, however, is that other histories often move within etymological histories.

"Angel" comes from the Old English *engel* and the Old French *angele*, both of which derive from the Late Latin *angelus*, itself tied to the Greek *angelos*, meaning "messenger," which was used by 70 C.E. to translate the Hebrew *mal'āk*, short for *mal'āk-yĕhōwāh*, "messenger of Jehovah." How did a Latinate word find its way into English, and a Greek word into Latin, and a Hebrew word into Greek? I lack the means to answer such a question adequately, but a simple observation on such translations will prove sufficient to make my point. While Christianity is central to the history of "angels," so too is the Roman Empire, with its curious form of *pax*—the many conquests that brought Latinate terms throughout Europe prior to and irrespective of the spread of Christianity. This is not to say that "angel" is one of those terms, but the spread of Christianity was bound to the continued existence of the Holy Roman Empire (which itself grew out of earlier Roman conquests). I take this to mean that a mother tongue is sedimented not only with meanings,

---

6. In Leo Rauch's translation, Hegel writes: "But as we contemplate history as this slaughter-bench, upon which the happiness of nations, the wisdom of states, and the virtues of individuals were sacrificed, the question necessarily comes to mind: What was the ultimate goal for which these monstrous sacrifices were made?" (Hegel 1988, 24).

sounds, and grammar but with the flow of blood as well, for words move with armies as well as with missionaries and their scriptures.

In the discussions that make up what has come to be known as his *Theses on the Philosophy of History,* Walter Benjamin (in a passage curiously left out of the standard translation) writes: "Do we not, ourselves, touch a breath of air that surrounded those who came before? Is there not in voices to which we give our ear an echo that has been muted until now? Do not the women whom we court have sisters whom they have come to no longer recognize? If so, there is a secret agreement between past generations and the present one" (Benjamin 1974–89, 1:2:693–94).[7] While Benjamin takes this agreement to be ripe with messianic promise, we need not follow him down that path in order to note the following about Simic's allegories of poetizing's place in and confrontation with history. Recall the repetitions of traditional sayings or figures that drive poetizing in general, ur-poetry included. By setting such efforts within a mother tongue drawn off the slaughter-bench of history, Simic's poem opens itself—and thereby us—to what percolates throughout its inheritance, should we care to attend to that surfeit. One might indeed hear the march of Roman legions in a figure like the "angel," even if it appears in a context such as Rilke's *Duino Elegies,* seemingly far-removed from those conquests.

This is not to suggest, however, that only etymologies carry history in this way. In contemporary American usage, regardless of the context, one can hear in words such as "red" and "scalp" the protracted war waged by the United States against the indigenous peoples of North America. Likewise, in the wake of the Shoah, those who write in and work with German (and the point is not limited to poets) are confronted with the very same language in which genocide was drafted, ordered, and carried out. In that mother tongue, then, trains still rattle along toward oblivion.[8]

---

7. Benjamin seems to be inspired, in part, by a teaching attributed to the Besht, a grand figure of Hasidic Judaism. "Man is not alone. . . . God makes us remember the past so as to break our solitude. Our forefathers stand behind us, some of them tested or chosen by God. Whatever they did, they did for us. Whatever we do, we do for them. Long ago, in Egypt, every one of us strove for the preservation of the holy tongue, the names of our ancestors and their descendants, and the memory of the Covenant. Each one of us sat at the Prophets' feet. . . . Every one of us marched through the desert, to Sinai and from Sinai. . . . And this is why we must stay together" (Wiesel 1978, 7–8).

8. In the introduction to his translation of Adorno's *Aesthetic Theory,* Robert Hullot-Kentor captures this sensibility well. He writes: "The historical breach on the other side of which German now stands makes even this translator involuntarily prefer to say [of the lan-

To a greater degree than "Poem Without a Title" or "Empire of Dreams," "Mother Tongue" reminds us that within its repetitions, voices and struggles echo. We can also say, I think, that its lines not only carry the struggles of history but also participate in them. As I noted, in Christian mythology, an angel can be a soldier in the army of "God."[9] In a way, I am claiming that the word "angel" is also a soldier, but not in a war between Jehovah and Satan. Rather, this war occurs between cultures, subcultures, and peoples, and it concerns the ways in which they perceive, engage, and live with one another. If I call a young woman an "angel," I set her upon a pedestal and elevate her above the merely human. Such is the suggestive power of the word, and the idiom explicitly trades on it. But I also deny her the full range of her being, i.e., her desires, foibles, and lived body. Angels are not mortals. It is thus unsurprising that a woman who is termed an "angel" is also often told not to worry her "pretty head" about mundane matters, as if she were too good for labor and should be freed from anxieties. *Qua* "angel," her role is not only to be admired and flattered but also to be admonished, should she allow her feet to touch the earth. Aside from the issues we have already discussed (e.g., the way in which a lineage speaks in the traditional sayings replayed in the language of the poem), the scenario I have conjured suggests that repetitions of received figures can also enter into new historical battles, such as that over sexism. The context of their deployment, through a facet of some figure, may thicken the bars of oppression.

We have not yet finished reading "Mother Tongue" nor gauged the full brunt of what is poetized there. And thus we have not yet mined what is to be found in Simic's two-handed ur-poetry. Beyond the clamor of buried histories, the poem suggests that further mediations and conflicts run through its language. Note that the butcher wraps the severed flesh in newspaper before handing it over.[10] The image suggests that the

---

guage in which *Aesthetic Theory* was written] the 'original' rather than German, and made it necessary to say page by page, that it is, or was, a Jewish language, too" (Adorno 1997, xix).

9. There are Milton's angels, described in Book VI of *Paradise Lost* in stark, military terms. God says: "Go, Michael, of celestial armies prince, / And thou in military prowess next, / Gabriel, lead forth to battle these my sons / Invincible, lead forth my armed saints / By thousands and by millions ranged for fight" (lines 44–48). But note also biblical cases, e.g., the four angels of *Revelation* released by the sixth of the seven trumpets bound to the last of the seven seals. "They were released, who had been held ready for the hour, the day, the month, and the year, to kill a third of mankind" (Rev. 9:15).

10. Note also that the tongue comes without a mouth and would not be able to speak on its own. One could read this as a nod back to *White,* for a mother tongue still needs the white,

severances whose traces have been left on the tongue are themselves handed down within current contexts of use, even within the chatter of the day (to take a less-than-generous stance vis-à-vis newspapers). I take this to mean that the language of the poem does not receive a mother tongue in isolation from reigning habits of usage. Atop the histories inherited, one also finds rules of the day concerning diction, construction, and the like. Is a given word slang? Whose? In what kinds of poems does it show up? Or what of prose lines? Are they suitable for a "poem"? Who is writing sonnets these days, and why? These questions, rhetorical at this juncture, direct us into a contested scene of usage, a scene wherein poems are gathered and a mother tongue lives.[11]

The newspaper image suggests something else as well. Amid its many stylistic habits, the writing one finds in newspapers is purposive (which is not to say biased, although it may be that as well). Editorials aim at persuasion, as do advertisements, in their own way. Likewise, stories are often selected with an eye toward influencing policy. Given the scene at work in "Mother Tongue," a scene wherein some nascent "I" awaits a voice of its own, I take this to mean not only that a mother tongue is subject to contemporary habits of use but also that such usages belong to larger, purposive contexts, e.g., persuading people to vote for X, to reject prose poems, to buy Y, or to notice how well- or ill-mannered the police have been lately. In other words, a mother tongue arrives already caught in the struggles of contemporary life—already a participant. If we take this point to the language of the poem, another level of struggle becomes apparent. Within its various elements, down to its words and rhythms, and *qua* "poem" (and then as the kind of poem it is, and then with regard to the subject matter it treats), the language of the poem, perhaps only inadvertently, champions certain things. Perhaps it embodies and thus promotes a self-described "high culture" and the learning

---

which is nearer to the language of the poem than its own breath and in which the differentiated dimension is opened wherein beings, poems, things, and worlds arise.

11. After Simic won the 1990 Pulitzer Prize for his prose sequence, *The World Doesn't End*, a terse editorial in *The New Criterion* objected, suggesting that prose poems were not verse (which, the editors argued, the prize was designed to reward) and that in rewarding a prose poem such a prestigious prize, the Pulitzer board did "considerable harm to poetry" ("A Pulitzer for—What?" 2). While the argument is far from clear, I take the point to be that in eschewing traditional forms, *The World Doesn't End* eschews poetry. This goes to show, I think, that insofar as mother tongues involve forms, genres, and the like, they will also involve conflicts over the nature and proper use of those forms and genres. To inherit a mother tongue is to inherit those conflicts.

its survival requires. What is a sonnet? Who wrote them? Or it might celebrate a particular language, say Spanish, and then alongside English, thus calling for (and favoring) bilingual readers.[12]

Now, one might think that an emphasis on purposive contexts undermines or even contradicts the earlier claim that in ur-poetry's first repetition, a traditional saying is replayed as a poetic figure freed from other ends, i.e., simply as something to be said. "Mother Tongue" does not deny that initial translation. What it insists, however, is that such translations, like it or not, participate in the struggles of those traditions with which they engage in dialogue, e.g., struggles over the nature and status of verse, the identity of "America," and so on.

Mediation upon mediation, struggle within struggle. This is what "Mother Tongue" opens up within itself, within the "I" that spoke in "Poem Without a Title" and "Empire of Dreams," and within all who speak. The maelstrom, so remarkable when read beside the silent, empty reaches of *White*, brings to mind a short poem from *Hotel Insomnia* (Simic 1992b): "War."

> The trembling finger of a woman
> Goes down the list of casualties
> On the evening of the first snow.
>
> The house is cold and the list is long.
>
> All our names are included.

If the white is always the first snow, and it must be, then in its wake Simic's ur-poetry prepares for another wake. The point does not simply concern mortality, however—the inevitability of our passing. Entitled "War," the poem insists that each of us is a casualty of the struggles that are our world. Now, one does not have to die in order to appear on this list. Not everyone dies of war, and yet we are all casualties of the conflicts raging in our mother tongues, inseparable from them. It is as if struggles

---

12. Here I have in mind the work of Guillermo Gómez-Peña, who explores questions concerning hybrid identities through multilingual poems, essays, and performances. For a selection of written pieces, see his *New World Border* (Gómez-Peña 1996).

ensue at each instant of presencing, as if originary occurrence were itself bellicose, much as the language of the poem is.[13]

In large part, the power of "Mother Tongue" stems from the intensity and range of the struggles that it admits into its own inception. And that intensity is only furthered by the fact that the butcher's scale from which a mother tongue is handed down is rusted. First, the rust suggests that for some time, mother tongues have been dispensed without recourse to a measure. Second, now that a measure is sought—one that will give a sense of what is being received—the scale may no longer weigh properly. At the point where mother tongues are received, we must make do without a reliable, external measure for what this "you" acquires. Not that the poem defends a claim that such is lacking; rather, it presents such a measure as part of the ensemble with which history's butcher doles out mother tongues, the very tongues, I would add, within which claims are marshaled, defended, and revised.[14]

We are still not finished with "Mother Tongue," with all of the exhortations that Simic's ur-poetry contains. In the second stanza (and only now am I really turning to it), a future unfolds for the "you." A black cat awaits him or her, ready to eat what is bundled in history's copy. Now, there is an ambiguity in the last line. The "you" is told that the cat leaps off the stove "At the sound of her name" (line 8). Is that the cat's name, or someone else's, perhaps someone who might be able to make use of the tongue? If the former, the prized tongue only serves to feed the age-old image of ill fate, and it appears that the "you" willfully keeps her fat. If the latter, ill fate still threatens the gift, the presence of the cat

13. In a suggestive passage from a lecture on sociology, Adorno writes: "Essence itself... is not identical with meaning, is not a positivity *sui generis*, but is the context of entanglement or guilt in which everything individual is entwined, and which manifests itself in every individual entity" (Adorno 2000, 21). We will return later to this thought of bellicose presencing.

14. Here one might expect an argument on behalf of the view, current since Jean-François Lyotard published *The Postmodern Condition: A Report on Knowledge* in 1979, that the metanarratives by which we might measure our actions, interpretations, evaluations, and prescriptions have proven incredible. This is not to say that metanarratives are not part of various cultural conversations or that they do not exist, but that (and this is a descriptive claim) they no longer have the force they once had. Moreover, and this is a prescriptive claim, they no longer should be interpreted or defended as if they were able responses to crises of legitimation or identity. They should be heard as part and parcel of the struggles they once sought to regulate. In this context, however, I think that such an argument would be out of place, for we are still working with how the language of the poem articulates and contests its situatedness in history. I have, in addition, argued this point elsewhere and will not pursue it again here, preferring to maintain our focus upon Simic's poetry (Lysaker and Sullivan 1992; Lysaker 1996, 1999a). Thanks to Jena Jolissaint for her thoughts on the image of the rusty scale. I am indebted to her.

thus underscoring an extremely bleak possibility in either case: journeys for a mother tongue and all that such enables for the language of the poem may only fuel ill fate, not remedy it. That is, what we gather from the slaughter-bench of history may only add to what will later cross it. Who knows for certain what casualties will issue from the wars raging inside mother tongues?[15]

Speaking from the point at which a poem is gathered into its poetizing, or, more precisely, from where its ink pools, allotting it a kind of density, a determinacy that helps poetizing redetermine other elements entering into the language of the poem (e.g., "angel," "lead," and "butcher," for instance), "Mother Tongue" allegorically unveils a wild scene of overdetermination. First, such density requires a mother tongue. Acquiring a mother tongue is no simple matter, however, and it does not emerge *ex nihilo*. Rather, one draws such a tongue off the slaughter-bench of history and thus receives a part and parcel of the contestation. Third, it arrives wrapped in the struggles of contemporary social life, struggles concerning the subject and manner of one's speech. Fourth, no external measure seems to exist that might enable one to legitimate or purify one's inheritance. Rather, one remains bound to the struggles one inherits. In fact—and this is the fifth point—one may even contribute to causes one would have hoped to avoid or even counteract.

Amid all these pressures, one has to wonder whether an "I" ever emerges. Perhaps the language of the poem never escapes the haughty, cocksure instructions of the voice that addresses the "you" moving from the butcher shop to a whisker-licking cat. Because a first-person voice never appears within the language of this poem, what are we to say? The point is not that "Mother Tongue" has something definitive to say on the matter, such as "History crushes poetry." Rather, it exposes in the gathering of a poem the presence of factors that might very well prevent a poem from translating traditional sayings into something else.

And what, then, of ur-poetry? Would it be possible under such conditions? Perhaps the ventures made with a mother tongue are so overdetermined, so bound to inherited figures, forms, and operations, that a language of originary occurrence is never broached. Perhaps the language of the poem merely repeats a traditional saying, translating it into a figure

---

15. Here I cannot help but think of Nietzsche's fate. A relentless critic of herd mentalities, anti-Semitism, and resentment, Nietzsche's texts were nevertheless put in the service of National Socialism, despite the fact that it bore all of the above-mentioned traits Nietzsche loathed.

of poetizing without reaching into and exposing the region of its saying. I think that this is the fate that "Mother Tongue" invokes, a fate wherein a "you" lives out the plays provided by an authoritarian speaker whose cocksure voice pronounces on what is what.

Recall that in *White*, poetry remains at the mercy of whatever is scratched upon sleep's blackboard. That is—as if being itself were muse-like—sense is neither conjured nor made by us, but sent, released, and in a riddlesome manner, i.e., without an apparent ground. Here we are once again in a receptive position, but the voice addressing us is far less gentle than the murmuring ventriloquism of "WHAT THE WHITE HAD TO SAY." Instead, it is authoritarian, and, perhaps, utterly leveling. Perhaps it will only enable obedience. This is, I think, why the speaker is afraid to don the mask needed in order to move about the "Empire of Dreams." Knowing about the conflicts that are part and parcel of any mother tongue, even an adopted one, the speaker must wonder what voice will squeak through the slit pretending to be a mouth. "Mother Tongue" thus not only poetizes a fate that threatens the "I" of those poems claiming to speak for themselves, that is, asking to be taken on their own terms (and that includes ur-poems), but it also suggests that the arrangements required by sense itself may be blind or even oppressive and murderous.

But perhaps I have been unfair in my reading of "Mother Tongue," rushing past a possible reading of this "you" whose fate we have been tracking, supposing it to entail the fate of the language of the poem. What if we take "you" to be the reader? The "you" would then not be simply a generic "you," but readers, although anyone who had read the poem could play that role. What if we read "Mother Tongue" in this way? Such a reading, I think, hauntingly leads us back to where we have just been, thus exposing the full reach of "Mother Tongue."[16]

Suppose that the reader is being told about a mother tongue that she or he, at some point, supposedly lacks. (Whether it is the present of the address does not matter, for at some time, the reader must gain a mother tongue and find him- or herself at the butcher's shop.) Like the nascent poet, "you" would belong to an intersubjective community and would be able to hear and respond to second-person addresses. But "you" would lack the "I," and thus the same dramas noted above would unfold:

---

16. As we bring the reader into the poem, we add another exhortation to Simic's work. In the wake of "Mother Tongue," readers should recall the shop at which they acquired their native language.

history's butcher would hand to "you" a tongue severed but not free from struggle and strife, one wrapped in newsprint and thus in habits tied to purposive efforts. And it would have been weighed upon a rusty, unreliable (even unsanitary) scale, so "you" will not really know precisely what "you" have received. Then, when "you" return home, the cat awaits "you," perhaps to feed upon "your" tongue, perhaps to spread ill fate. In other words, on this reading, "your" fate is as nebulous and sinister as the fate of the nascent poetic "I." History might run over "you," too. Left without an "I," "you" would be at the mercy of another voice—and a voice whose goodwill ought not to be supposed, for one must suppose that the owner of the voice goes to the same butcher.

In the case of the nascent "I," the collective fate of a mother tongue signaled the possible dissolution of ur-poetry into history, the collapse of ur-ventures into stale repetitions and the loss of an exposure of all that is said via traces in the language of the poem. What, though, does failure at this juncture signal for the reader? First, note that "you" is an abstract universal, applying to anyone who chances upon the poem. Without an "I," however, a reader is nothing more than the abstract addressee, for here, at the point before a mother tongue is acquired, the personal side of the second person (the "me") is nothing but an amalgamation of reports and orders received from another. In other words, in "Mother Tongue," the addressee, if we read it as a reader, cannot exclaim, "This poem has been addressed to me," for that degree of reflexivity has yet to coalesce. It thus makes no difference whether we take the "you" in line four to be singular or plural. Without mother tongues, the field of possible readers has yet to individuate.

If a reader amounts to nothing more than an abstract addressee, several fates unfold. First, one would be hard-pressed to claim that anything like reading is taking place. Just as the poetic "I" loses its ability to struggle with what moves in the lead of a pencil, so too a reader, *qua* empty addressee, lacks the ability to interpret the language of the address, to move between whatever sense she or he might make of the address and the language of the poem. Lacking what we might call an interpretive "I," that reader will never have "my" interpretation, a singular interpretation to bring back to the language of the poem for comparison. Instead, the reader will take dictation, and that is all.

Without the possibility of interpretation, critical engagement also disappears as an option for those addressed. Questions such as "What have I (or we) just heard?" are preludes to "And is it true?" If one cannot even test an interpretation, how can one scrutinize the veracity of what has been said? One cannot. Nor can one reflect upon matters of import as we did in Chapter 2. "What does this mean for me (or us)?" and questions similar to it require just as much critical distance as questions about truth and falsity. If "you" are overrun by history, therefore, "you" will find yourself locked into a position of obedience, just like the nascent "I" of the poem. Thus one can see that if we read "you" through the language of the poem or in terms of a reader, we end up in the same subordinate place.

A third fate awaiting "you" burrows nearer to the heart of ur-poetry. If one can only take dictation, how might one follow out the language of the poem as it recoils upon what is said into the how of its saying? Again, one cannot. The power and import of ur-poetry hinges upon its reflexive plays, on its turn back toward its origin. Of course, one could be told, "Turn back toward the origin of saying," but insofar as one could not do so with that very address, one cannot broach the origin at all. Instead, one will have taken at face value what is presented in the address. Bound to the fate of a merely abstract addressee are thus the fates of poetic building and dwelling. If one cannot follow the language of the poem back to its *Ort*, the site at which it may turn into a language of originary occurrence, one will not stand exposed to traces of being in its presencing, to beings at the originary point of their occurrence, or to the manner in which humans (in what Heidegger terms "dwelling") exist within a dimension that is neither world nor thing, but part of the difference between them.

In 1913, in "On the Addressee"—and here one can already see why he will perish under Stalin—Osip Mandelstam insists: "Without dialogue, lyric poetry cannot exist" (Mandelstam 1979, 72). With "dialogue," he has in mind an address whereby a poet sends a poem into the future, bound for a *secret addressee*. "And so, although individual poems, such as epistles or dedications, may be addressed to concrete persons, poetry as a whole is always directed towards a more or less distant, unknown addressee in whose existence the poet does not doubt, not doubting in himself" (Mandelstam 1979, 73).[17]

Given "Poem Without a Title," "Empire of Dreams," and "Mother Tongue," I think that Simic's work calls into question Mandelstam's faith

---

17. Note that in rejecting the subordination of poetic address to determinate parties, Mandelstam signed his death warrant. In Stalin's USSR, one had to know for whom one wrote.

in the secret addressee, and on either side of the equation. In "Mother Tongue," both the nascent poet and the reader become mere functionaries of the cocksure voice addressing us in the poem, a voice less that of a peer than of total authority. In the poem that many believe sealed his fate (although he only read it aloud in Pasternak's apartment!), Mandelstam (1991) writes:

> We are alive but no longer feel the land under our feet,
> you can't hear what we say from ten steps away,
>
> but when anyone half-starts a conversation
> they mention the mountain man of the Kremlin.
>
> (lines 1–4)

The poem is horrible and its fate difficult to imagine, even though it and its author were to live out the scene the poem depicts. Here, conversations can only half start, for "the mountain man of the Kremlin" enters before they can become something unto themselves and follow their own momentum. Moreover, that carrion-loving man might interrupt at any time, pointing, thundering amid the pitiful murmurings of what may no longer be a group of peers but of hirelings. "Mother Tongue" gestures toward a similar situation, but perhaps an even more thorough one, one in which authority not only begins every conversation but continues and ends it as well, for if the "I" dissolves into second-person addresses, the authoritative address is all that speaks.

Now, one might object that by undermining the credibility of poetic address, "Mother Tongue," insofar as it is a poem addressing readers and thus implicitly bound to the second person, also negates its ability to communicate the oblivion toward which it gestures, an oblivion wherein impersonal forces (those accounted for in the third person, e.g., history, fate, and the like) speak for us by speaking *through* us. That is, if the voice addressing the nascent poem or the reader is itself nothing but a function of history, does the poem not collapse under the weight of its own doubt and suspicion? Yes, in a way. But then, that is the point—although not in a propositional sense. Rather, "Mother Tongue" begins to perform the collapse of poetic address into bare semiotic transmission, that is, it begins to perform what it cannot represent, even allegorically: a moment when the language of the poem is so overdetermined by history that its address as something singular is neither sent nor received.

Rather, the relay of pre-fab language takes over what would be a language coalescing into a unique instance of saying. But in suggesting this, does the poem not fall into performative contradiction? I will concede the point, but then underscore that such a contradiction is part of the brilliance of "Mother Tongue," for the charge only sticks as a criticism if one wishes to maintain the integrity of poetic address in and following the pronouncement. If the point is to expose the impossibility of that address, then such a contradiction, one that cripples poetic address, is precisely the way in which a poem might announce (perhaps in final desperation, perhaps with a final hope) the approach of its own death.[18]

Earlier we noted how a contrast developed between the silent emptiness with which *White* shrouds what comes to presence and the din of historical strife that poems such as "Poem Without a Title," "Empire of Dreams," and "Mother Tongue" find in the language of the poem. If anything, that contrast has only darkened. Perhaps it has even solidified into an opposition. After all, the poems we have considered here have opened wickedly onto fates that call into question the very possibility of ur-poetry. They depict a world wherein the language of the poem amounts to nothing more than the stale repetition or meager semiotic transfer of a traditional saying whose tradition is simply reinscribed in the language of what persists, almost lifelike, as a poem.

One has to wonder, therefore, whether Simic's two-handed corpus is hopelessly at odds with itself. One hand writes in response to Joseph Cornell's eerie boxes, "Cosmogonies are soap bubbles. . . . A soap bubble has no content. After it has burst, there's nothing left of it" (Simic 1992a, 54). In the wake of *White* (and we are always in its wake), I take this to mean that discursive productions such as cosmogonies or ur-poetry, irrespective of their breadth and ambition, remain bound to the breath that inflates them, and thus to what is nearer to us than breath itself: the empty nest cradling sense itself. Another hand insists, however, on introducing the work of Aleš Debeljak: "The poet who is not sensitive to the enormity and complexity of our historical and intellectual predicament is not worth reading" (Simic 1994a, 119). In *White*, I think

---

18. We begin to see that death when it strikes us that the voice speaking in the poem (I do not say "the speaker" here) may be neither an address to a reader, nor a generic "you," nor a nascent poetic "I." Instead, as if over a loudspeaker, it might simply be a proclamation. No poem could actually say that fate, however, for it would still be addressing a reader with news of a state that has yet to totalize thoroughly its administration of social life. It could signal the approach of that end, however, and that is one of the fates I hear emerging in "Mother Tongue."

we are working with what Simic terms our "intellectual predicament," a predicament exposed in the double repetitions of ur-poetry. In "Poem Without a Title," "Empire of Dreams," and "Mother Tongue," the complexity of our historical predicament unfolds as Simic's poetizing offers allegories of poetic repetitions that cut against the grain of the traditions out of which he cannot help but write, traditions he must repeat if he is to venture ground figures or poetize at all. But how are we to understand a corpus seemingly written at cross-purposes? And what import do these tensions have for how we live our lives? Can a life heed both exhortations—namely, to attend to a silent, white, empty dimension of presencing and to the slaughter-bench of history?

5

Characterizing the Cosmos

Ur-poetry's power lies in its ability to expose and figure the origins of sense. By "sense," I mean the manifold ways in which beings come to presence, the ways in which they come to be there as beings. One might regard a teacup as an object, for example, and identify its many traits: a porcelain container with a handle, and so forth. One would not be exploring it *qua* sense, however, for one would be presuming its presence *qua* object in order to identify its characteristics. In order to engage the question of its sense, one would have to inquire into, among other things, its presencing *qua* "object." One would ask: "What does it mean to presence as an object replete with qualities, and what enables it to be there in that manner?"

In its own way, ur-poetry takes up such questions. But it does so nonpropositionally, offering instead a language of originary occurrence that, through the interplay of various reflexive figurations, directs and even exhorts us toward the ground of those figurations, unveiling within poetizing the clearing of the open dimension that the presencing of sense requires—an open dimension that nevertheless only takes place in and through differentiated, determinate arrangements. What results is not simply a language concerning the originary occurrence of poetizing, however. In broaching the grounds of poetizing, the language of the poem exposes and figures the limits of sense, thus announcing the fate of all determinate presences, not simply poems.

Concerning lyric poetry, Charles Simic writes: "Both poetry and philosophy, for instance, are concerned with Being. What is a lyric poem, one might say, but the recreation of the experience of Being. In both cases, that need to get down to essentials, to say the unsayable and let the truth of Being shine through" (Simic 1990c, 60). As usual, Simic is to the point. In saying that ur-poetry is able to expose and figure the origins of sense, I am claiming that it creates for those who read it an "experience of being," by which I mean an experience of the way in which sense comes to presence.

With regard to Simic's own ur-poetry, we have undergone a complex, multifaceted experience. On the one hand, we found, cradling sense, a silent, empty whiteness whose radical anteriority prefigures all presences and relations, including those of ur-poetry. On another hand, we found anything but silence. Instead, a din of historical relations, some violent and oppressive, raged atop the silent whiteness. But how are we to think these two hands in relation to one another? The question arises because the determinate, bloodied fingers of Simic's historical hand seem different from his silent white ones. While both are exceptionally dexterous, recoiling upon their own poetizing, the latter writes out a language of originary occurrence that speaks beyond the reach of metaphor and allegory. The former, however, through allegories of poetic transpositions, unearths within the very repetitions presupposed and performed by the language of the poem a manifold of historical sedimentation. In addition, the allegorical hand clearly writes over the white that it requires (as relations of historical forces, like all presencing, demand an open, differentiated dimension). And yet, given the possible weight of historical events, e.g., totalitarianism, it would seem that a hand in search of the white might fail in its efforts to retune traditional sayings such that they expose the open, differentiated dimension underwriting their own presencing.

While we confront these tensions, we also need to gauge the import of Simic's ur-poetry, to follow out some of the ways in which it displaces and recasts our lives. And we must do so with Simic's double-handed writing firmly in our minds and attempt to make sense of how the groundless presences that are our world are also sites of historical articulation. In other words, we need to consider the implications of *White* and of "Mother Tongue" for each and every burst of presence, including our own. The remaining three chapters will pursue both goals simultaneously—that is, reconciling Simic's two-handed poetry and gauging its import. Concretely, this means that as I weave together the script of either hand, I will try to articulate some of its import along the way, allowing it to thicken as our feel for Simic's ur-poetry thickens.

Let us begin by relating *White* to poems like "Mother Tongue." In order to do so, which amounts to thinking the play of the white alongside of and in the struggles and losses of history, I want to make use of Reiner Schürmann's discussion of terms we have already encountered. In thinking about Heidegger's notion of poetic building, we considered two terms relating to the origins of sense: "origination" *(Ursprung)* and "inception" *(Anfang)*. I return to them because Schürmann's reading of them holds a key to the crisscrossing script of Simic's ur-poetry.[1]

In Simic's ur-poetry, origination is marked by the white, a radically anterior event that has always already transpired by the time sense is present. I say "event," because as we saw in *White*, the white is a "bullet / That has gone through everyone already" (lines 205–6). We observed in Chapter 3 that this anteriority underwrites self-relations, self-world relations, and ultimately any relationality whatsoever, underwriting the birth of sense itself, as ubiquitous as it is anterior. Recall, for example, the ways in which it enables writing, speech, and thought. The white must be there in order for the blank ink to appear with the separation and distinctness writing requires. Likewise, the white proclaims, via proxy, "I am nearer to you than your breath" (i.e., the breath that carries speech [line 215]). Third, "I thought of you long before you thought of me" (line 207). That is, thinking, a soul's purported discussion with it-

---

1. Because my concerns differ from Schürmann's, I will not engage *Heidegger on Being and Acting* (Schürmann 1987) in any systematic fashion. He focuses on the history of being and the ways in which Heidegger remains a transcendental phenomenologist even while developing an account of the history of being. But I am no longer specifically concerned with Heidegger, and thus I prefer to build upon and confront the general direction of Schürmann's reading rather than engage it in a detailed fashion.

self, requires an open self-relation and thus also comes to pass along corridors papered in white (line 207). The white is not simply a facet of intellection, however. Self-world relations, from sensation on up, also require the white, the "bullet / That has baptized each one of your senses" (lines 225–26). As a relational event, sensation not only involves two presences but the between of their engagement as well. It is there that the white—or rather, its wake—lies.

Because it comes to pass prior to the self-relational labors of the subject, pre-reflective or otherwise (and thus is not a function of those labors), and because it enables relations between distinct presences, the white underwrites all of presencing. In *White*, we read:

> Steadily, patiently I lift your arms.
> I arrange them in the posture of someone drowning,
> And yet the sea in which you are sinking,
> And even this night above it, is myself.
>
> (lines 221–24)

Not only does the white exceed interiority, coming before it, nearer to us than breath, but it underwrites each point of exteriority as well: the abysses of sea and night, the far reaches of the earth and heavens. It enables the sense that a self might encounter and the sense of the world itself, a world that includes selves surrounded by and even drowning in presence.

The white is so anterior that, in its own way, it surrounds us, above and below, inside and out, like a kind of "emptiness that tucks you in like a mockingbird's / nest" (lines 232–33). I think the trope of "emptiness" appears because the white is not a thing, an object, or a ground, nor is it ultimately some present energy or force. One might prefer to speak of an absence—namely, the absence of an event that has always already occurred by the time the present has emerged—but we do not strictly have an absence here, for the ubiquity of the white remains traced throughout whatever is present. Moreover, these traces are not mere voids or gaps, but an enabling openness that allows one to be suspended in a world of sense. The white thus unfolds along the lines of Heidegger's dimension of difference (as we saw in Chap. 3), enabling relations while keeping instances of sense just far enough apart to be singular. That is, the sea of sense in which one sinks is such that one can be there as "one." One might say, keeping to Heideggerian terms, that the white event of "origination" is an event of the clearing of the open dimension preceding any burst of sense. And the ubiquitous traces of the white, what the bullet white leaves in its wake, are also the dimensionality that enables relations in the first place. Given these traces and what they enable, then, "absence" seems to miss the mark. "Emptiness," however, is not entirely inappropriate. The wake of the white's arrival and departure does seem to blanket sense in an openness that is no-thing and that, in opposition to absence, makes all the difference in the world.

Thus far we have explored the event of origination in order to fathom the radically excessive side of sense, the open dimension into which sense arrives on the heels of an anterior, ubiquitous event. I think the German *Ursprung* can also help us to think the arrival of sense into this open dimension, for sense "leaps forth" out of the white emptiness in which it is cradled. I speak of a leap because in Simic's language of originary occurrence, sense is not the consequent of a ground. Rather, it flashes into the open dimension without an antecedent that can be designated or identified. In that sense, sense *at* and *of* the origin, presencing cannot be thought with recourse to causality. When one considers origination, one has followed the birth of sense beyond the explanatory power of causal concepts.

Causality—and not only when limited to efficient causality—concerns present forces influencing one another. For example, one billiard ball redirects another (efficient causality), atmospheric conditions influence what life-forms can develop (material causality), or a function and a design organize the production of some tool (final and formal causality). But precisely because these concepts concern present forces influencing one another, causal notions fail to think origination even if they necessarily gesture toward it. In other words, causal forces (or better yet, relations in general) presuppose the open dimension that is cleared in an event of origination and thus they cannot fathom the emptiness within which the relations they name come to pass.[2] Instead, one must make do with exhortative gestures, writing, for example, of a "zero burped by a bigger zero."[3]

---

2. In a somewhat similar manner, Heidegger interrogates the phenomenon of causality in "The Question Concerning Technology" (Heidegger 1954a, 11–16). I have explored this discussion in "Heidegger's Absolute Music" (Lysaker 2000).

3. An entire problematic of freedom opens here, one pursued by Heidegger on various occasions—e.g., in "On the Essence of Truth"—as well as by Jean-Luc Nancy in *The Experience of Freedom* (Heidegger 1976, 187–91; Nancy 1993b). I can only wave at it, however, in the discussions that follow.

Because it has no antecedent, I am inclined to follow Schürmann in claiming that the event of origination has no history.[4] One can make this point in at least two directions. First, the very thought of origination eludes historical or genealogical circumscription: no attempt to locate the emergence of the concept historically can exhaustively account for it. Why? It reappears within the very notion of historical emergence or production that such an account presumes, as one can see in Foucault's essay "Nietzsche, Genealogy, History." In an attempt to explain the point or scene wherein historical energies and forces interact, e.g., the warriors and priests in Nietzsche's *Genealogy of Morals,* Foucault has recourse to: "What Nietzsche calls the *Enstehungsherd.* . . . It is nothing but the space that divides them, the void through which they exchange their threatening gestures and speeches. . . . it is a 'non-place,' a pure distance, which indicates that the adversaries do not belong to a common space. Consequently, no one is responsible for an emergence" (Foucault 1984, 84–85).[5] But then, this non-place is precisely what we have been thinking in terms of the white, a differentiated dimension whose emptiness preserves the distances or differences that relations require. As you can see, then, the thought of the *Ursprung* as whitely poetized in Simic's language of originary occurrence will reinscribe itself in any attempt to delimit historically the emergence of historical relations. One cannot explain the phenomenon away, therefore, by regarding it as the product of particular historical relations.

Now, one might suggest that "history" is a positive state of affairs, not simply what historians or genealogists tell us. But (and here it does not matter what drives the wheels of history) any such notion still fails to fathom origination, for it will, in the end, come round to some notion of causality whereby historical force X produces historical force Y, thus

---

4. Schürmann makes this claim while arguing, compellingly, that Heidegger did not limit presencing—what we are treating as the birth of sense—to epochs within the history of being (Schürmann 1987, 140–42). Note, though, that while the claim is Schürmann's, the arguments that follow are my own.

5. One might object that Foucault distinguishes his genealogical understanding of "origin" from *Ursprung*, favoring instead thoughts of *Enstehung*, "emergence," and *Herkunft*, "descent." True, but when we flesh out these terms, I do not think (with the possible exception of this rhetoric of "purity") that Foucault sounds all that different from Heidegger in the opening lines of "The Origin of the Work of Art." "Origination [*Ursprung*] here means that from which and through which a matter is what it is and as or how it is. That which something is as or how it is we name its essence. The origination of something is the source or descent [*Herkunft*] of its essence. The question concerning the origination of the work of art asks after its essential descent [*Wesensherkunft*]" (Heidegger 1977a, 1).

entering into the origins of sense too late to catch and explain the event of origination.

But have I not claimed that history moves throughout Simic's ur-poetry? I have, and it does. My argument, though, is not that history has no place in Simic's language of originary occurrence. Rather, I claim that an unfathomable distance (or better still, a difference) separates origination from the histories it originates, including the histories that are repeated by and echo in ur-poetry. Or, viewed from the other direction, a crack or fissure (two other meanings of *Sprung*) moves through those histories much as it does through ur-figures, all the while underwriting their manifold work. I invoke "unfathomable" here because, as we have seen, origination cannot be discursively apprehended except in a self-effacing exposition that is not a modality of the proposition. Origination is thus not a product of history in any sense of historical production. Instead, it precedes and originates the histories of sense that we tell and live, histories that "leap" out into the open dimension of presencing.

And yet, this is not to say that origination is ahistorical. Although not a product of history, it is of history insofar as it is the origination of history and its traces are borne by determinate presences and their relations. Moreover, because origination has always already come to pass, it is only thinkable through a kind of historical recollection or repetition of what has occurred that follows out the traces of difference and distance left upon what has occurred—a fact evident in the recoiling repetitions of ur-figuration. I think we would do better, therefore, to regard origination as extrahistorical, not ahistorical. Origination is bound to history but, in a certain way—in an anterior way—it is also beyond it, marking its limit.[6]

As the extrahistorical, empty white ground of sense, "origination" marks a decisive moment in Simic's ur-poetry, but only one moment. Let us now turn to another facet, one we will mark with the term "inception" (to employ again Schürmann's translation of *Anfang*). One speaks of inception because origination is inseparable from determination, that

---

6. Schürmann does claim that origination is ahistorical (Schürmann 1987, 141). I do not think he would be adverse to my rewording of the claim, however, as it appears true to the spirit of his discussion. How Heidegger stands on the matter is complicated, for he claims in a seminar on "Time and Being" that "the sending as appropriation is itself not-historical [*ungeschichtlich*], or better, without destiny [*geschichtlos*]" (Heidegger 1969, 44). I cannot pursue this matter here, but if I were to do so, I would also have to explore Heidegger's remarks on eternity and being in *Contributions to Philosophy*, section 238 (Heidegger 1989, 371).

is, there is no presencing per se. Rather, as sense leaps into presence, it does so with character. In *White,* this is marked in various ways. For example, neither the pure whiteness of the Arctic nor lines of infinity enable the flash of sense. Contrast (or difference) is the rule. The white needs the ink, the color of blindness, as much as the ink needs the white. To recall another image, one could say that origination is always coupled with those scratches on sleep's blackboard with which the white calls us into the open dimension of presencing. And it is these scratches that are there at the inception of sense, just as an arrangement is always there as the dimension is cleared and opened.

Interestingly, Simic's ur-poetry does not limit the inceptual to mere scratches and scrawls that bear the traces of the event of origination. Instead, origination is set into the everyday. In "WHAT THE WHITE HAD TO SAY," we read:

> One sun shines on us both through a crack in the roof.
> A spoon brings me through the window at dawn.
> A plate shows me off to the four walls
>
> (lines 216–18)

Origination is everywhere in Simic. The open is always being cleared and arranged, even in a breakfast room. Vis-à-vis inception, this means that every facet of presence is inceptual, part and parcel of the arranged fabric of origination, that which origination fissures and enables. One need not turn to the history of metaphysics in order to think presencing, therefore. Like a sea, presencing surrounds us: a roof, its crack, four walls, a plate, and a spoon. In other words, Simic's language of originary occurrence, in exhorting us to attend to the event of origination, draws us not only toward the event of origination but also into the everyday, where sense is born.

In this turn toward the everyday, what one might term "facticity," Simic's language of originary occurrence distinguishes itself from Schürmann's. The latter limits the inceptual to epochal "categories of presencing," such as "will to power" or *"phusis."* In Simic's ur-poetry, one simply does not find the mediating step of what, for Schürmann, is best thought of as the history of being, i.e., a history of categories that define how beings presence in a given epoch. I consider Simic's turn to the everyday an advantage because it disentangles his ur-poetry from the constructivism to which Schürmann remains bound, a bind evident in his belief that epochal categories lay claim to or seize human thought that thereby, through those very categories, constructs the world.

I find constructivist positions troublesome because, like all Kantian positions, they are forced but never seem to account for some pre-reflective grasp of an indeterminate presence (whether of epochal-categorical stuff or of determinate presence stuff, presuming that determinate presences are not simply moments within epochally outfitted self-consciousness). The problem is not simply negligence, however. Once one explains how thought receives and is constituted by the categories through which it later constitutes experience, one has doubled the inceptual into "how it is received by us" and "how it is in itself," thus repeating the Kantian problem of the thing in itself at the level of categories. Second, the constructivist doubles the factical into how it appears to a given epoch and what it is in itself, that is, beyond any epoch or in a period of transition. The constructivist thus remains bound to a kind of idealism vis-à-vis beings, even if the categories through which thought constructs beings are themselves more than ideal at their point of origination.

Two other problems are perhaps less easy to see but nonetheless significant. Note that for the constructivist, some facet of existence must become what exceeds the categories, or else they would not be categories but determinate presence itself. Second, for the most part that excess remains the mere matter of the categories. Not only does this render the matter of determinate presence a residual category, thus saddling the account with a concept that does nothing but gather together what it has yet to explain, but it also subjects the account to a distinction between form and matter, thus unveiling a metaphysics buried within what purports to be originary: categories of presencing (or whatever it is that informs presencing) leaping out of emptiness. Thus, in relying upon an event of construction in order to explain determinate presencing, presencing itself remains unthought as long as one has yet to explore how categories and their respective matters come to share the open dimension of presencing that their engagement and its resulting constructions require.

Given its shortcomings, I would eschew constructivism altogether with regard to matters of origination and inception and follow Simic instead. In setting origination directly into the everyday, he avoids the conundrums that plague constructivism and leaves us with (or rather dwelling amid) a factical world, shrouded in emptiness and leaping into presence.

One might object: "everyday," "factical world," are these not just abstractions, that is, are they not on a par with "will to power" and *"phusis"* as historical categories? If they were left to stand on their own, I would concur. But Simic's ur-poetry does not work with the "everyday" as an abstract category. Rather, its exhortations lead us into the factical, unveiling for us the manifold density of the inceptual world. One can see the beginnings of this density in an early version of "Spoon," from *Somewhere Among Us A Stone Is Taking Notes* (Simic 1969).

> An old spoon,
> Bent, gouged
> Polished to an evil
> Glitter.
>
> It has bitten
> Into my life—
> This kennel-bone
> Sucked thin.
>
> Now, it is a living
> Thing: ready to scratch a name
> On a prison wall—
>
> Ready to be passed on
> To the little one
> Just barely
> Beginning to walk.

Note that we could be back in *White*, except now the spoon that "brings me [the white] through the window at dawn" is glittering in a different way. Like many of Simic's early poems, "Spoon" presents us with a fully animate world—silverware glaring, a "living / Thing."[7] Now, one might consider Simic a metaphysical animist, one who believes that things are animated by some spirit or energy, but I find no evidence to support that view. Rather, poems like "Spoon" bring us into a world of determinate presencing wherein things have character—even "presence," in a more colloquial sense.

---

7. I am thinking of the accompanying poems "Table," "Knife," "Fork," and "Needle," all of which can be found in *Somewhere Among Us A Stone Is Taking Notes* (Simic 1969).

But this animate world does not only encompass things. Even our own bodies (and even parts of our bodies) come to presence in their own, determinate way. In "Bestiary for the Fingers of My Right Hand" (see Simic 1969)—a title that compels us to wonder whether things are otherwise on the left—we read about the ring finger:

> The fourth is mystery.
> Sometimes as my hand
> Rests on the table
> He jumps by himself
> As though someone called his name.
>
> (lines 26–30)

Note that the matter here is but one finger on one hand, a fact that implies that the remaining fingers and all the body's parts deserve their own place in this bestiary of determinate presence. This is quite provocative, for it suggests that the body is a maelstrom of sense (or a kingdom of beasts). No doubt, the various determinate presences that make up and continue to swirl about this maelstrom align themselves in certain ways, that is, they may co-presence in manners that appear cooperative, but rebelliousness is not out of the question. There is the jumpy finger noted above. But think also of tumors, of so-called renegade cells, of the way in which they turn an instance of growth into a growth, and a malignant one at that, or so we insist.

Lest we exempt the mind from this maelstrom (let alone suggest a dualism), I should stress that thoughts and feelings are no less a matter of animate flashes of sense. In Simic's "A Letter," from *The Book of Gods and Devils* (Simic 1990a), we read:

> Dear philosophers, I get sad when I think.
> Is it the same with you?
> Just as I'm about to sink my teeth into the noumenon,
> Some old girlfriend comes to distract me.
> "She's not even alive!" I yell to the skies.
>
> (lines 1–5)

As Nietzsche might say, we do not think thoughts (or re-collect them in any obvious sense). Rather, they come to us, take hold of us, and often in overlapping and disruptive ways.[8] Thought is not synonymous with white noise, but ideas, feelings, memories, and so on flash in determinate ways, instances of sense alongside others.

I introduce figures of fingers and various thoughts into this reading of "Spoon" because, as with origination, it is not as if what I have termed the "everyday" (which, as inception, shadows the event of origination) is a matter of exteriority or interiority. That everyday includes each flash of determinate sense, from a clumsy finger to a malignant spoon to an erotic recollection. And each flash is animate, that is, all instances of sense presence in a determinate manner, and to that degree, they have a way of being, a character, even a life. This is not to say that all existence is "vital," that some animating principle of "life" courses through all things. Such principles strike me as unduly mysterious; moreover, we are not concerned here with present beings and their traits, hidden or otherwise. Instead, through Simic's language of originary occurrence, we are thinking about how determinate sense comes to presence, how it leaps out of a white emptiness. And what we have seen is that sense happens in determinate, animate ways, which is to say that at the inception of sense, presencing has character, something of a life of its own. I thus find it starkly compelling when I read in a second version of "Spoon," from *Selected Poems* (Simic 1990b), about an "evil-eyed" spoon that is "Eyeing you now / From the table" (lines 5, 7–8).

In the preceding paragraphs, we have been exploring, if implicitly, the import of Simic's ur-poetry, the way in which it recasts the supposedly inanimate world, our thoughts, our bodies—or, more generally, our everyday. The moral I have drawn from "Spoon," reading in the folds of *White*, is that in having a characteristic way of being, the presences of our world address us (and one another, for that matter) in characteristic ways. Thus they are able to "bite into our lives" in virtue of their own.[9]

---

8. In *Beyond Good and Evil*, Nietzsche writes (in Kaufman's translation): "With regard to the superstitions of logicians, I shall never tire of emphasizing a small, terse fact which these superstitious minds hate to concede—namely, that a thought comes when 'it' wishes, and not when 'I' wish, so that it is a falsification of the facts of the case to say that the subject 'I' is the condition of the predicate 'think' " (Nietzsche 1966, 24).

9. The earlier version of "Spoon" is actually somewhat ambiguous on this matter. After the utensil bites into the speaker's life, the speaker says: "*Now*, it is a living / Thing" (emphasis mine). This seems to suggest that the spoon only comes to life after it comes into contact with a human subject, a thought in step with the philosophy of consciousness evident in Simic's prose. And yet, note that the speaker also says: "*It has bitten /* into my life" (emphases mine). This suggests that even prior to contact with a human subject, the spoon already has a life of its

In other words, the everyday is not a mute repository of potentialities for our representational or constructivist efforts but a surfeit of characters addressing us on all sides: my desk, this cat at my feet, my neighbors Sue and Steen calling from their windows, and the great California bay tree rustling out back.

Two aspects of this address bear notice. First, it is constitutive; determinate (or animate) instances of sense are not atomistic, only addressing one another from time to time. In fact, these relations are originary. The argument is dialectical. To term something "determinate" (a spoon, say) is to acknowledge that it has a characteristic way of being, that it is singular in some sense, that it presences in its own way, even if there are other spoons. If something is to be singular, however, it cannot be solitary. If it were solitary, one would not say that it "presences in its own way," for its mode of presencing would be the only way in which presencing would occur. In fact, its presence would be the only presence, that is, a truly solitary presence would be the world, and an inarticulate world at that, for its seamless unity would prohibit the relation required by articulations such as "X is singular" or "X is a function of a larger whole." Determinate presence thus co-presences among other singularities, sharing, as we have seen, a dimension enabling those relations yet maintaining the distance and distinction that singularity requires.[10]

Earlier, we noted that origination underwrites any relation between a subject and an object such that the distinction is displaced from any originary site. Regarding the inceptual world (and this is my second point), that distinction is again displaced, but in a different sense. If we take "object" not simply as an object of cognition but also as some state of being, then with regard to originary occurrence, there are no objects in Simic's ur-poetry. Rather, presence itself, in being determinate, is animate. But then, this is not to say that there are only "subjects," for as noted earlier, the suggestion is not that "determinate" means "ensouled." Rather, being determinate entails a characteristic way of presencing, irrespective of whether a given X can be characterized as having a soul or a mind. Simic's ur-poetry thus draws presencing and what is

---

own. Needless to say, I find the latter account more compelling, and thus I have allowed it to guide my reading. The ambiguity should be considered, however.

10. I have translated and condensed an argument that can be found throughout the work of Jean-Luc Nancy, particularly in his *Inoperative Community* and *The Experience of Freedom* (Nancy 1991, 1993b).

present outside of the subject/object distinction, leaving us instead among co-presences with whom our fate is intertwined.[11]

With an eye on import, let us render more concretely the notion of co-presencing characters. Because they are not consequents of a ground, bursts of presence are singular. None can take another's place. If beings were the consequences of a ground, they could conceivably be reproduced if their ground were reproduced. But the origination of presencing occurs outside of a causal register, and thus each burst of presence is thoroughly unique. Now, I have tried to capture this facet of presencing by construing uniqueness as character, the suggestion being that each burst of presence has its own character and addresses us as such. Interestingly enough, we are often happy to regard human children in this manner. Each is unique. Each has its own way of being. We marvel before the uniqueness of a child but seem content to regard the rest of the cosmos as replaceable. As Ronald Reagan reportedly said: "A tree is a tree—how many more do you need to look at?"[12]

Recall that we need to gauge the import of ur-poetry through its displacement and recasting of the sense of sense. In Simic's ur-poetry, Reagan's view is thoroughly displaced. No being can stand in for another. One thus needs to look at every tree if one wishes to know that tree, and so on, into the furthest reaches of the cosmos. No doubt we resist such a notion because we are used to limiting character to the animate, if not the ensouled. But Simic's ur-poetry pushes us past these prejudices, displacing them as it recasts the cosmos in terms of an ensemble of singular, irreplaceable characters. And it does so without anthropomorphizing the whole of what presences. Not only does ur-poetry not work via analogical arguments, claiming that other beings are like us—e.g., in being able to suffer pleasure or pain, in being the subjects of a life, or in being teleological centers of life—but it also exhorts us to

---

11. I take these reflections to address, if only obliquely, David Abram's account of the more-than-human world. In *The Spell of the Sensuous*, he argues that plants, trees, spiders, and so on are animate beings that intelligently address us, should we care to listen (Abram 1996). I share and have learned from his view, but I would downplay the rhetoric of the "animate" in favor of a language of "character." (The former, down to its etymology, leads us to seek out an animating force, thus risking a dualism.) Also, I take every flash of sense to have character, whereas Abram seems to suggest that only regions of being have character (e.g., the organic), and then only when they are wild. We would have to part company on that point, albeit amicably.

12. I came upon this remark in Carol Bigwood's provocative and reflective *Earth Muse* (Bigwood 1993, 145).

attend to each presence in its singularity, demanding that we not limit our view of things to analogical accounts.[13]

Given its resistance to treating beings analogically, one should not expect Simic's ur-poetry to change our lives through some grand narrative concerning beings in general. In fact, at this point, the point of origination, Simic's work actively resists generalizing the fate of presence. The force of "Spoon" does not lie in a universal claim concerning the nature of beings, e.g., "they bite," or even "they are animate," as if ur-poetry were assembling surrogate metaphysics. Instead, poems like "Spoon" direct us toward the world in its presencing. Or, better still, they turn us around; they turn us away from categorical generalizations and toward beings in their uniqueness. In this reading of "Spoon," therefore, one should be less concerned with the concept of "singularity" and its import than with the gesture it makes toward the world in its presencing, toward mugs, wet rags, and wrinkling fingertips. But then this is what I have said all along: ur-poetry does not offer each being a new name, proper or otherwise. In recasting the sense of sense, it exhorts us instead to attend to the world in a new way, to see unique characters addressing us in their characteristic ways.

Having found ourselves amid irreplaceable characters, we need to avoid rendering their ensemble in terms of a spectacle of singular objects that live out lives independent of our own. I have argued that singularity does not entail a metaphysical atomism; instead, singularity requires relations. This is not to say, however, that singularities are mere functions of larger wholes. In marking X as a function of a larger whole, one fills the empty, differentiated dimension that enables singular beings to presence in the first place. Sense is thus neither a part of a whole nor an atom. In presencing within a white dimension of difference, each burst of sense both shares a world and remains more than a facet of that world. In relation to other beings, therefore, each burst of sense has what one might call a shared alterity. Its difference from its peers is a relation, not an oppositional affair; a bond, not a monadic isolation chamber. And that holds for us as well. I am the singular being I am only because I am differentiated from those beings with whom I presence (and here the personal "whom" is quite fitting). My being is thus of the relations

---

13. Drawing from Peter Singer (1974), Tom Regan (1980), and Paul Taylor (1981), respectively, I refer to characterizations of the more-than-human world that anchor a good deal of debate among environmental ethicists.

within which I co-presence, relations with friends and foes, neighbors and nuisances. And the whole cosmos can play these roles: humans, cats, a rooster, a tree, or a chainsaw. These relations are interanimating, that is, the ensemble of characters that co-presence at a given time characterizes our relations as well (and this is a truly plural "our"). If one were to ask, therefore, "Who am I?"—and to do so within the folds of Simic's ur-poetry—one's response would have to begin with a look around, a look into the various relations to which one is inextricably bound.

Now, one might object that surely one can enter and withdraw from relations. For example, one can begin a friendship or kill a weed. True enough; if one pursues an explicit relation with another being, however, one is able to do so only because of an already extant relation. As I have said, relations go all the way down. We less initiate or end relationships than transform them.

One should also note that because they involve singularities, our relations are singular as well. The characters in this drama are unique, but so is the play—each scene unrepeatable, each exchange one of a kind. In assessing one's prospects, therefore, one should find no shortage of novelty.

As we move further into the inceptual world of Simic's ur-poetry, the character of origination merits repeating. Because presencing is ultimately groundless, one cannot speak of necessity here (or of the kind of freedom that entails being one's own ground). Should one, then, strictly speaking, do without the concept of contingency as well? Normally, one terms some X "contingent" when it is not self-caused but owes its presence to something other than itself, that is, when it is dependent upon something else for either its existence or its character (or some element of that character).[14] Here, however, a causal register is not in force: determinate presence is not the consequent of some ground that it is not. But neither is it the case that determinate presences are self-caused, and I do not just mean that by way of further negating the rhetoric of causality vis-à-vis the birth of sense. In Simic's ur-poetry, sense—wrapped in an emptiness—arrives, presences; it owes its being to that emptiness as that which enables it in its singularity. In a certain way, then, determinate sense does seem contingent, particularly when we recall that singularity

---

14. One could say that the "contingent" is coextensive with the "insubstantial," not in a colloquial sense, but in the sense of not being "that which is in itself and is conceived through itself," to cite Spinoza's definition of substance (Spinoza 1992, 31).

also requires synchronic relations, that determinate presence or sense is always co-presence or co-sense. What, then, to do?

First, just as Simic's language of originary occurrence displaces the distinction between animate subjects and inanimate objects, so, too, with regard to origination, it displaces the opposition between contingency and substantiality (and the necessity toward which both move). This is not to say that presencing splits the difference between the two, being a bit of both. Rather, insofar as that opposition is oriented around the trope of grounds and their consequents, it sets contingency and substantiality aside as far as inception is concerned and replaces them with what one could term a thought of underdetermined presencing (or rather, underdetermined co-presencing, given the synchronic webs operative in and at the inception).

I think that one might speak of determinate sense as underdetermined for three reasons. First, sense has a singular character that is not self-derived, and thus we can speak of it as "determined." Second, those determinations are in relation to other instances of determinate sense. Therefore, any instance of sense is determined by its peers, i.e., those relations are part and parcel of its character—they help make it what it is.[15] And yet neither of these facets of determination exhausts the nature of determinate sense, for each instance and its relations bear the traces of an enabling event of origination. And precisely because that event is not itself a determinate ground but the opening of an emptiness, determinate sense, lacking a necessary ground of which it would be a mere consequent, is not determined. Instead, it is presencing, and at any instant it may (that is, it is able to and it might) presence in a manner at odds with its past behavior.

Now, one might think that a rhetoric of underdetermination marks a feeble attempt to elude a contradiction, namely, that sense is both determined and not determined. I would agree, except that a contradiction only arises if one presumes the opposition between contingency and substantiality. (The presumption is evident once we realize that the apparent contradiction only arises if one affirms both sides of the opposition.) But

---

15. As a dialectical argument, this claim is indebted to the "Perception" chapter of Hegel's *Phenomenology*. There, the point is that things exist in virtue of what they are not (Hegel 1977, 67–79). Here, the point does not concern qualities or even things, for that matter, because determinate presence does not equal the thing of perception. Still, if we shift our focus from a present thing of perception to presencing, we see that a determinate presence is what it is only through what it is not—and that is another determinate presence.

that opposition is no longer operative here. Rather, without a ground of which sense would be a consequent, we face a phenomenon that requires thought of an entirely different order—one I would term "the order of presencing" to acknowledge my deep debt to Schürmann's work. Regardless, once we step outside the opposition between substantiality and contingency, "underdetermination," *qua* concept, is no longer self-contradictory.[16]

Within the inceptual world, underdetermination translates into change and flux as well as into unpredictability. In "Comedy of errors..." from his long prose poem, *The World Doesn't End* (1989), Simic captures this side of determinate sense in a humorous vignette.

> Comedy of errors at an elegant downtown restaurant.
> The chair is really a table making fun of itself. The coat tree has just learned to tip the waiters. A shoe is served a plate of black caviar.
> "My dear and most esteemed sir," says a potted palm to a mirror, "it is absolutely useless to excite yourself."
>
> (60)[17]

Again, the scene is animate, full of characters. Determinate sense flashes, changes, shifts; X seems to be something it's not. A comedy of errors? Not in any epistemological sense. As far as we can tell, in this scene the mirror is working well, even if it is anxious. It is the world that is uncooperative, refusing to stay still, to accept allotted determinations. The point, then, is not that we misjudge, although we do. In fact, insofar as judgments engage an originary scene of determinate presencing, they do so only after the comedy has transpired. Or, because judgments are also instances of presencing, perhaps it is better to say that insofar as they play a role on this stage, they do so as straight men for what they

---

16. As I have suggested, one gauges the import of an ur-poetry partly through its displacements. From the vantage point of Simic's language of originary occurrence, causality seems to demand a fresh look, one that not only overcomes modernity's obsession with efficient causality but also begins to think causal relations from the order of presencing rather than thinking presencing from the order of causality. What would that entail? I am not sure. I suppose, though, that one might begin to think causal relations as patterns of co-presencing, as part of the polyphony that singularity paradoxically is, and set aside the thought that causality entails one being limiting another.

17. One finds a similar poem in *Charon's Cosmology* (Simic 1977), in which a bear eats with a silver spoon, a bedbug suffers, and rats do calculus.

presume and conceal: the underdetermined, flashing inceptual world cradled in an emptiness that is the wake of a white bullet that has always already arrived.[18]

As a concept, unpredictability orients itself toward whatever presences from the vantage point of a predicting subject. Therefore, we might do better to regard unpredictability and instability in terms of an ongoing creation. Children of silence, cradled in emptiness: this is a world created again and again, a world that refuses to sit still. Without an enduring ground of which it is a consequent, each burst of sense arrives in an underdetermined (which is to say, possibly novel) manner. To my mind, this only intensifies the singularity within which Simic's ur-poetry casts the cosmos. Not only is each being singular, not only are the relations to which it is beholden singular, but at every instant singularity also reasserts itself such that the cosmos becomes a comedy of errors, a drama of ceaseless formations and transformations, reversals and inversions.

This intensification of singularity is extremely significant for the import of Simic's ur-poetry. I suggested earlier that ur-poetry changes our lives through exhortations that provide us with the task of translating the world into the registers opening through and within ur-poetry itself. In exhorting us to attend to the singularity of presencing, however, Simic's ur-poetry provides us with an infinite task: the task of attending ever again to what has grown familiar. Why? The comedy of errors in which we are involved persists through the very fabric of sense (and again, the personal pronoun is decisively appropriate). One can even say that in Simic's ur-poetry, various senses of sense are displaced—for example,

---

18. These farcical elements are complemented by Simic's often-remarked-upon debt to surrealism. The images in Simic's poems seem to stare at us from the most unusual places, including storefronts, street-corners, tree limbs, mannequins, aunts, and silverware. But then, this is how sense often unfolds: obliquely. J. D. McClatchy fails to appreciate this in his review of *Classic Ballroom Dances*. He complains of what he calls the "drabbest kind of automatic writing," and he hopes that in the future, Simic will pursue "fresher" paths (McClatchy 1981, 235). But this supposes that Simic's "surrealism" (McClatchy employs the term) is some abstract technique rather than an aspect of his relentless attempt to expose our cosmological and historical predicament. Perhaps McClatchy should have consulted David Gascoyne's *Short Survey of Surrealism*: "I should like to make clear, as I tried to do in my original 1935 preface to this book, that the Surrealist movement was and remains radically different from all other contemporary movements in the arts because its most serious undertaking is literally *to change life*, as Rimbaud at the height of his visionary power declared. . . . Surrealism was and is prepared to leave behind the old tradition of 'literature,' *belles-lettres,* and paintings for rich collectors and State-supported museums" (Gascoyne 1982, vii). My thanks to Robert Bernasconi for introducing me to Gascoyne and to Kirstin Larson for a brilliant seminar paper on farce in Heidegger's "On the Essence of Truth."

the world of a divine creator or one represented by either a personal or collective subject—and the cosmos is refigured as an event of ongoing displacement or even conversion. In directing our attention toward events of ongoing displacement and conversion, Simic's ur-poetry exhorts us to turn again and again, to keep pace with the conversions that not only surround us but also embrace us, making us the beings we are.

Despite the concept's apparent risks, I elected to construe the life changes that ur-poetry effects in terms of conversion. The risk lies in the suggestion that ur-poetry offers a quasi-religious dogma to which one converts. At this point, it should be clear that nothing of the sort occurs in an engagement with Simic's ur-poetry. First, in exposing a world of singular co-presencing characters, its sets dogma aside. In fact, if anything, this language of originary occurrence undercuts dogma, turns us around as incessantly as the world that it figures turns. It thus asks us only to convert to the ongoing conversions that we are, as this page from *The World Doesn't End* indicates.

> I was stolen by the gypsies. My parents stole me right back. Then the gypsies stole me again. This went on for some time. One minute I was in the caravan suckling the dark teat of my new mother, the next I sat at the long dining room table eating my breakfast with a silver spoon.
>
> It was the first day of spring. One of my fathers was singing in the bathtub; the other one was painting a live sparrow the colors of a tropical bird.
>
> (5)

The earlier passage about a comedy of errors unveiled instability at the heart of the inceptual world. Here, the emphasis seems less on instability than on a kind of synchronic polyphony. At the outset, the speaker's parents are distinguished from thieving gypsies, and the speaker is tossed back and forth between those competing to rear him or her. But in the second paragraph, two men bear the title "father," and the speaker has come to regard him- or herself as the child of both. I take this to mean that the speaker is not determinate in any univocal sense, that neither familial unit is the true progenitor, but that, from minute to minute, the speaker moves from one family to another, equally their child. In other words, we could say that the speaker is singular, presencing determinately, but not one, not a being unto itself occasionally entering into relations.

Burrow into a singular character and one will discover that, as Simic writes at the close of *The World Doesn't End:*

> MY SECRET IDENTITY IS
>
> The room is empty,
> And the window is open
>
> (74)

Isolate a burst of sense, and one will find an open window en route to elsewhere. In the opening poem of *Night Picnic* (Simic 2001c), "Past-Lives Therapy," Simic replays this theme. The speaker says of his therapists:

> Some days, however, they opened door after door,
> Always to a different room, and could not find me.
> There'd be only a small squeak now and then,
> As if a miner's canary got caught in a mousetrap.
>
> (lines 17–20)

Given the current discussion, I take this to mean that determinate presences, because they belong to synchronic webs, come to presence along various axes of co-originary relation. A hand, for example, can be—all at the same time—a part of a human body; a collection of cells, living, dying, often battling; and a host to some fungus alongside a nail. Note that I am not claiming that a hand serves many purposes, although it does. It holds a telephone, caresses a cheek, writes a card, and so on. Rather, as a determinate presence, it relates to multiple determinate presences other than itself. It is thus a polyphony unto itself (that plays into others), a polyphony we must track if we are to keep pace with the ongoing conversions that we are.

In this chapter we have considered the world figured in *White*, a world beginning in an extra-historical event of origination that gives ongoing birth, beyond the reach of causal notions, to an interanimating, polyphonic world of underdetermined, singular characters. As we have seen, such a world is thoroughly animate, addressing us on all sides in ways that constitute who we are (given that we, too, are children of this riddlesome event cradled in emptiness). And it is a world of thoroughgoing uniqueness, each character, relation, and moment an irreplaceable one. But the force of Simic's ur-poetry does not lie in the production of a new categorical apparatus with which to cast the world. Rather, each of these terms is better understood as a gesture, even as the performance of an exhortation. "Consider the spoon." "Consider it again." "Turn, turn, turn." Here, then, we are decidedly not asked to change our lives once and for all. Rather, the conversions initiated here never end, for this world never ends.

6

"Then Came History"

We have been thickening our feel for Simic's ur-poetry and what it entails—endless tasks of converting ourselves into the conversions that we relentlessly are, that is, into the polyphony of underdetermined, singular, co-presencing characters that surround and permeate us, rendering us a polyphony unto ourselves. We could continue reading Simic's worldly poems—poems like "Spoon" that open for us various facets of the world of determinate co-presencing—and try to gauge their import for how the world strikes us, for the sense of the sense that we try to make and that swarms our sight, hearing, taste, touch, and smell. In doing so, we would be trying to catch up with the ways in which it has asked us to change our lives, meditating upon the ways in which its ur-poetic address has thoroughly sounded us out, leaving us exposed to a world through which we had been traipsing clumsily, a world resistant to an ontological distinction between subjects and objects, one without grounds and their consequents. But let us pause and reflect instead upon a question that remains in play, unresolved: the question of history. How, as the inception of presencing, does it relate to origination?

Initially, we took "inception" to mark both that which arranges the open dimension cleared in the event of origination and that through which that event is traced. But given the limits of constructivism, we have denied that the inception plays a categorical role, one that mediates between the event of presencing and concrete, determinate presences. In fact, we have gone so far as to equate the inception with the world of underdetermined, unstable, singular characters reciprocally addressing one another, i.e., co-presencing. But this suggests that the inception is not only *(a)* that which arranges the open dimension of presencing and *(b)* that through which the event of origination is traced, but also *(c)* that which comes to presence in the open dimension of presencing. It seems redundant, therefore, and even possibly misleading to speak of an inception at all. In the thought of origination, both the clearing of the open dimension and its differentiation through determinate arrangements is marked.[1]

If we do away with the notion of an inception as some categorically unique facet of the origin of sense, how then are we to think the historical relations allegorized in "Poem Without a Title," "Empire of Dreams," and "Mother Tongue"? The question arises because, at least in Schürmann's reading of Heidegger, the inceptual categories of presencing bear the historical determinations that cloak and overdetermine events of sense or presence. But if there is only a world of underdetermined, unstable, singular characters addressing one another—i.e., co-presencing within an empty, differentiated dimension—it is no longer clear how we are to think history, whether in terms of a past that still echoes in a mother tongue or with regard to the ill fate that seems to await so much of what travels down history's various tributaries.

1. The German *Ursprung* can help us think origination without the notion of a categorically distinct inception, particularly if we opt for the graphics of an *Ur-sprung*. "Ur" marks the silent anteriority of the event that clears the open dimension of presencing, whereas "sprung" marks the trace bearer of the "ur," standing as both what arranges and differentiates that dimension as well as what comes to presence within it. And then, not unlike the ":" in *Garbage*, the "-," the hyphen, could mark the immeasurable distance that distinguishes yet aligns the extrahistorical clearing of the open and the world that comes to pass therein, thereby arranging it. Moreover, the "-" could remind us that what comes to presence is always fissured—that is, not self-sufficient but underdetermined and thus unstable.

Consider "History," from *Unending Blues* (Simic 1986):

> Men and women with kick-me signs on their backs.
> Let's suppose he was sad and she was upset.
> They got over it. The spring day bore a semblance to what they
>   hoped.
> Then came History. He was arrested and shot.
>
> Do they speak in heroic couplets as he's dragged away looking
>   over his shoulder?
> A few words for that park statue with pigeons on it?
> More likely she wipes her eyes and nose with a sleeve,
> Asks for a stiff drink, takes her place in the breadline.
>
> Then the children die of hunger, one by one.
> Of course, there are too many such cases for anyone to be
>   underlining them with a red pencil.
> Plus, the propensity of widows to flaunt their widowhood:
> Coarse pubic hair, much-bitten breasts.
>
> History loves to see women cry, she whispers.
> Their death makes Art, he shouts, naked.
> How pretty are the coffins and instruments of torture
> In the Museum on the day of free admission to the public!

This is a remarkably rich poem. Note first that the figure "History," appearing in line six and marking the title of the poem, is not an object of theoretical concern; the poem does not offer theses concerning history. Rather, history is poetized through the impact of its arrival upon a scene of other figures: a couple, a statue, a red pencil, a museum, and so on. And what is most evident in that impact is its suddenness, unpredictability, and murderous force. "Then came History." The line arrives within the poem much as the figure arrives within the narrative: it stops all that comes before it and reassembles the situation. And note the matter-of-fact tone: this is not an event out of the ordinary. Not that people can predict its ETA. These folks have "kick-me signs on their backs." But that History holds something in store, that it will arrive, seems certain.

Interestingly, we're considering again the slaughter-bench poetized in "Mother Tongue," except here the bench does not lie in the prehistory of the poetic and interpretive "I." Rather, the speaker is moving about its grooves, bringing us into the co-presence of slaughters unfolding. "Then came History. He was arrested and shot." And later: "Then the children die of hunger, one by one. / Of course, there are too many such cases for anyone to be underlining them with a red pencil." Not only tongues are severed upon this bench, then, but an entire host of characters as well—some quite young. If the poem would have us think history in terms of its impact, here we would have to say that at times its arrival is murderous.

Murder is not all that arrives in this poem, however. Poetry itself moves about this terrible scene.[2] As the man is taken away, the speaker asks: "Do they speak in heroic couplets as he's dragged away looking over his shoulder?" First, the "they" is ambiguous. Does it refer to all the men and women noted in the first line, some chorus for this tragedy, or just to the couple upon whom the poem focuses? Either way, the irony is palpable. What is "heroic" about couplets as a man is being dragged away to be shot? Might the suppleness and musculature of a rhythm save him? Might the certain, well-rounded lines that heroic couplets offer bring order to this scene? Or might their Augustan grandeur reassure the protagonists that they at least have parts in the great drama of History's unfolding? Apparently not. While Orpheus purportedly charmed Hades until he released the soul of Eurydice, here nothing seems to stem the tide of History. It arrives, and that is that. In other words, while poetry is possible in this scene, it remains but one possibility coming to pass among other presences—some intractable, no matter how sweet the lyre.[3]

How, though, does poetry arrive in this scene? A man is arrested. The question of couplets arises. It would appear that poetry, at least in this

---

2. If the lyric "I" spoke in poems such as "Poem Without a Title" and "Empire of Dreams," here a narrator addresses the reader. This formally draws narrative poetry into the fate being poetized, although as I argued earlier, all forms of poetic address have been in question all along, given that questions about the nature of poetizing have been part and parcel of the language of the poems we have been considering.

3. It is worth underscoring that in mocking the heroic couplet, Simic is mocking the seventeenth- and eighteenth-century English delight in its "fashionable, tight enclosure of sense and sensibility" as well as the classical aura that poets such as Johnson and Pope felt it conveyed (Strand and Boland 2000, 122–23; Hollander 1981, 15). The force of the jab lies in its denial that History can be poetically subdued (a notion suggested in these lines from Pope: "Of all the causes which conspire to blind / Man's erring judgment, and misguide the mind, / What the weak head with strongest bias rules, / Is pride, the never-failing vice of fools" (see Strand and Boland 2000, 129).

scene, responds to History's arrival. In a way, this is not surprising, given that poetizing commences with repetitions. I would add, however (and the point is a dialectical one), that a response is bound to that to which it responds, and thus poetry is part and parcel of the arrival of History, another facet of its unfolding, not its other. The poem itself makes the point when, after his lover whispers that "History loves to see women cry," the prisoner, now naked, shouts: "Their death [presumably women's] makes Art."[4] Again, the irony is thick. Is this a form of recompense? A husband or lover murdered, children dead—but do not worry, you will star in a poem as a "victim"? If the limits of art's power are underscored in the ironic mockery of heroic couplets announcing the arrival of violence, here it becomes evident that poetry is not only surrounded by History but also of it, another swell in its ever-arriving waves, thus recalling "Empire of Dreams." Here, too, poems commence in scenes already set by what has yet to be a poem.

I have been suggesting that History is a figure for the arrival of poetry and the world within which poetry occurs. If so, then the poem "History" cannot help but be implicated in the scene it presents, thus marking it as a poem of poetry and casting its efforts in an ur-poetic light. More precisely, this means that rather than simply being about History (which it no doubt is, employing the term both in the title and as a principal figure), the poem also, by allowing the figure of History to mark the grounds of its own poetizing, opens us to a thought of History arriving in and surrounding the figure of History as well as the poem entitled "History." In other words, History is a ground word, a figure of poetizing that draws one of its own enabling events into the language of the poem, marking it as of that language while simultaneously underscoring that History, as what enables this very figuration (the trope, the surrounding syntax, the type, and the like), arrives in the language of the poem as something manifest rather than represented, as something to which the poem belongs, even in its most autofigurative moments.

If we read this exposition alongside of *White,* and we must, for the question of the *Ort* emerges here among the various relations poetized and presumed (e.g., among the figures of the poem, between the poem

---

4. This sentiment is certainly not unique to this poem. Many view art as the translation of tragedy into something finer. For example, in her biography of Anna Akhmatova, Roberta Reeder speaks often of the poet's "ability to transform tragic circumstances into works of great art" (Reeder 1994, 175). Part of the power of "History" is its ability to recall us, with humility, to what such transformations are in fact transforming.

and the traditions it repeats), then the figure of History replays and enriches the figure of the scratch upon sleep's blackboard, a figure that marked the arrival of sense. In other words, together with *White*, "History" poetizes the fated arrival of sense out of and into a silent emptiness and the underdetermined scene of characters arranging it. "Then came History" thus announces not only a particular turn of events but the way in which sense leaps into presence as well, such that one could also say: "Then came sense," and suddenly, addressing us with its singularity. Put otherwise, History is a figure of fate, or better yet, a fated figure, and thus we could say of it, echoing *White*: "Say: There was never any real choice" (line 236).

In *White*, the ubiquity of the white is repeatedly underscored, perhaps most powerfully when we are told in the speaker's mock-song that the white is a sea in which we drown, surrounded on all sides by its emptiness (lines 221–24). It surrounds us, however, only insofar as it is arranged; that is, this dimension is differentiated, and in just as ubiquitous a fashion. If one thus encounters the white wherever and whenever one turns, so too one encounters History, that is, the flash of sense arriving from and as all quarters. History is just as much the sea of presencing in which we drown as the white is. And so throughout Simic's ur-poetry, at least with regard to what is poetized across it, the song remains the same, revolving around the ways and days of presencing in all of its concreteness, a concreteness that admits of the struggles poetized in "Mother Tongue" (e.g., among present interests) all the while exposing the emptiness that shrouds and enables each flash of singular sense. This is not to say that *White* and "History" duplicate one another. Whereas the ubiquity of the white is silent, the ubiquity of History is cacophonous, its arrivals roaring about us, a furious symphonic explosion racing to fill the silences and rests that each and every note requires. And yet, such contrasts (or better still for this ur-poetry, such differences) are integral to origination.

Now, one might want to ask: "Isn't the din of 'History' different from the silent reaches of *White*?" After all, it is not as if presencing necessarily requires a man to be arrested and shot or struggles to ensue at every (or any) turn, for if it did, presencing would be the consequent of some ground, and we have already shown that such a thought is inappropriate to the phenomenon of co-presencing, singular, underdetermined characters. And yet, the anteriority of the arrival of the white does seem to be a necessary aspect of presencing. A man might be shot or spared, and in either instance, the white will have rushed ahead of it all like a bullet. Why not distinguish, then, the ontological concerns of *White* from the ontic concerns of poems like "History"?

I appreciate the concern just noted, but the intuition behind it presumes a distinction no longer applicable. In order to distinguish the ontological from the ontic, one needs to distinguish structures of presencing from instances of presencing. But in eschewing any categorical understanding of the inception, I think one loses the ability to do so. If the inception is coextensive with the world of determinate presencing (or with History), then there are only instances of presencing, or rather, there are only men being dragged away and shot, mudslides burying villages in Colombia, tumbling trade centers, couples in love, a handshake, a hangover, and so on. Strictly speaking, there is no clearing of the open per se, no such event that is separable from gunshots, a request for spare change, or the ecstatic shake of an orgasm. What leaps into presence does not instantiate the white, therefore, as if the white had some being of its own. Thus there is nothing to term "ontological" in opposition to something that would be merely "ontic." Yes, the white is ubiquitous in a way that any singular character is not, and it appears to be a necessary facet of presencing. But this is only if we fall into the trap of speaking of presencing per se, and we should not, for as we have seen, presencing is shorthand for the History of co-presencing, singular, underdetermined characters. The ubiquity of the white does not entail, therefore, the presence of something that could be said to have a categorically different kind of being than some other kind of being.

Now, this is not to say in nominalist fashion that there are only particulars. In this language of originary occurrence, beings are only in virtue of what is decidedly not a being, the open, differentiated dimension of presencing. It is to say, however, that we misconstrue this dimension if we cast it as something ontological (as opposed to the ontic likes of you and me). I think the distinction between the ontic and the ontological maintains its intuitive appeal because of the categorical drift of concepts, that is, the fact that they refer to and represent certain things and not others, thus prompting us to hypostatize their references in their ideality. However, Simic's ur-poetry exhorts us to resist the representational features of language when it comes to originary matters. Those features hide their own origination even when they aim to name them. Therefore, when employing concepts like "open dimension" and "presencing," we should recollect that they are further bursts of History, leaping into presence even as they arrange it in their own singular fashions.

Once again, I find myself arguing against categorical language with categorical language. Luckily, Simic's ur-poetry fares much better in this regard, particularly when we think of the world of underdetermined, co-presencing, singular characters within the reach of the ground word "History." Consider, for example, how the silence of the white rings differently when heard from atop History's bench. At the end of *White*, the speaker is confronted by a white tooth grinning silently and ironically at one who had sought to name the grounds of presencing: "the most beautiful riddle has no answer" (line 231). Now, in its own way, the History of Simic's ur-poetry unveils a silence as well, first by refusing to subordinate to any epic teleological or eschatological narrative the fateful bursts of presence that, cradled in emptiness, are History unfolding, and second, by underscoring the silences that reign when plaintive voices reach past what is present and scan the heavens for a "why," whether final or efficient in its causality. One finds the latter silence just as *The World Doesn't End* opens.

> My mother was a braid of black smoke.
> She bore me swaddled over the burning cities.
> The sky was a vast and windy place for a child to play.
> We met many others who were just like us. They were trying to put on their overcoats with arms made of smoke.
> The high heavens were full of little shrunken deaf ears instead of stars.
>
> (3)

Note how the stars sought and praised in *White* have turned into "little shrunken deaf ears." When the poet raises a glass, therefore, a poetic word in which to capture the shimmering stars, the silence that rings in the crystal bowl may prove awful, for these scratches upon sleep's blackboard are lives begun and ended. As Simic notes: "The death of God, you may say, is no big deal if everybody behaves well, but once the slaughter of the innocent starts, how do you catch any sleep at night?" (Simic 1997, 75). Seen through the ur-figure of History, then, a grinning tooth may mark more than an irony for those seeking to begin again from the origin.

More than the sounds of silence thicken, however, when we give History its due place in Simic's ur-poetry. Let us look again at "History." Its opening scene is endearing and fragile. A couple quarrels. Perhaps he is drifting, incommunicado. The indulgence of it may be what angers her. But they "[get] over it." And between their own desires and the budding eroticism of spring, what is and what is hoped for seem closer to one another. Something rare, no doubt, a time when time present is not only bound by the weight of time past, but, clock hand to cheek, also pushes us toward a budding future.

We are once again considering the import of Simic's ur-poetry, this time from the vantage point of love's labor. Simic draws our attention (particularly in recent works) to moments when eros propels us toward something more than we had thought possible, or, more humbly, into moments of ecstatic respite.[5] I want to consider one such poem—"Crazy About Her Shrimp," from *A Wedding in Hell* (Simic 1994b)—in order to see what might be at stake in the opening lines of "History."

> We don't even take time
> To come up for air.
> We keep our mouths full and busy
> Eating bread and cheese
> And smooching in between.
>
> No sooner have we made love
> Than we are back in the kitchen.
> While I chop the hot peppers,
> She wiggles her ass
> And stirs the shrimp on the stove.
>
> How good the wine tastes
> That has run red
> Out of a laughing mouth!

---

5. In *Walking the Black Cat* (1996), Simic explicitly sets the power of eros within the historical landscape (to which eros no doubt remains oblivious while passion pulses and clothing is cast aside). "Shadow Publishing Company" opens with a couple strolling in a world of their own. It closes: "Lying there, closing one's eyes in revery, / A figment among figments / Living one of their blessed moments / Without recognizing the century, / Only the scent of the lilacs on the pillow" (lines 26–30).

Down her chin
And onto her naked tits.

"I'm getting fat," she says,
Turning this way and that way
Before the mirror.
"I'm crazy about her shrimp!"
I shout to the gods above.

The drive of the poem is hard and plain: love and sex breed play, drive the everyday away, set us dancing naked in a kitchen, and compel our voices to testify toward a heaven we might otherwise think sealed, deaf, uncaring.[6] As "History" opens, then, we should see eros assembling a day into something that bears a semblance of what we hope for—nakedness, laughter, pulls of pleasure, or even just the knowledge that this moment is one well shared.

"Then came History." The man, nameless, is arrested, dragged away, shot. The children die, one by one. No one takes special notice. There have been so many, after all. And the wife? The mother? Also nameless, she "[flaunts] her widowhood" as widows are wont to do, although here the issue is not mourning. Rather, she bares her "[c]oarse pubic hair, much bitten breasts"—the marks of one forced to barter with all that history has left her, a body whose labor power she might sell on her back. "Then came History." The force of the arrival is said through what it wrecks (promise) and what it bestows (murder, death, prostitution). "Then came History." As I see it, we should not regard co-presencing as some state unto itself to which other relations adhere. Rather, it is concrete through and through, and thus, *qua* concept, "co-presencing" is only a stand-in for relations such as desire among creatures that go hump in the night.

In "Notes on Poetry and History," Simic writes: "If history, as it comes through the historian, retains, analyzes, and connects significant events, in contrast, what poets insist on is the history of 'unimportant' events. In place of historian's 'distance,' I want to experience the vulnera-

---

6. The poem is complicated by the fact that the woman is not opened up to heaven but to a mirror that convicts her of failing to maintain an ideal of sorts—and a sinister one at that. I cannot address this matter here, however, except to say that it speaks precisely to a fact already noted: poems, or any action, may contribute to fates against which they would rather have fought.

bility of those participating in tragic events" (Simic 1985, 126). Simic's ur-poetry remains true to this desire because it sets history (via the ground figure of History) into the very fabric of presencing. Not that it suggests that history makes us who we are by constructing us out of some mysterious fabric termed "historical forces." Rather, in this language of originary occurrence, History is simply the world *as* singular characters unfolding through a cleared, open dimension of co-presencing, unfolding beyond the draw of age-old oppositions such as contingency and necessity, animate subjects and inanimate objects, grounds and consequents. In place of a historian's distance, therefore, Simic's ur-poetry presents us with lived history, or rather, history as lives unfolding in their concrete singularity—which is also life in its thoroughgoing vulnerability. These characters can break, and they do.

Note that the vulnerability of singular characters in (and *as*) history is intimately bound to their underdetermined, unstable nature. The underdeterminacy of what comes to presence introduces an instability into the heart of things, for any burst of sense might always presence in a novel fashion, that is, exemplify a new character, given that it is neither self-caused nor the consequent of some ground but tucked in emptiness. This is not to say that it might manifest new characteristics, but its essential character might change over time. Now, it is precisely this nature, free of necessity, that exposes singular characters to relations and their attendant risks—i.e., transformation. After all, if a character were complete unto itself, that is, truly substantial, it would not admit of any relations whatsoever but exist solely through itself, thereby bringing the whole of the cosmos into itself. However, insofar as it is open to relations (or rather, insofar as it is relational in itself, always co-presencing), any burst of sense risks sharing presence with another singular character, for better or for worse.

In the eighth of his *Theses*, Walter Benjamin has suggested that "[t]he tradition of the oppressed teaches us that the 'state of emergency' in which we live is not the exception but the rule. We must attain to a conception of history that is in keeping with this insight" (Benjamin 1968, 257). Written when Europe lay almost entirely in the clutches of fascism, Benjamin's suggestion is that disaster (even barbarism) has dominated the lives of the characters we ourselves are and that we need to think of and comport ourselves toward the world with this in mind, as if it and we were in a state of emergency. Simic's ur-poetry contributes to such a conception of history, and on a remarkable scale, as if sirens were ringing down the white streets into which co-presencing spills from emptiness. Thought in terms of the ubiquity of History, the world unfolds along the incisions and revisions that are History's arrival, not unlike a relief map of famous and not-so-famous battles. Not to say that disaster is a necessary aspect of presencing. There is no presencing per se, bearing either necessary or contingent aspects. Instead, there are co-presencing singular characters, and their lives have largely been ruled by disaster.

One finds just this ubiquity of disaster in "Paradise Motel" from *A Wedding in Hell.*

> Millions were dead; everybody was innocent.
> I stayed in my room. The President
> Spoke of war as of a magic love potion.
> My eyes were opened in astonishment.
> In a mirror my face appeared to me
> Like a twice-canceled postage stamp.
>
> I lived well, but life was awful.
> There were so many soldiers that day,
> So many refugees crowding the roads.
> Naturally, they all vanished
> With a touch of the hand.
> History licked the corners of its bloody mouth.
>
> On the pay channel, a man and a woman
> Were trading hungry kisses and tearing off
> Each other's clothes while I looked on
> With the sound off and the room dark
> Except for the screen where the color
> Had too much red in it, too much pink.

The poem recalls "History." History arrives and gobbles up refugees who, in vanishing, recall the nameless victims of the earlier poem. But here, millions are dead, not just a father and his children. And all are innocent, a fact not stressed earlier. (Note also the irony here. No one will take responsibility for these deaths, and thus in another sense, everyone is "innocent.") Moreover, whereas History broke in upon love in "History," bringing it to a halt, here eros and History's bloody arrival intertwine. War appears as a fierce aphrodisiac, and behind a hotel room's soft-porn parade, blood seeps into the chromaticism of passion.

As the overwhelming presence of disaster dawns upon the speaker glued to a television, astonishment fills his or her face. But this is not what the poem would impress upon the reader—astonishment that right now, people are being killed. As astonishment sets in, the speaker catches her or his countenance in the mirror: a twice-canceled postage stamp. The image is precise. Astonishment is no longer worth anything. Having been used and reused, it might serve as a collector's item, but nothing more. In that sense, it is merely an aesthetic response to atrocity, like a shudder that evaporates as the ambulance passes. Moreover, astonishment can no longer claim to be a genuine response to disaster. Used and reused, it has become a worn, clichéd flutter of feeling, almost a matter of decorum. Later in his eighth thesis, Benjamin writes: "The current amazement that the things we are experiencing are 'still' possible in the twentieth century is *not* philosophical. This amazement is not the beginning of knowledge—unless it is the knowledge that the view of history that gives rise to it is untenable" (Benjamin 1968, 257). At this juncture, I think Benjamin and Simic are of one mind. The point is not to be astonished or outraged, but to realize that in the ubiquity of its violence, the world is anything but astonishing. All one has to do is look carefully at a television and one will see blood flowing, blurring even what is offered as intimacy. True, one may be living well at the moment, but any degree of acumen will make plain that "life is awful," that History's arrival is murderous, a disaster unfolding, a slaughter-bench (although not necessarily, for necessity is no longer an appropriate concept with which to think presencing).

Disaster is not simply a matter of villains and victims, however—some agents with smoking guns, others with clean hands. As suggested in "Mother Tongue," any burst of sense, i.e., any life, may contribute to an ill fate (poetized in terms of a black cat hoping to feast upon some tongue). And if we reflect upon the ways of History, we can see how this is so. Because History's arrival is underdetermined and always a matter of co-presencing, any singular character, a polyphony unto itself, may be enmeshed in any number of worldly fates. For example, Nietzsche's texts may re-present within the deadly rhetoric of National Socialism, regardless of their stated contempt for herd mentalities, resentment, and anti-Semitism. Or, driving, one might run over a bicyclist who has run a red light. Or a five-dollar bill, handed to an overly weathered man, might help him acquire a final and fatal dose of heroin. Such fates are possible because every burst of presence is a matter of co-presencing, bound to the world wherein it arises. So bound, it both contributes to and shares a variety of fates, part and parcel of the world therein and thereby taking place in ultimately unpredictable ways (for as underdetermined, each burst of sense is ever open to ever new twists of fate).

Allow me to bring the point closer to home, to allow myself to be turned around by Simic's ur-poetry in order to fathom part of that into which I am being converted. We are thinking about co-presencing, about the ill fates in which our polyphony rings. While researching this book, I often admired a view from the Knight Library at the University of Oregon. This university, along with many other schools, found the 1990s particularly difficult. Changes in Oregon's tax structure radically transformed the university's financial structure. Its budget once relied upon one out of every three dollars from the state, which now provides only one out of every six dollars. And yet during that time, Oregon enjoyed its most successful period of fund-raising, thanks in large measure to the generosity of Phil Knight—who not only remodeled the library but also gave $25 million for distinguished chairs and underwrote the building of a new law school. No one can or should deny that the University of Oregon (and that includes its administration, faculty, staff, and student body) is indebted to Phil Knight and his remarkably vital company, Nike. I note this because as I follow out the exhortations of Simic's ur-poetry, I turn to see what colors line my television set or what precisely stuffs the chairs in my campus library. Here is what I find.[7]

In 1988, Nike, seeking cheaper labor markets, moved much of its production from South Korea and Taiwan to China and Indonesia. That year, workers in West Java, Indonesia, earned 83 cents per day, a sum able to satisfy only 56 percent of their minimum physical needs as measured by nongovernmental agencies. (Such wages were typical of most shoe manufacturers, not only Nike.) In 1992, after protests and strikes, the Nike workers' pay rose to $1.30 per day, and in 1996, to $2.80 per day. As of 1993, however, it was supposed by most nongovernmental estimates that $4.00 per day was needed to meet the minimum physical needs of the workers.[8]

---

7. My source for information about Nike is a collection of research papers published in the late 1990s (Ballinger and Olsson 1997).

8. In order for this figure not to remain abstract, one should note that a 1988–89 study in Jakarta found that 88 percent of women earning the minimum wage were malnourished.

Across these years, Nike flourished. In 1993, the gross export value of products made in Indonesia was $268 million. In 1995, that figure had risen to $546 million. And in 1996, the Nike Corporation reported an overall profit of $670 million. But none of this found its way into the hands and mouths of Indonesian workers. In fact, in 1993, the daily wage paid by Nike was three times less than what the Beta company paid through their contractors, even though Beta's profits paled in comparison with Nike's. True, Nike *often* paid the minimum wage across these years (although in 1994, Nike admitted to some violations, including an illegal practice known as "training wages," wherein new workers are paid 20–25 percent less than minimum wage). But these wages are far from living wages and could be increased without significantly undermining Nike's profit margin.

A polyphonic being, I am a creature of multiple entanglements. In recasting the world in terms of synchronic entanglements beyond the explicit pursuits of subjects, Simic's ur-poetry refigures how I move about the world. Whereas I once entered and exited libraries without a thought beyond securing texts, I now (as I take a seat before an on-line catalog), consider the meaning of a living wage, consider who makes one, think about who does not. As I check out a book I also consider the length of a workday, the condition of a workplace. I live well, but the world is awful. Not that Simic's ur-poetry tells me this. Rather, it directs me into the folds of my world, where the conclusion seeps through my manifold relations.

We are thinking through History's arrival. And yet, we should not take History to involve only the co-presencing of present disasters. Many voices speak in the birth of sense, resounding in the polyphony of co-presencing characters. Take "Emily's Theme," from *Walking the Black Cat* (Simic 1996).[9]

> My dear trees, I no longer recognize you
> In that wintry light.
> You brought me a reminder I can do without:
> The world is old, it was always old,
> There's nothing new in it this afternoon.
> The garden could've been a padlocked window

---

9. The title recalls Emily Dickinson's sense for the age of the world and the fleeting, almost silly attachments of humanity. One of her poems (no. 345), for example, begins: "Funny—to be a Century— / And see the People—going by— / I—should die of the Oddity—" (lines 1–3).

> Of a pawnshop I was studying
> With every item in it dust-covered.
>
> Each one of my thoughts was being ghostwritten
> By anonymous authors. Each time they hit
> A cobwebbed typewriter key, I shudder.
> Luckily, dark came quickly today.
> Soon the neighbors were burning leaves,
> And perhaps a few other things too.
> Later, I saw the children run around the fire,
> Their faces demonic in its flames.

Like so much of Simic's work, "Emily's Theme" draws the exterior in, true to its manifold addresses, and flings the interior out, true to the rule of co-presencing as the way of the world; trees bring reminders, for example, and thoughts open onto what exceeds their indexicality. More remarkable here, however, is how the age of the world co-presences in the shadows of bare trees, how ghosts speak in the speaker's thoughts. Alongside the synchronic polyphony of the world, one also finds diachrony, at least in Simic's ur-poetry. But what an odd thought: the past co-presencing, arriving in and as History. Note, the point is not that some vista into what had been opens on a cold, late afternoon, affording one a journey back in time. Rather, here the past haunts the present, woven through it, as in a mother tongue, to recall our brief foray into etymology from Chapter 4. But what could it mean that the past co-presences?

One might suggest that the diachronic dimensions of sense are simply instances of memory projected upon determinate presences. I do not think so. One need not, in the representational sense, have experienced an event in order for its marks to appear in the present. (I think here of the geological record or, more banally, of silt at the bottom of a stream, or dead leaves beneath a tree that one has chanced upon for the first time.) In addition, the poem does not speak of memory. The trees themselves return the speaker to an awareness of the age of the world. But how are we to understand this kind of address, one in which a past enters the present in and through the underdetermined address of co-presencing characters?

One might think that a past only arises when a judgment is made to that effect. On this view, the past presences only insofar as something like an indentation is judged to be a gouge, taken as evidence of some event, some synchronic relation that had been. In itself, however, the indentation simply would be a part of the determinate presence of a spoon (to recall an earlier poem), an aspect of its shape, as a rim belongs to a bowl. Note how this concern brings us into the lines from "Emily's Theme" in which the speaker tells the trees, "You brought me a reminder I can do without: / The world is old" (lines 3–4). How might trees bring a reminder? Do they bear their age in and of themselves? Or do they simply serve as an occasion for a judgment that imagines (perhaps through comparisons with other trees, present or recalled) how things might have been prior to this moment of determinate co-presencing?

I think we need to clarify what we mean by "past." If we mean "what has been but is no longer occurring," then nothing of the sort arises in the world of co-presencing characters. By definition, "what has been but is no longer occurring" is not of the co-presencing world. If it were, it would occur in some fashion. The realm of "what has been but is no longer occurring" is thus a posit of some judgment, implicit or explicit.[10] Such judgments may seem to take their leave from traces of what has been: a gouge on a spoon, or a leafless tree near a leaf pile. And yet why do we regard these as "traces" of what has been, not as characters leaping into and arranging, for the first time, the open dimension of presencing? If the world were the consequent of a ground, we might refer each character back to its antecedent cause and talk about how past causes co-presence in the world through their effects. But as presencing cannot be regarded as the consequent of a ground, riddled as it is by an emptiness in which an open dimension of presencing is cleared, one cannot presume that what has been lives on in its consequences. In other words, the rhetoric of trace, *qua* remainders of causes, begs the question.

Suppose, though, that we think the past as part and parcel of presencing, not simply as the negation of the present (i.e., as the no-longer-now back toward which we might like to travel). Three thoughts come to mind, two in support of the claim that one cannot have the presencing of singular characters without diachrony. First, the clearing of the open dimension of presencing has always already occurred by the time that some underdetermined, unstable character comes to co-presence. Second, the logic of the "always already" entails a diachronic series of events

---

10. I must leave as an open question *(a)* how recollection functions (or historiography more generally), *(b)* that from which it takes its leave, if anything, and *(c)* what epistemic challenges it faces given the co-presencing, underdetermined, singular lives we often wish to recount.

of which it is the first. This becomes evident when we recall that the clearing of the open is not itself presencing but only its initial moment. As we have seen, there is an open dimension of presencing only insofar as it is arranged by differentiated, determinate presences, presences that leap forth (or arrive as History) on the heels of the clearing of the open. Viewed from the vantage point of what comes to presence, therefore—that is, from within the world—there remains the trace of an event that has always already happened, a trace that stands as the co-presence of a past. Built into presencing, therefore, is the co-presencing of a past, a white past, a past that lingers as an emptiness in which the world's characters are suspended.

But is this what "Emily's Theme" proposes, a world old in the sense that it has whitened in what underwrites it? Yes and no. Insofar as the clearing of the open is part and parcel of what comes to presence, then one cannot separate out what comes to presence from the anteriority of its presencing. But the extrahistorical vanguard of presencing is not "old" in any usual sense, and that is the sense running through "Emily's Theme," the sense that the world itself in its underdetermined singularity has been presencing for ages, that it has been around longer than this moment no "this" can catch, as Hegel has shown.[11]

Perhaps we might do more justice to "Emily's Theme" if we think presencing from the side of what comes to presence. As we have noted several times, what comes to presence always arrives within determinate arrangements. Now, these arrangements cannot be the result of a onetime event of co-presencing, as if a self-relating totality were to come into being all at once and remain there, static, some colossal geometric figure. First, such a world is not only foreign to our experience but also to experience per se. Even when thought of as an undergoing (as opposed to something represented to a subject), experience suggests temporal duration. It commences and passes away or is displaced by a new experience.

Second, and more decisively, upon its emergence, an indefinitely enduring synchronic world would congeal into a seamless whole. In its stasis, its supposed singular characters would dissolve into mere parts, like the interior angles of a square, for they would remain locked within

---

11. I refer to the demonstration in the "Sense-Certainty" chapter of the *Phenomenology* that the now of a "this" supplants the now to which any "this" might refer, thus rendering the referent not-now, or no longer now (Hegel 1977, 62–64).

their initial positions *ad infinitum*, functions rather than unstable, underdetermined characters. But even "parts" says too much, for X is a "part" only for one who perceives it as such (distinguishing one angle from another, for example), and such distinctions could never arise in a static world. As part and parcel of the world that they perceive and judge, they would occupy temporal locations, occurring now (perceiving and interpreting the first angle) and later (perceiving and interpreting the second angle), locations that would have to arrive after the initial establishment of a fixed pattern of co-presence. The very notion of a part thus introduces diachrony into what would remain pure synchrony, as does, for the very same reason, the claim that the world is an indefinitely enduring, synchronic web of relations (for there is always the arrival and hence the time of the claim).

One can conclude, therefore, that sense is not born all at once, ever to remain the same, for in suggesting that it is, one falsifies one's own pretensions. My point is not that the claim is incoherent (though it is), but that its presencing *qua* claim gives evidence for the determinate diachrony that is part and parcel of presencing. More precisely, its own arrival makes plain that sense is born in an event of displacement: an already determined world is set aside in favor of what arrives in and as History. (For example, in "History," a couple's reconciliation displaces a breach, and then the man's arrest displaces that reconciliation. Or, less dramatically, a claim responds to a question.) When scrutinized, the arrival of singular sense unveils a diachronic as well as a synchronic difference at play throughout the open dimension of presencing. Not only is presencing always co-presencing, but it is also a matter of underdetermined, singular characters displacing others and then only after the open dimension has been always already cleared.

What, then, of "Emily's Theme," the address of its trees, and the co-presencing of the past? First, to experience or be addressed by the arrival of History is also to experience or be addressed by its passing away, for the two are inseparably bound. The passage of time is part and parcel of the birth of sense. As we drown in presencing, the relentless, fleeting quality of the world is thus made plain. Thought in terms of *White*, this means that with each scratch upon sleep's blackboard, one is drawn into an exposition of the passage of the world or even the world as passage, as arrival, displacement, and departure.

Second, insofar as the arrival of History entails the displacement of what came before it, then (and my reasoning is dialectical) the sense that is born in the arrival of X remains bound to its predecessor Y. The point is akin to the earlier claim that in a world of co-presencing singularities, each singularity is a polyphony unto itself, bound to those with whom and among whom it presences; so, too, within the diachronic dimensions of presencing. In the birth of sense, within an underdetermined, unstable, singular character echo the other singular characters displaced by its arrival.

One might take this to be a formal, logical point, a point pertaining to a general structure of presencing, but as we have seen, there are no general structures of presencing because there is no presencing per se. This means that the displacements in question are always concrete. I take it, then, that the diachronic bonds of co-presencing, like its synchronic ties, are also only ever concrete. More precisely, what is displaced in History's arrival remains part and parcel of the characteristic way of presencing that is every burst of sense, for its character involves, among other things, having displaced a concrete arrangement of the open dimension of presencing. In other words, in its arrival, the arrest poetized in "History" (*qua* burst of sense) is bound to and even preserves the reconciliation it renders empty. One could equally say that an ur-poem is bound to and preserves the traditional sayings it repeats en route to autofiguration.[12]

It is this recuperative, preservative side of presencing that accounts for how the past co-presences—how a tree might inform us that the world is old—and is not simply relentlessly arriving and fleeing. The past, as that which is displaced in the arrival of History, radiates throughout the world, arriving as displaced in each new burst of sense. Recall a passage from Benjamin's *Theses:* "Do we not, ourselves, touch a breath of air that surrounded those who came before? Is there not in voices to which we give our ear an echo that has been muted until now? Do not the women whom we court have sisters whom they have come to no longer recognize? If so, there is a secret agreement between past generations and the present one" (Benjamin 1974–89, 1:2:693–94). From within Simic's ur-poetry, I would cast the agreement between past generations of sense and a present one as a matter of origination, of how singular characters co-presence—namely, in an arrival that displaces yet preserves those sin-

---

12. In the idiom of dialectics, one could also say that the arrival of History is always the determinate negation of its earlier arrivals. Negativity, however, would not be the activity of a subject, i.e., not the "energy of thought, of the pure 'I,'" as it is in Hegel's *Phenomenology*, but the anteriority of a white event whereby an open is cleared (Hegel 1977, 19).

gular characters that arrange the white, open dimension wherein we dwell.

As with the synchronic webs in which it recasts sense, the diachronic folds of sense disclosed by Simic's ur-poetry further thicken the polyphonic strands of our lives. Earlier I wrote of the many determinations that run through the library I used to research this book. With "Emily's Theme" in mind, permit me another reflexive exercise prompted by the exhortations of Simic's ur-poetry.

In 1931, Franklin Delano Roosevelt said: "There can be little doubt that in many ways the story of bridge building is the story of civilization. By it we can readily measure an important part of a people's progress" (Steinman and Watson 1941). If we look briefly into the history of the Brooklyn Bridge, we may be inclined to agree, albeit not without a certain irony. In May 1883, the Brooklyn Bridge opened. Numerous figures spoke that day, and their sentiments presaged Roosevelt's. The Reverend Richard S. Storrs termed the bridge a "durable monument to Democracy itself." It embodied, he thought, all that a people could accomplish through collective efforts (Trachtenberg 1979). And Abram S. Hewitt saw in the cables holding the bridge aloft the weave of a future harmony between labor and capital. For both men, the bridge marked not only a technical advance but an economic and political one as well, an advance symbolically present in the bridge itself.

One has reason to pause amid all this steel and praise, however. While the bridge was funded in part by public money (some 60 percent), the charter was secured from the State of New York through a bribe. Boss Tweed, the now infamous leader of Tammany Hall, required $65,000 from State Senator Henry C. Murphy in order to back the project. Likewise, graft drove the awarding of contracts, graft that often fell into the pockets of the New York Bridge Company's directors, the body of public and private officials who directed the company that initially owned the bridge.[13] As Alan Trachtenberg notes, "in the long run the bridge was surely a social good, a public service (only ferryboat operators continued to oppose it); but in the short run it seemed to serve the pocketbooks of some notoriously private citizens" (Trachtenberg 1979, 99–100). In other words, the markets surrounding the bridge's construction were anything but free, and politicians were embroiled in the machinations.

---

13. The bridge became a public work in 1875, although many of the original directors of the New York Bridge Company continued on as trustees of the project.

Concerning Hewitt's vision of intertwining interests weaving themselves into the bridge's suspension wire, one should note that of the six hundred or so workers who helped assemble the bridge, twenty died. Moreover, workdays were long, wages low, benefits unheard of, and workman's compensation a pipe dream. Unsurprisingly, none of the directors of the New York Bridge Company met his death in the project, although the principal designers of the bridge, John and Washington Roebling, were both injured on the site. John, refusing medical attention, eventually died from his injuries; he thus left the project to his son, Washington, who—exploring the site—was crippled shortly thereafter.

I have invoked the Brooklyn Bridge because it stands as an engineering feat of some magnitude and as the work of two great minds, those of the Roebling father and son. Moreover, the bridge was and remains as much a symbol as a passageway. Even in 1941, one could read that "the Brooklyn Bridge is more than a structure to span a river; it is a symbol of victory, of man's [sic] conquest and achievement" (Trachtenberg 1979, 207). What is in question, however, is what announces itself in this "symbol," what we should hear therein. And that is a matter for which Simic's ur-poetry has great import: it tells us to look for diachronic relations echoing among a synchrony of co-presencing characters. In the Brooklyn Bridge—and not just as a philosophical example but also as a structure I drive across or admire from a pier—I find less an emblem of democracy than its subversion, one favoring the interests of economic elites at the level of legislation and commerce. And inside Hewitt's temple of progress, I find not only steel but the crushed fingers, legs, and bodies of laborers as well. And even in the bridge's symbolic function I find (as Benjamin no doubt would) a history of ideology, of mystifying accounts that bury vanquished bodies beneath the accumulating rubble of progress. The point is not that the Brooklyn Bridge is not an engineering achievement but that such achievements are far from victimless, a fact we are loath to ponder and recall, preferring as we do the history of the victors. Simic's ur-poetry helps us hear a different history by exhorting us to listen for what is not ostensibly present.

"Then came History," the co-presencing of underdetermined, unstable, vulnerable, and singular characters, living out an ongoing disaster, haunted by the pasts that each arrival relentlessly displaces. Wrapped in emptiness, in a white anteriority that opens the dimension of History's arrival, this is the cosmos that Simic's ur-poetry unfolds, that which its address presents to us. In its language of originary occurrence it runs over every burst of sense and sounds us out, head to toe. Here "there is no point / that does not see you," to recall yet again Rilke's "Archaic Torso of Apollo." The ubiquity poetized across Simic's corpus, in all its wonder and terror, in all of its birth and death, touches upon every aspect of life: if we hear what is found there, the world will never remain the same.

Once touched by this poetry, one can no longer consider the cosmos to involve so many consequents of a ground. No longer will the world, at the scene of origination, be thinkable between the poles of contingency and necessity or within a register of causality. Rather, in its singularity, each flash of sense will address us (and not only us) with its singular, characteristic manner of presencing, a manner misunderstood by a discourse built upon the distinction between subjects and objects or a vitalist sense of the animate and inanimate. Dwelling in what this ur-poetry builds, one no longer will take the past to be simply past. Instead, one will begin to see how it arrives with the future as History, how it echoes within the co-presencing world of underdetermined, unstable, and vulnerable characters. And if one should push past the drama of History's arrival, of a world of characters unfolding, if one should work one's way toward that point where grounds were supposed to rest, complete in themselves, one will find instead a silent emptiness that, rather than lying behind what comes to presence, surrounds it, part and parcel of History's arrival. And yet this emptiness is extrahistorical: its silent, anterior arrival does not come to presence as an underdetermined, singular character but in traces of a silence that shrouds the co-presencing of the world.

7

Preserving the Possible

Introducing poems by Aleš Debeljak, Simic writes: "My sense while reading Debeljak is that this is what pondering one's life feels like in this waning century" (Simic 1994a, 119). Less than a decade later, the century having waned, my thought while reading Simic is that this is what pondering (or better yet, experiencing) the birth of sense is like. Through several poems and the interplay of multiple figures of poetizing, such as the white and History, Simic's ur-poetry offers one an experience of sense at the point of its origin, of beings within the scenes out of and into which they emerge, loci we have regarded, following Heidegger, as pertaining to origination, to how beings presence.

Thought most generally, Simic's ur-poetry casts the emergence of sense in terms of the arrival of a History of singular, underdetermined, co-presencing characters. History is a figure for the arrival of sense out of and into a white, empty dimension that cradles it as the difference between singularities. That dimension itself is extrahistorical, however, for the event of its opening never arrives into presence. Instead, it has always already happened by the time singular bursts of sense co-presence. This fact is traced through the synchronic and diachronic manifold that does arrive as History. Moreover, the empty, differentiated dimension of presencing is such only in virtue of the singular characters that cascade through it. The dimension of presencing, arranged by the white and other figures of poetizing, is thus part and parcel of History, even if it never arrives as a singular, underdetermined character.

"Sense," "synchrony," "diachrony," "presencing"—these categorical terms are somewhat misleading. As we have seen, there is no sense or presencing per se. It is difficult to overestimate the import of this disclosure, for it turns the entire cosmos into a whirl of singular characters addressing one another in their own unique ways. "Interlude," from *Austerities* (Simic 1982), captures and provokes this thought as well as the astonishment it brings.

> A worm
> In an otherwise
> Red apple
> Said: I am.
>
> It happened on a chipped
> China plate,
> At a table
> With twelve empty chairs.
>
> The rightful owner
> Of the apple
> Had gone into the kitchen
> To get a knife.
>
> She was an old woman
> Who forgot things easily.
> Dear me,
> She whispered.

In Simic's ur-poetry, the cosmos, at the point of origination, the *Ursprung*, cannot be neatly carved up into subjects and objects, into those who can claim their being for themselves as opposed to some vast range of mute presences that only articulate their essence through narratives scripted by the former. No, here we find ourselves amid a fully animate cosmos. Each burst of sense has its own character, its own way of being, its "I am"—that is, its characteristic address through and in the synchronic and diachronic webs that arrange the open dimension of presencing.

This is not to say that each being has subjectivity in the sense of self-relation (i.e., an awareness of its own polyphonic co-presencing) as either a capacity or a distinguishing trait. Simic's animism, should we retain the term, is thoroughly non-vitalistic. Beings are not rendered animate in virtue of some enlivening power, e.g., "consciousness," from which they acquire cognitive capacities. As a child of History, sense is not the consequent of any ground, but a leap out of a white emptiness into a differentiated dimension of co-presencing that comes to pass in an underdetermined yet characteristic fashion. The character with which sense occurs is not, however, the characteristic of some substratic entity, a mind or brain's consciousness. To speak of an animate cosmos, therefore, is not to fill each corner with ensouled matter but to underscore the singular nature that each burst of sense brings into the webs of co-presence that are integral to it and its world.

It would seem, therefore, that an apple has once again brought startling news: singular characters abound. And it is through this news that I would begin to read the old woman's "Dear me." Given the knife, she no doubt had hoped to eat the apple, and that does, to some extent, explain her surprise. But that cannot be all there is to the matter, for this is a worm speaking in the first person. It is not merely a lost snack that troubles her, therefore.[1] But what else? Her forgetfulness is underscored, and thus there is reason to think that her surprise stems in part from recalling what she had forgotten. Perhaps she had grown deaf to the address of her world; confronted with its "I am," she returns to it with a start. If so, we need to reread the poem, but this time from the restrained

---

1. The Christian themes running through the poem are not lost upon me: the apple, "I am," the table set for a twelve who, for some reason, are absent. I would suggest that the play of these themes throughout the poem, when read within the thoughts I have just developed, bring the sacred into every corner of the cosmos in a way that refuses to oppose birth and death (for a worm-god is as much a symbol of decay and corruption as it is a living being).

amazement of her "Dear me." For in a cosmos full of singular characters addressing one another, one must think differently the poem's sharp details, e.g., the thoroughly red apple, the chipped plate. Each facet stands as a burst of sense, a "self" presenting within a world. In other words, on a second reading, the force of the worm's "I am" runs over each image, eventually spilling over the page and the type until the whole world rises into a startling conversation.

This is the cosmos that Simic's ur-poetry opens. This exposition does not arrive in the form of a thesis, however. In fact, it undermines the authority of propositional thought by disclosing what a proposition can only presume: the empty dimension of presencing that is cleared in a radically anterior event and persists as the difference between co-presencing characters. Nor does Simic's ur-poetry address us through allegories of the birth of sense, as if various ur-figures were stand-ins for sense in general. In fact, with regard to the birth of sense, ur-poetry does not represent, metaphorically or otherwise, any state of affairs coming to pass beyond the language of the poem. Instead, by figuring and exposing its origination (a dynamic explored in Chaps. 1 and 2), a language of originary occurrence results, one that touches upon the coming-to-pass of each and any instance of underdetermined presencing.

Because it poetizes the birth of sense, one can say of Simic's ur-poetry, "there is no point / that does not see you." Like Rilke's torso, it has the power to sound us out and even change our lives. In reaching into every place (and time), every flash of sense, into every relation, Simic's ur-poetry retunes the cosmos whenever and wherever sense is born—which is every "where." And this is not to say that it offers us a new worldview. "There is no point / that does not see you," and that goes for metatheoretical registers as well, registers that would delimit the reach of poetic language within an author's intent, a reader's response, the unconscious, interstices of social labor, cultural metabolism, and so on. This poetry spans the cosmos, and it is limited only by the limit of sense itself, though even that limit is traced and exposed herein with startling rigor.

What, though, of the allegorical poems we read in Chapter 4—"Poem Without a Title," "Empire of Dreams," and "Mother Tongue"? How do they read within Simic's ur-poetry? Recall that they allegorized the repetitions poetizing seems to entail, that is, they offered allegories of the transpositions that occur when a traditional saying is repeated as a poetic saying. More precisely, and with specific regard to ur-poetry, they refused the second repetition of ur-poetry, the one whereby a poetic saying becomes a figure that poetizes the grounds of poetry. Moreover, they wrote over the white, apparently ignoring it, preferring instead to confront their sociohistorical present, including totalitarianism. These poems embrace allegory where ur-poetry seems to eschew it, and they do so in order to pursue ends that would seem to run counter to that for which ur-poetizing is, i.e., autofiguration and a language of originary occurrence.

Suppose, however, that we read these allegories within the cosmos opened by Simic's ur-poetry. What then? True, they would not return to the originary grounds of their birth in a thorough fashion. Instead, they would move among the various elements at play in a mother tongue in order to allegorize them and it (and thus themselves). Still, why not regard such a concrete confrontation with the language of the poem as another wave in the arrival of History? Recall that "History" closes with the ironic observation, "How pretty are the coffins and instruments of torture / In the Museum on the day of free admission to the public!" With vigor, the poem underscores how often violence and suffering are aestheticized, as does the earlier line in which the prisoner shouts that the death of women makes art. Read more generally, the suggestion extends to the violence of history itself, and thus the observation recoils upon this very poem, emphasizing the way in which it remains parasitic upon events like execution, forced prostitution, and starvation. Is that not what transpires in poems like "Mother Tongue"? While the thought is not poetized in the same manner, both poems suggest (reflexively) that a poem is made out of a history of suffering and violence. The only difference is that "History" extends its reach into the ways in which sense leaps into presence, whereas "Mother Tongue" limits its efforts to the notion of a mother tongue and the rich and terrible choirs in which it sings. This difference does not seem to problematize the claim, however, that even in their refusal to carry out the repetitions required by ur-poetry, Simic's allegorical efforts can be read within his ur-poetry. "History" poetizes a full range of fates, from arrests to allegory.

Given that they are to be read as arrivals of History, Simic's allegorical efforts need not be read in opposition to *White* and the scenario it unfolds, despite their overt concerns with the world presently engulfing them. Once they are set within the context of Simic's ur-poetry (and by the ur-poem itself, for it is a poem of poetry, after all), it becomes apparent that the white moves silently through each phrase, beneath every scratch and scrawl. I thus wish to repeat my suggestion from Chapter 3: every one of Simic's poems needs to be read through what *White* has to say, within the registers or "ranges of vibration" it opens. Simic's allegories thus remain cradled in emptiness despite their insistent attention to co-present forces at the expense of the presencing of those forces.

To situate allegories such as "Mother Tongue" within Simic's ur-poetry is not to deny their import, however. Even within the folds of History, these poems retain their power to expose us to what might be co-presencing within and alongside the language of the poem, e.g., in the paper upon which the poem has been written, the ink with which it has been printed, and so on. Consider an older poem from *Dismantling the Silence* called "Butcher Shop."

> Sometimes walking late at night
> I stop before a closed butcher shop.
> There is a single light in the store
> Like the light in which the convict digs his tunnel.
>
> An apron hangs on the hook:
> The blood on it smeared into a map
> Of the great continents of blood,
> The great rivers and oceans of blood.
>
> There are knives that glitter like altars
> In a dark church
> Where they bring the cripple and the imbecile
> To be healed.
>
> There is a wooden slab where bones are broken,
> Scraped clean:— a river dried to its bed
> Where I am fed,
> Where deep in the night I hear a voice.

Like the other allegories we have read, this poem explores a range of presences that speak through the "I" of the poem. And, more concretely, the prevailing image of the butcher block recalls the slaughter-bench of "Mother Tongue," i.e., history in its manifold violence, its "great continents of blood, / The great rivers and oceans of blood."

These connections aside, I think the poem focuses itself in the final stanza, when the speaker (peering through the window at the "slab where bones are broken") hears a voice. Several things merit our attention. First, this is a site at which the speaker feeds. Second, even though the slab has been scraped clean, a voice resounds. Now, one might think that this is merely the speaker's voice, but the poem does not specify this and even avoids the possessive "my voice" in favor of the indefinite "a voice." I think, therefore, that we have to regard this voice as more than that in which the poem's "I" speaks. This is not to say, however, that it is unrelated to the "I" of the poem. After all, this is where the speaker feeds, and thus what passes across this slab courses through him or her. The voice that arrives here is bound to the speaker's voice in an intimate way. The ambiguity of the indefinite article is thus felicitous, for it cannot be said to be the voice of some *this* versus some *that*, but only a voice owned by no one particular presence, a voice that resounds upon the slab (echoing what has transpired there, e.g., "bones are broken") and in the speech and poem of the "I" that feeds there.

There is more to say about this poem—about the knives shining like altars, say—but allow me to break off my reading in order to explore the import of such a poem within the folds of Simic's ur-poetry. "Butcher Shop" arrives as an exhortation that would have us follow, like convicts, a light out of the prison of an everyday, a prison that obscures what the deep night allows us to hear: the voice of what we feed upon, perhaps worms that say "I am," but then, as I suggested in the last chapter, not just that. Such an exhortation is not somehow other to History, however, and I think the confession that anchors "Butcher Shop" concerning the "river dried to its bed / Where I am fed" underscores the point. Rather, it is an event within History that would expose a bloody facet of History's arrival, much as "Mother Tongue" would alert us to that which passes over our lips.

Along with exhorting us toward a greater circumspection, allegorical expositions such as "Butcher Shop" also fight the categorical drift of figures—"voice," "I," "white," and "History," for example. They underscore that each is, as an arrival of History, caught in the fully concrete, synchronic and diachronic polyphony of that arrival; each is a co-presencing, singular character. These allegories have such power within Simic's ur-poetry because poems like *White* and "History" deny any burst of sense a purely categorical status that would somehow allow it to elude ontic entanglements (and thus not be part and parcel of the world of sense whose birth they figure and expose). In the cosmos unfolding here, ontic entanglements are all there are. It thus no longer makes any sense to speak of them as ontic. In sum, Simic's allegories do not repudiate or even contradict his ur-poetry. Instead, they belong to it, move and speak within it, and offer complementary expositions, perhaps even intensifications of what his ur-poetry already makes plain. Each burst of sense is polyphonic, from hands to trees to pork chops to ur-figures.

The fate of these allegories within Simic's ur-poetry is particularly fascinating once we realize that what holds true of them holds true of all the engagements with present (or presencing) circumstances that arise in his work: they come to pass as History cradled in emptiness. This fact throws into relief a marvelous facet of Simic's poetry. Not only does it open up a cosmos, it lives in it as well. Allow me to explain with two points. The first concerns a confrontation of totalitarianism.

Recall our discussion of "Mother Tongue." In Chapter 4, we drew several conclusions from reading this poem (alongside "Empire of Dreams" and "Poem Without a Title"). First, poetizing requires a mother tongue, but one can only draw such a tongue off the slaughter-bench of history, thus participating in that contestation and carnage. Second, a mother tongue arrives caught within the struggles of contemporary social life over how one speaks and about what, struggles that bring poetizing into contexts it might rather avoid. And because of this entanglement, poetizing always seems to contribute to certain futures and not others, some of which may produce suffering. Fourth, no measure exists that might legitimate one's inheritance. Rather, one remains bound to the struggles one inherits. Fifth, one might dissolve into one's inheritance and thus only ever be the recipient of second-person addresses, thereby losing one's singularity. This extreme fate would involve the dissolution of poetizing, for the language of the poem only repeats tradition.

Looming large in "Mother Tongue" (and the "occupied territory" engulfing "Empire of Dreams") is the threat of totalitarianism. In fact, among the various specters haunting the slaughter-bench of "Mother Tongue" and the slab in "Butcher Shop," it is totalitarianism above all else that shades the corridors of Simic's work. And yet, despite its palpability, Simic's fear of authoritarian rule is hauntingly elusive. What forms will the censor take? How will the poem police find their way into the first pages of our dreambooks? I think we might gain better access to Simic's understanding of totalitarianism if we note his insistence that the singularity of lyric poetry is staunchly political. In "Elegy in a Spider's Web," he writes: "The lyric poet is almost by definition a traitor to his own people. He is the stranger who speaks the harsh truth that only individual lives are unique and therefore sacred" (Simic 1994b, 38). Now, this declaration that individual lives are sacred decries any who would willingly sacrifice individuals to some systemic religious, political, or philosophical end. But such sacrifices cannot be the sole threat that looms here. "Empire of Dreams" and "Mother Tongue" suggest that the secret police can not only compel conscription in some (un)holy war but also work their way into our thoughts and dreams, such that, without our knowing it, our first person might not be ours. If this is so, then the war that Simic's ur-poetry fights against totalitarianism involves more than affirmations and defenses of the value of individuals (and individual poems). It takes place at the point of the genesis of some burst of sense we might term "individual."

Two questions are in play. First, what understanding of totalitarianism is appropriate to the fears that manifest themselves in poems such as "Empire of Dreams," "Poem Without a Title," and "Mother Tongue"? Second, how does Simic's work confront those fears, if it does? That is, how does it resist totalitarianism? In order to appreciate the depths of Simic's fear, we need to come to terms with the kind of totalitarianism that moves across the pages of dreambooks with the speed of neural transmissions. To this end, consider Philippe Lacoue-Labarthe and Jean-Luc Nancy's analysis of "new totalitarianism" (Lacoue-Labarthe and Nancy 1997, 126–28). Unlike "classical totalitarianism," which seeks to subordinate particularities to some transcendental end—e.g., the drive of reason in history or the destiny of a *Volk*—new totalitarianism obliterates transcendence altogether, subjecting every moment of presencing to a coercive logic attempting to totalize the range of its extension. The difference is decisive. Whereas appeals to transcendence allow one to test their legitimacy (if only formally), opening regimes to normative spheres beyond the naked power they wield, new totalitarianism denies the existence of an "outside" altogether.

Hannah Arendt argues:

> The fundamental reason for the superiority of totalitarian propaganda over the propaganda of other parties and movements is that its content, for the members of the movement at any rate, is no longer an objective issue about which people may have opinions, but has become as real and untouchable an element in their lives as the rules of arithmetic. The organization of the entire tex-

ture of life according to an ideology can be fully carried out only under a totalitarian regime. In Nazi Germany, questioning the validity of racism and anti-Semitism when nothing mattered but race origin . . . was like questioning the existence of the world. (Arendt 1958, 363)

On the surface, this kind of self-evidence, one that protected Nazi racial theories from scrutiny, gives us an example of new totalitarianism at work. But certain facets of Arendt's account suggest that Nazism, at least on this analysis, failed to employ the wholesale immanence of new totalitarian politics. First, new totalitarian proclamations are not "propaganda." "Propaganda" connotes "lying": Stalin routinely rewrote Russian history to suit his needs. As Osip Mandelstam suggests in his fatal portrait of the tyrant (see Mandelstam 1991): "He forges order after order like horseshoes, / hurling them at the groin, the forehead, the brow, the eye" (lines 13–14). Under new totalitarianism, however, given the supposed rigors of neopositivist methodologies, ruling regimes would simply traffic in the "real." In fact, I would even hesitate to refer to new totalitarian ideologies as "theories." "Theory" suggests a qualification at odds with the kind of purported necessity that organizes new totalitarian regimes. Established along positivist lines, they trade in facts, ever committed to no-nonsense realism, inflecting their proclamations with the cocksure tone of "Mother Tongue." As such, their theories are limited to inductive predictions, and thus, as the positivists would have it, they are *practically* devoid of theoretical content, content one might call into question or explore (in either a dialectical or deconstructive fashion) as the trace of an unacknowledged origin.

Second, there is an ambiguity in Arendt's account. It is not clear whether Germans refrained from questioning National Socialist racism because they took it to be true or considered it idle to oppose it. If the latter was the case, then what remained self-evident was not the truth of Nazi ideology but the fact that disagreement was pointless. Under conditions of new totalitarianism, however, reigning ideologies do not appeal to a cynical reality principle, stick in hand; they present themselves as reality itself. One has to reason to suppose, therefore, that forces such as the secret police might prove anachronistic in a new totalitarian regime. In the face of what we take to be reality, we would police ourselves.

With extreme concision, "Mother Tongue" opens us to the nightmarish endgame of a thoroughly totalitarian present, one wherein the poetic "I" and the interpretive "I" prove mere functionaries of an immanent reality wherein whatever comes to presence is an expression of laws already ascertained, such that speech about what is entails only the banal repetition of what "we" (i.e., the seamless community of knowledge) already claim to know. As Adorno and Horkheimer would say: "Factuality is confirmed, cognition is restricted to its repetition, thought proceeds toward empty tautology. The more that this thought-machinery subjects a being to itself, the more blindly it contents itself with its reproduction" (Horkheimer 1987, 49). Or, to use the vocabulary I have been employing throughout—and to shift our focus away from propositions to poems—in a seamless totalitarian present, poems become copies of traditional sayings. Thus one can speak of poetic machinery, although its products would not be tautologies but forgeries. But then, rather than betraying the spirit of art, such reproductions would embody a thorough loyalty to all that their mother tongue had accomplished.

Addressing the city of Bremen, Mandelstam apparently on his mind, Paul Celan remarked: "The poem can be, because it is a manifestation of language and thus dialogical by nature, a letter in a bottle sent with the faith—certainly not always full of hope—that it might sometime and somewhere wash ashore, perhaps on the land of the heart" (Celan 1983, 3:186).[2] I do not want to dispute that such a faith is part and parcel of poetic address (and not only when delivered in the second person). Even a poem like "Mother Tongue" has still been written and published. Even though it may arrive like a self-immolation, it does so as a warning: "This may happen to you." "Beware the voices hidden in your tongue." But as we saw in that very same poem, the "I" that would address another might dissolve into the "you" addressed by the state, or destiny, or a nebulous but quite effective reality principle. In other words, its greeting might just be a formality among those following orders. Likewise, the "you" addressed by the poem might be no more than the plural "you" of an obedient herd. But then whoever picked up the bottle thrown by

---

2. I think Mandelstam was on Celan's mind that day, because his Russian predecessor also imagined poems to be messages in bottles. "At a critical moment, the seafarer tosses a sealed bottle into the ocean waves, containing his [sic] name and a message detailing his fate. Wandering along the dunes many years later, I happen upon it in the sand. I read the message . . . I have the right . . . I have become its secret addressee" (Mandelstam 1979, 68). One should also note that in 1958, Celan was most likely working on the translations of Mandelstam's work that he published in 1959.

the poet would not undergo the "shiver of joy" that Mandelstam underwent when he chanced upon a poem by E. A. Baratynsky: "My gift is scant, my voice lacks force behind it," but "some far descendant possibly may find it" (Myers 1988, lines 1, 4). In response to this, Mandelstam writes: "What reader of Baratynsky's poem would not shiver with joy or feel that twinge of excitement experienced sometimes when you are unexpectedly hailed by name" (Mandelstam 1979, 69).[3] Under thoroughly totalitarian conditions, one cannot be hailed by name, however, for functions do not have proper names. Nor, for that matter, do they have hearts in which to receive bottles thrown by the likes of Celan. Instead, when opened, their contents are fed to cats. But this is not to point out anything that Celan did not know. As Celan writes to Hans Bender in May 1960: "We live under dark skies, and—there are so few human beings. That is why there are probably so few poems. The hope that I still have is not great" (Celan 1983, 3:178).

And yet I would insist that Simic's ur-poetry, while not ballast for hope (presuming hopefulness concerns a calculative regard for the likelihood that that some X will occur, e.g., the emergence of human beings), still tears at the closing canopy of new totalitarian regimes. On the side of poems like "Mother Tongue" and "Empire of Dreams," totalitarian forces are allegorically depicted, suggesting that the present is not free of such threats. Second, these allegories exhort the reader to attend to such threats, and they even guide one to points of vulnerability and hence possible resistance (e.g., poetry, a mother tongue, and so forth). Third, given that totalitarianism would script the whole of social life, such depictions, daring to speak for themselves and reveling in their singularity, stand as protests against the order that threatens singularity at every turn.

Do not forget, however, that these concrete engagements remain shrouded in an emptiness they also expose. I recall this point because I think that *White* is also an aspect of Simic's confrontation with totalitarianism. Where new totalitarianism would erect the walls of a *real* governed by necessity, those attentive to the white that underwrites all articulations hear only the winds of underdetermination and the instability it (perhaps ironically) ensures. In other words, *White* makes plain that no system is ever complete unto itself or grounded in necessity, be that

---

3. Mandelstam's claim that each poem has a "secret addressee," and that any of us can be that addressee, has been recently reasserted in Ed Hirsch's *How to Read a Poem* (Hirsch 1999, 1–30).

necessity bio-psychological (as maximizers, humans are egoists or even capitalists by nature), historical (the contradictions afflicting human modes of production must and eventually will resolve themselves into a communist society), or economic (the value of beings can be "dollarized"). To draw a poem from *The World Doesn't End:*

> Things were not as black as somebody painted them. There was a pretty child dressed in black and playing with two black apples. It was either a girl dressed as a boy, or a boy dressed as a girl. Whatever, it had small white teeth. The landscape outside its window had been blackened with a heavy and coarse paint brush. It was all very teleological, except when the child stuck out its red tongue.
>
> (41)[4]

But the point is not just that epistemic and political orders are underdetermined. The very beings such regimes would define and regulate are unstable through and through, and they demand the renewed attentions of any order irrespective of its self-conception.[5]

To live in a world figured by Simic's ur-poetry is to live in a world opposed to totalitarianism from the "ground" up. This may be why, as "Empire of Dreams" suggests, totalitarian regimes would keep us from the street-corners where poems and poets convene. The threat is not simply posed by poems of agitation and protest, though so-called committed work may offer some measure of resistance. Rather, the challenge issues forth from that originary corner itself, its whiteness barely visible beneath the yellowing rubble. As the ur-poet opens the white pages of his or her dreambook, exposing an event of origination running through and along the bounds and grounds of sense, the closing canopy of totalitarian rule is punctured, its claims to necessity thwarted by a sense of sense that refuses to render itself transparent to those who would lay claim to the laws of the real.[6]

It is worth pointing out that Simic's ur-poetry does not confront to-

---

4. While the red tongue ruptures the teleology smothering this scene, do not forget the white teeth, for they are, I think—if we set this poem within Simic's ur-poem—the trace of what enables the co-presencing of a red tongue amid all this blackness.

5. Elsewhere, I have explored the import of this instability for political regimes predicated upon recognition and representation (Lysaker 1999a, 1999b).

6. Here my reading again draws upon the work of Jean-Luc Nancy, particularly his meditations upon community and his invocations of a literary communism (Nancy 1991).

talitarianism in the form of a normative critique. It neither offers arguments—either against what it interrupts or in defense of what it discloses—nor confronts other languages of originary occurrence, or their derivations, in the form of a moral judgment. Third, it does not presume to proceed on the basis of a standard by which one might weigh the merits and validity of its figurations versus the explanations and justifications of totalitarian regimes. In fact, Simic's ur-poetry calls such a presumption (and the rusted scale it relies upon) into question. But how then does it confront a presence (or co-presencing polyphony) such as totalitarianism?

As we have seen, Simic's allegories, arising within an ur-poetic language of originary occurrence, confront totalitarianism by disclosing its presence, presuming, I take it, that their readers already regard such institutions and discourses as anathema. In addition, Simic's ur-poetry draws totalitarianism into its language of originary occurrence and exposes it (and us) to our polyphonic, underdetermined, unstable nature. Now, given that totalitarianism requires the repression of its underdetermined nature through the rhetoric of necessity (in order to lay claim to all of social life), such an exposure has the force, if not the form, of a critique. In other words, the effect of such an ur-poetic exposure should be "Dear me"—the realization that one had been misconstruing oneself and the world all along.

Because it lacks the form of a critique but nevertheless has the potential to compel a change in self-understanding through its displacements, we could say that ur-poetry involves an oblique immanent critique, one that engages a regime from outside the purview of its self-understanding while nevertheless laying claim to whatever sense it might make of itself. Such a critique is immanent because it claims to confront a regime with itself. It remains oblique, however, because it does not take that regime's self-understanding at face value but confronts it with an ur-poetic figuration of the matter. This is not to say that it ignores a participant's perspective in favor of its own third-person account, for it is precisely the origination of participation, person, and address that is at stake here. It is to say, however, that ur-poetry, in poetizing the sense of sense, will never engage another language of originary occurrence (or its derivations) except according to *its* own lights.

Despite its distance from critique proper, one might think that this kind of wholesale destabilization of totalitarianism, when carried to its logical extreme, reduces to an indeterminate negation of politics per se and produces a skepticism with regard to any course of action.[7] With regard to Simic's ur-poetry, I think such a worry is misplaced. First, it is true that, because it engages all of sense, Simic's ur-poetry poetizes all political regimes in the same manner. But note that its impact changes given the presumptions of those regimes. The logic of totalitarianism is devastated by Simic's ur-poetry because it is predicated upon a kind of self-possession and constancy that seems utterly misguided within the ranges vibrating in poems such as *White* and "History." Liberalism, on the other hand, finds itself mired in an altogether different issue. Rather than destabilizing the rhetoric of necessity, Simic's ur-poetry drags the liberal subject to a point where its univocal, isolated self evaporates in the face of an apparent co-presencing polyphony. Simic's ur-poetry does not, therefore, indeterminately undercut any form of politics. Rather, it transforms a politics whose presumptions about the origins of sense run counter to what manifests itself within the language of the poem.

Simic's ur-poetry has a varied impact upon political regimes because it does not exhaust itself in the banal proposition that discursive and institutional orders are contingent or even, to be more precise, underdetermined. Not only is it not propositionally derived but it also opens up an entire language of originary occurrence, thus redetermining (or overpoetizing) existing patterns of sense rather than simply negating them. It is thus not a skeptical force but an abundance—an overflow of sense that washes over every burst of sense.

Amid the abundance opening in Simic's ur-poetry, one element bears special notice: possibility. In returning us to a scene of wild underdetermination and instability, in dislodging the sclerotic density of what passes for the real, Simic's ur-poetry continually exposes the persistence of possibility. This is not to say that it offers or recommends particular possibilities (although it might). It is to say, however, that ur-poetry keeps the scene that makes possibilities possible ever open, underscoring the ways in which that scene cradles each burst of sense in its emptiness.[8]

---

7. I note these objections, given the concerns expressed by Thomas McCarthy with regard to deconstruction (McCarthy 1991, 111). This is not to suggest that Simic's ur-poetry deconstructs anything. Such a suggestion would conflate the strategic interventions of a kind of criticism with the repetitions, transformations, figurations, and exposures of ur-poetry. And yet, the play of the white does have a destabilizing power akin to deconstructive readings. It thus seems reasonable to consider McCarthy's worries in this context even though they arose in another.

8. On the basis of her responses to deconstruction and other so-called post-structuralist phenomena (responses that have inspired McCarthy as well as Habermas), I think that Nancy Fraser would ask that we not conflate an ur-poetic preservation of possibility with "politics

Now, because it preserves possibility in this manner, Simic's ur-poetry remains possible under any conditions that allow poets to write, speak, read, or even imagine. By engaging origination, Simic's ur-poetry is able to reach past any force that would overdetermine it (no matter what the status of its mother tongue) and bring to light the underdetermination and possibility that run through the fabric of the world. One might object, of course, that possibility is precisely what does not make its way into "Poem Without a Title." Instead, the lead the poem addresses and hopes to retrieve from a bullet life remains lead, the language of the poem unable to draw it back into the scene of its origination. Does this not suggest that ur-poetry might fail when faced with an overwhelmingly overdetermined traditional saying, operation, or element? I would suggest that this poem remains "without a title" because, for all its reflexivity, the "I" of "Poem Without a Title" cannot secure the conditions of its possibility on its own. As we saw in *White,* the speaker could not play the role of the white (by freezing his breath in the cold air) and produce poems. Instead, poetizing requires that the white has always already arrived, bullet-like, baptizing the sense of sense. That is, the language of the poem, irrespective of its density, of its power of translation and determination, remains dependent upon what remains anterior to subjects and their powers of translation. It is at its limits, therefore—where its "I" both begins and ends—that the language of the poem opens onto originary possibility. And as long as that limit is broached, ur-poetry can arise.

My concerns about the originary status of the lyric "I" return us to a problem broached earlier. Simic writes: "In the beginning were the epic and the folk song. Then came the lyric poem. Someone said, 'I exist,' and wondered that it should be so. The world hasn't been the same since. Lyric poetry remains the place where the individual asserts himself or herself against the gods and demons of history and the tribe. In that sense the lyric poem remains potentially the most subversive of literary

---

proper," i.e., normatively and empirically driven arguments, strategies, and enactments concerning what is to be done (Fraser 1989; Holland 1997). I would agree but also add that Simic's ur-poetic labors are neither irrelevant nor incompatible with such efforts. I thus find Fraser's suggestion that the kind of work pursued here and elsewhere is little more than "quasi-Heideggerian speculation" unfair and naïve (Fraser 1987, 86). The matter at hand, i.e., the birth of sense, is not an object of speculation (and particularly in ur-poetry, although, to be fair, Fraser is not addressing that phenomenon). And, because it engages the origination of the agencies with which "politics proper" concerns itself, it remains a matter that no worldly comportment can set aside or overcome through some supposed theoretical or practical advance.

forms" (Simic 1994a, 118). Note again that my issue is ur-poetry, not lyric poetry, and for reasons I have already given: the figure of the lyric fails to capture the originary, autofigurative power of the kind of poetizing at stake here. That point aside, the real question is whether ur-poetry's subversiveness requires the figure of the individual.

As you might surmise, I would rather speak of singularities than individuals, and not just in order to ensure that the underdetermined character of every facet of sense (not just the human) is underscored. To my ear, "individual" connotes a philosophy of the subject, that is, a philosophy that treats the birth of sense, thought either as sense in general or a peculiarly human sense, as a function of the creative or representational capacities of a subject, conscious or otherwise. It thus prevents the language of the poem or any language of originary occurrence from opening onto what exceeds any self-relation, even in the deepest regions of first-person speech, i.e., "I am." For Simic, this "I am" throws off whatever yoke totalizing narratives would lay across the shoulders of unique lives. But this is true whether we treat the "I" as the self-assertion or self-presentation of an individual or as the co-presencing address of a singular, underdetermined character, for the latter is precisely a life in its utter uniqueness. And given that the latter preserves the most radically originary disclosures of Simic's ur-poetry, it seems prudent to allow that ur-poetry to draw, as radically as possible, the figure of the individual into its language of originary occurrence such that it opens onto the diachronic and synchronic polyphony that is more than the product of the sense-making efforts of a subject.

Now, one should not exaggerate the power of Simic's ur-poetry. After all, oblique negations of totalitarian rhetoric will neither topple walls nor halt the cruel swiftness of unconverted lead. But I would caution against underestimating the force of an event that lays claim to each and every instance of sense. True, the weave of Simic's ur-poetry is not Kevlar. Moreover, and this was apparent in *White*, the street-corner at which poem, poet, and reader meet can often point toward exile, or worse. And yet, recall again Rilke's "Archaic Torso of Apollo": "there is no point / that does not see you. You must change your life." My claim has been that ur-poetry (and Simic's ur-poetry in particular) has that power, for there is no nook or seam of sense in which to elude its reach. It lays claim, as Heidegger says, to the whole of being as well as to particular beings at the point of origination, including us. And if that claim insistently draws its readers back behind whatever curtains cloak our world in some faux fate, then it will do so wherever its sense of sense washes ashore, to recall Celan and Mandelstam.

One may doubt, of course, others' ability to receive or engage such a claim. But one will have similar doubts with regard to any event, whether it is a poem, a policy, or a plea. In other words, such a risk is unavoidable, not a shortcoming that plagues ur-poetry alone. However, if the language of the poem has the power to reach the ends of the cosmos in the most thorough way, then Joseph Brodsky's remark, offered while introducing Alexander Kushner, is relevant here: "I do consider it my duty to warn you that an encounter with poetry in its pure form is pregnant with far-reaching consequences, that this volume is not where it will all end for you" (Kushner 1991, ix). Far-reaching consequences? Even psychologically speaking, I do not consider this hyperbole. In a small apartment in Leuven, Belgium, I first read Rilke's "Archaic Torso of Apollo." At twenty, I had no idea how long these lines would stay with me, how intricately they would weave and worm themselves through and into what have come to be intuitions. I had no idea how far-reaching the consequences of that encounter would be, how they would still be unfolding over fifteen years later, for I am still trying, even now, to fathom that encounter, to fathom what Rilke's poem unveiled to me with remarkable reflexivity—the potential force of and in the work of art.

But if matters remain so open-ended even in the psychological realm, one overdetermined at the metatheoretical level, then what are we to say about Simic's ur-poetry, about a figuration and exposition that lays claim to the sense of sense, unveiling at its heart (and thus at the heart of whatever comes to pass) underdetermination, instability, and possibility? How could such an exposition end? Where would it end, and when? Could such matters ever settle? Or would not such an "ending" go the way of all presencing, the way of instability and eventual displacement at the hands of History's ongoing arrivals?

Alongside its confrontations with totalitarianism and its recoiling invocation of possibilities without end, Simic's ur-poetry also addresses the reader with a kind of humor that arises less in the form of jokes or gags than in a kind of comportment. In an interview from 1972, he tells Wayne Dodd and Stanley Plumly: "Humor. Why humor? I guess when you think of classical comedy, humor seems to be a temporary interruption of harmony, the great harmony. The audience knows better. I think in the twentieth century humor has become ontological. It's a permanent disruption . . . a philosophy of life" (Simic 1985, 19). What does it mean for humor to become ontological? To my mind, the point is not that Simic's humor entails a set of explicit beliefs or observations about the world—e.g., history is a tragicomedy—if only because it is difficult to imagine how such a position would fit into a Simic poem. How could a poetry whose language is so circumspectly non-propositional pursue humor through a series of propositions? Moreover, humor, at least as poetized by Simic (and this will become evident shortly), involves a pre-reflective comportment toward the world, a way of receiving its impress. It is not a matter of presenting to a reader the multiple ironies that plague us. The point is that for Simic, humor persists as way of receiving and engaging the address of History's arrival out of and into the white. In other words, it is "ontological" (although I would do without the term) insofar as it relates itself to the birth of sense.

As a kind of comportment, Simic's humor moves about his ur-poetry much as his confrontations with totalitarianism do. Like his allegories, his humor responds to History in the concreteness of its arrivals, engaging the flashes of sense that are, for the moment, the underdetermined world. And, as we shall see, like those very same allegories, his humor remains attuned to History's arrival. Simic's humor is thus another example of how his work both engages the whole of the cosmos at its limit while continuing to live with all of its concreteness.

Simic's funny bone can be felt in the opening lines of "History": "Men and women with kick-me signs on their backs." Here the humor is plain, even coarse. Humans are dupes for the fates in which they (or we) are entangled, and that is why, clown-like, History can sneak up and kick us in the ass. As Simic writes, reflecting on the work of Saul Bellow: "No one who has been thus sent adrift by one of history's practical jokes is a great believer in Reason. One can say anything about history except that it gives a hoot what happens to one person or another. It's tough for anyone to figure out why his or her life turned out the way it did. . . . The absurd is the only reality there is, so for an individual, life is all about luck" (Simic 2001a, 13). The humor running through Simic's ur-poetry bears an attunement to the instability or "luck" that underwrites (and often undermines) the characters that arrive in and as History—or what *The World Doesn't End* presents as a "comedy of errors." One can see, therefore, why Simic considers "ontological humor" disruptive. It sees through the consistencies of the everyday into scenes of radical underdeterminacy and vulnerability. Furthermore, one can see how Simic's humor complements his resistance to totalitarianism: it undermines what presents itself as secure, even self-possessed. As he writes in "Cut the Comedy," echoing Eco's *The Name of the Rose:* "It is impossible to imagine a Christian or fascist theory of humor. Like poetry, humor is subversive" (Simic 1997, 41).

Despite its ability to chuckle as ill fates tumble all around, Simic's work does not laugh at the victims of History. As he goes on to tell Dodd and Plumly: "the person, the victim of a joke as well as the person who cracks a joke—they both sense themselves defeated" (Simic 1985, 19). Or, rather than defeated, we might say that this kind of humor recognizes that everyone is thoroughly vulnerable. This humor is not a self-congratulatory cynicism, one that draws pleasure from being in the know, even if "the know" proclaims that everything is going to hell. Rather, it regards our sorry lot with tenderness, recognizing its own fate among those blind to the kick-me signs upon their backs.

Consider "Blindman's Bluff" from *Walking the Black Cat.*

> Death's an early riser.
> You've got to be real quick
> To slip under his arm
> Stretched toward you in the street.
>
> His nails brushing you,
> Press yourself against the wall,
> Eyes wide open,
> While he spins around,
>
> In his white blindfold,
> Arms like a Dutch windmill,
> Or like huge scissors
> On the pavement already crowded
> With schoolchildren.

Note first that the comic principle operative here complements the one at work in "History." There, protagonists are blind to an approaching fate. Here, blindness is again in play, but now fate is blind, thus bringing perpetrator and victim into the same comedy of errors. (And given the poem's second-person address, the reader is brought into the whirl as well.) Note also how a chilling, harrowing image (children waiting to be cut down) closes the curtain on a slapstick scene: death, blindfolded, spinning around like a clumsy fool, no doubt tripping over himself while slicing and dicing away. One almost expects him, black hair slicked back, to shout "Hey, lady!" The scene is absurd and it's hard not to laugh, as if death's scythe swung like a long two-by-four to knock over anyone approaching. But the scenario is also awful, and perhaps, like me, you feel a rush of compassion for the assembled, oblivious (and most likely playing) children, perhaps even a desire to leave the safety of the wall "you" are pressed against in order to scoop up as many as you can. Simic is thus more akin to Walter Benjamin's Proust than to a cold, detached nightclub comedian: "His style is comedy, not humor; his laughter does not toss the world up but flings it down—at the risk that it will be smashed to pieces, which will then make him burst into tears" (Benjamin 1968, 207).⁹

For all its tenderness, there is also coldness in "Blindman's Bluff"—as there is to all black comedy. Along with interrupting would-be grand harmonies and underscoring the instability of you, the cosmos, and me, Simic's humor also offers some defense against the blind onslaughts of History. Recall that in *White*, the speaker refused to relinquish his mortality when marrying fate. I think something along those lines occurs with Simic's so-called ontological humor. Humor can be a kind of bravado, one by which we flip a finger at fate even as it runs us over, one through which we affirm our mortal singularity despite its fragility and transience. In *The World Doesn't End*, we find:

> From inside the pot on the stove someone threatens the stars with a wooden spoon.
> Otherwise, cloudless calm. The shepherd's hour.
>
> (69)

On the reading I am offering, Simic's humor is much like the "someone" in this vignette, shaking a spoon even as it floats about History's boil. (And thus this brief poem draws humor humorously.) It senses its own futility, but it rages (and laughs) anyway, refusing to relinquish its singularity, to diminish the wealth of what has been given. This is a humor of dignity, an oblique way of taking oneself and the world seriously even while appreciating the pratfalls that are the birth of sense.

---

9. As his plain from his remark to Dodd and Plumly, I do not think that Simic distinguishes between comedy and humor, and we should not presume that Benjamin's distinction implies that Proust's comedy is categorically other to what I have been calling Simic's humor.

It is not only Simic's humor that shakes a spoon at heaven, however. All of his ur-poetry shares the same boat (or pot). For all its recoils, its mimicry of the labor of self-possession, Simic's ur-poetry never exceeds the insight offered in *White*: "Well, you can't call me a cook / If the pot's got me under its cover" (lines 113–14). Even as this ur-poetry drapes the cosmos with interanimating tropes like History and the white, it also makes evident how it remains at the mercy of what is exposed in the interplay of those figures. Simic's humor is thus not unlike his allegories when thought in relation to the ur-poetry to which they belong and within which they speak. It infuses the various ur-poetic repetitions that drive the corpus with a bit of their own medicine, underlining the way in which they too are children of the fates they trace and expose. As if aware of the irony written through the fate of his ur-poetry, Simic notes: "What a mess! I believe in images as vehicles of transcendence, but I don't believe in God!" (Simic 1990c, 92).[10] It is precisely this kind of mess that is the true marvel of Simic's work—to continue on with living even as the grounds of a cosmos are displaced in the arrival of a History that draws the birth of sense away from the thought of grounds (and their consequents) altogether.

Now, one might fear that Simic's humor leads to a kind of comic resignation, one that prefers a knowing (albeit somber) laugh to an engagement with the fray. I think, though, that Simic's work eludes such a fate. Recall "Blindman's Bluff." Even as it comically depicts the indiscriminate and incalculable arrival of death, it unveils what happens before and around those who, in an effort to avoid death, keep to the wings: children are cut down. In other words, the poem shows us what inaction entails, and thus, as I suggested earlier, it tugs us away from whatever point of safety we think we might have found (e.g., comic detachment) and back to center stage. This is not to say, however, that the poem compels or calls for engagement in place of ironic detachment. Rather, it drives home the fact that we are always engaged, ever on center stage. In a cosmos of thoroughgoing co-presencing, resignation is out of the question.

Another concern. Amid all this laughter, might not Simic's humor prevent his work from mourning the victims of History? Again, I think

---

10. One can find a similar remark in "Charles the Obscure" (Simic 1997, 19). These disavowals appear to retract Simic's faithful testament in 1972: "But then I don't mind admitting that I believe in God" (Simic 1985, 6).

not. When in the early 1990s a crisis began to tear Yugoslavia apart, Simic (Serbian by birth) recounted a story told by Karl Jaspers in a letter to Hannah Arendt. Apparently, Spinoza used to "amuse himself by placing flies in a spider's web, then adding two spiders so he could watch them fight over the flies" (Simic 1997, 34). The image chills, and on two levels. First, it suggests the kind of detachment undermined in "Blindman's Bluff." Second, it suggests a mode of comportment for which the arrivals of History and the snips of death unfold as grand if not harmonious narratives. But Simic's ur-poetry denies one a leap to any plateau from which a burst of sense might arrive merely as an instance in some cosmological drama. In erasing the distinction between ontological conditions and ontic instances in favor of singular bursts of co-presencing, Simic's ur-poem opens us to flashes of sense, each of which is unique, such that its loss would be irrevocable. And Simic's humor remains true to this realization. In its empathy, it resists what we might term "ontological" *Schadenfreude*. It thus remains congruent with the decision to elegize without self-aggrandizing pathos those whose lines of fate have been snipped, who now only persist in the diachronic folds of History's displacing arrival. As he says, concluding his reflections on Yugoslavia's descent into genocidal conflict (and note the deadpan tone, even here): "So what's to be done? people rightly ask. I've no idea. As an elegist I mourn and expect the worst. Vileness and stupidity always have a rosy future. The world is still a few evils short, but they'll come. Dark despair is the only healthy outlook if you identify with the flies, as I do" (Simic 1997, 39).[11]

There is yet another side to Simic's humor, and we risk overlooking it if we remain bound to these justifiably dark remarks. Consider "The Road in the Clouds" from *Walking the Black Cat*.

> Your undergarments and mine,
> Sent flying around the room

---

11. Elsewhere, Simic writes: "I prefer Aristophanes to Sophocles, Rabelais to Dante. There's as much truth in laughter as there is in tragedy, a view not shared by many people. They still think of comedy as nose thumbing at the serious things in life" (Simic 1994a, 113). As I have tried to show, his humor is far from nose thumbing. And yet, this may be precisely because it makes room for the tragic at the level of the everyday. "You don't need Hamlet or Lear," he writes, "or an assassination of a president to experience the tragic" (Simic 2000, 45). I thus see no need to choose between Aristophanes and Sophocles, between comedy and tragedy, when Simic's ur-poetry seems to find room for both of them.

> Like a storm of white feathers
> Striking the window and ceiling.
>
> Something like repressed laughter
> Is in the air
> As we lie in sweet content
> Drifting off to sleep
> With the treetops in purple light
>
> And the sudden memory
> Of riding a bicycle
> Using no hands
> Down a steep winding road
> To the blue sea.

Not much despair here. In the wake of a possibly pillow-tearing bout of lovemaking, "Something like repressed laughter / Is in the air." The speaker and his or her partner are giddy with "sweet content," and with the sense, it seems, of how overtaken they were, how dispossessed. I say this because they are about to laugh after tearing off their clothes—and to laugh at each other. It is as if they are only now returning to themselves, and with good humor: "What the hell just happened? Wow!" And then consider the image that overtakes the speaker: riding dangerously, even recklessly down a hill—a hill "steep" and "winding"—and no hands on the handlebars. This is a poem of dispossession, of being scattered about like skivvies, and the humor that can well up when passion leads us by the nose. And in its building laughter, this is also a poem of affirmation, of welcoming what arrives even as we, perhaps desperately, cling to whatever will bear us (a bicycle, say, or, better yet, a generous, laughing body).

The repressed laughter that one finds in "The Road in the Clouds" thus shows us yet another side of Simic's humor. Like his darker, tender commiserations, it orients itself toward the scene where sense is born. But whereas poems such as "Blindman's Bluff" find vulnerability, even helplessness, "The Road in the Clouds" finds gleeful excitement before what History has to offer, before what arrives and washes over us, carrying us along. This is not to oppose the two, however. Like Simic's confrontations with totalitarianism, both are oriented toward possibility; both wiggle their way to the limit at which sense emerges. But because possibility (or instability) is double-edged, opening what occurs to growth *and* destruction, so too is Simic's humor. On the one hand, it empathetically attends to the absurd slapstick fate whirling around us, simultaneously laughing and crying, while on the other hand it cackles when the whirl takes us for a ride.

In tracing how Simic's work confronts totalitarianism and engages the co-presencing world with a doubly-tuned sense of humor, one consonant with elegy, I have tried to show some of the ways in which Simic's work moves about the cosmos it figures and exposes. As I have explained, this is possible because Simic's ur-poetry unveils a cosmos wherein every burst of sense arranges and throws the white, differentiated dimension of presencing into relief. Various poetic figures, forms, and themes can thus function as ur-poetry even as they engage the world wherein they co-presence. In fact, as Simic's allegories remind us, in their co-presencing and irrespective of their form, they cannot help but engage the world. But if this is so, then ur-poetry entails a third repetition, one we have thus far failed to note.

Recall that the initial repetition of ur-poetry occurs when a traditional saying, say "History" or "white" or "mother tongue," is set into a poem and rendered poetic. A second repetition occurs when the figure poetizes the grounds of poetry, that is, when its reach comes to include the language of the poem to which it belongs—such that the poem itself becomes, for example, a part of History. In this second repetition, figures that poetize the grounds of poetry come to be ur-figures or figures of poetizing, and in two senses: they both belong to the language of the poem and concern, through autofiguration, the language of the poem. Figures of poetizing do not limit their figurations to the language of the poem, however. Rather, their figurative interplay concerns the whole of sense, and thus these second repetitions produce a language of originary occurrence, one that overdetermines or overpoetizes the birth of sense.

In the case of Simic's ur-poetry, his language of originary occurrence denies categorical status to any burst of sense, ur-figures included. Instead, each burst of sense is itself a singular, underdetermined, co-presencing character. And in the thoroughly animate world that thereby arises, every burst of sense arranges and throws into relief what the ur-figures initially exposed: the white, differentiated dimension of co-presencing running through the synchronic and diachronic webs of relations in which these characters come to pass. Now, if one were to reread a poem like "History" at this very point, something remarkable would happen. The figure "History" would lose its status as an ur-figure, for it would no more throw the world and event of co-presencing into relief than any other figure, say "kick-me signs" or "back," or any burst of sense for that matter, say a period, the page, a hand holding the book, or a blinking eyelid. From within Simic's language of originary occurrence, therefore, a third repetition occurs. Ur-figures are returned to the world, once again just another facet of the cosmos into which they initially led us.

Now, the point is not that ur-figures are stripped of their disclosive power in this third repetition. Rather, it is that the power of ur-poetry is extended to every burst of sense. More precisely, in this third repetition, Simic's language of originary occurrence no longer addresses the reader through the interplay of a select number of key figures. Once the origin of sense is figured and exposed, in its ubiquity, the entire cosmos speaks in and as a language of originary occurrence, unveiling the emptiness out of which sense emerges and tracing the differentiated dimension through which sense co-presences.

At least two things follow when Simic's ur-poetry assumes this inclusive stance with regard to its language of originary occurrence. We are reminded, as we are by Simic's allegories, that ur-figures and the language of originary occurrence they enable are part and parcel of the world they refigure. Moreover, this third repetition counteracts whatever tendency we might have to fetishize the language of the poem at the expense of the cosmos into which it has led us and to which, on its own terms, it belongs. In exposing how each burst of sense is a harbinger of presencing in all its synchronic and diachronic polyphony, Simic's ur-poetry effectively insists that it no longer stands as a privileged guide into the scene where sense is born. Instead, it reminds us of its place within the cosmos and exhorts us to attend to the full polyphony enveloping us, not just to the language of the poem.

Simic writes: "To rescue the banal is every lyric poet's ambition" (Simic 1997, 92). With the utmost intensity, this is precisely what Simic's ur-poetry does, and most thoroughly when, in returning its ur-figures to the world, it sends us out into a world of bursting, underdetermined singularity, attuned to the uncanny marvel to which we, in our essence, belong. Not that Simic's ur-poetry praises the ordinary or offers an *apologia* on its behalf. If anything, it interrupts the hardened presumptions and seeming necessities of everyday life. As Simic writes in *The World Doesn't End*:

> A dog with a soul, you've got that? You apes with heads of Socrates, false priests' altar boys, retired professors of evil! I

> imagine cities so I can get lost in them. I meet other dogs with souls when I'm not lighting firecrackers in heads that are about to doze off.
> Blood and guts firecrackers. In the dark to see, you ass-scratchers! In the dark to see.
>
> (29)

But in drawing the ordinary up into its language of originary occurrence until the underdetermined, singular characters of that world are a language of originary occurrence in themselves, Simic's ur-poetry rejuvenates the banal, showing how even that which gleams dully is not only singular through and through but also occurs at a point of perpetual possibility.

Afterword

Our discussions began with Rilke's "Archaic Torso of Apollo," and I stated that I wanted to explore how a work of art might address us such that it could change our lives. With the help of Martin Heidegger, and limiting our attentions to the work of Charles Simic (thus forgoing any attempt to speak of art in general), we have considered the idea of ur-poetry. Ur-poems are poems of poetry, but they also address us with a language of originary occurrence, one concerning the birth of sense and thus the whole span of the cosmos, including the very sense of "cosmos."

In its three repetitions, Simic's ur-poetry is as much a journey through the language of the poem as it is a dynamic palimpsest of overlaid figures and operations, one in which various moments are multiply replayed. As readers, then, we need to regard ur-poetry as something undergone, a series of relations and transformation that one tracks, struggles to fathom, and gauges. Or, because we have just done precisely that, I think we should regard the preceding chapters as steps in a journey, as explorations of the riches of Simic's ur-poetry.

In the Introduction, we read several testimonies concerning the power of the work of art. The claim that I support is that artworks "engage" us in extraordinary ways. More precisely, as if we were engines, they set us in motion. At the level of pathos, this is a matter of feeling struck, compelled. In the case of Simic's ur-poetry, however, it is also a matter of beginning and pursuing a journey through a thicket of poetizing repetitions and transformations. The first repetition entices us, taking a traditional saying and presenting it to us as something slightly different: a moment in a poem. It catches our attention, buoyed perhaps by rhythm, a stark juxtaposition, or what appears to be a personal address. "In a forest of question marks, you were no / bigger than an asterisk" (Simic 1989, lines 1–2). Certain figures do not remain mere moments in a poem, however, but recoil upon the grounds of poetry. The very address that had initially proven so enticing thus leads us toward another thought, and so on. To be engaged by ur-poetry is to follow out these recoils, even to experience them by experiencing the changes they exact upon figures such as History, the white, the page itself, and the ink upon it.

To experience these changes is to undergo them, to be entangled (another sense of "engagement") in their various plays. When I say "undergo," I mean that once entangled, we begin to hear and see differently those words and operations upon the page, the ink with which they were printed, and the page upon which they stare back at us. But then this is just to say that to follow out the recoils of an ur-poem is to be transformed, changed, to no longer hear or see the world or part of the world in the same way. Heidegger claims that certain works "transport us out of the realm of the ordinary. To comply with this displacement means to transform accustomed ties to world and earth and, henceforth, to keep oneself from all well-known ways of acting and assessing, knowing and viewing" (Heidegger 1977a, 54). My claim has been that in poetizing the birth of sense, Simic's ur-poetry effects precisely this kind of transformation (or better still, conversion), though not by offering theses to which we give our assent. Rather, ur-poetry enables and encourages us, even exhorts us to hear differently the very sense before us, e.g., the sense that is the language of the poem, the chair at our backs, the brush and smell of cat fur, the light glaring upon the blue tarp outside an upstairs window. I should stress, though, that the kind of displacement at work here does not entail being transported to some realm of ur-poetry or pure figuration. Part of the power of Simic's ur-poetry lies in the way it displaces the everyday without discarding it in favor of a poetic Arcadia. Instead, it drags the mundane and extraordinary alike into its language of originary occurrence, eventually bringing the whole of the cosmos into the no-longer-plain sense of things with whom we co-presence. In other words, to be transformed within the ur-poetic journey that moves through Simic's work is less to leave the world behind than to begin to see, hear, and live within it in qualitatively different ways.

In the case of Simic's ur-poetry, the changes wrought upon the cosmos are enormous. Once Simic's ur-poetry sets to work on our "accustomed relations," the cosmos rises up in a rather novel manner. Beings, cradled in an extrahistorical, ubiquitous, white emptiness that surrounds them as the difference between and among them, come to presence as something other than the consequent of any ground. Rather, they leap into presence underdetermined. They are thus creatures neither of necessity nor of contingency, but unstable, vulnerable figures, wrapped in possibility, ever open to transformation.

Beings do not leap into presence on their lonesome, however. Instead, they co-presence polyphonically, arriving as History within synchronic and diachronic webs of relation that are integral to their being: a table and a chair, a cell of cells, a hand and a nail, a shirt and the hands that assembled it, a tree and the sunlight that fed it. Beings are not mere functions of these webs but singular characters uniquely and irreplaceably addressing the world within which they presence even as that world addresses them. At an originary level, therefore, it is misleading to carve the cosmos into subjects and objects, as if some creatures were mere expressions of laws whereas others had agency. Each burst of sense has its own character, its own unique way of presencing through the ubiquitous white emptiness that surrounds it as the difference between and among the whole ensemble.

It bears repeating that Simic's ur-poem does not offer these thoughts as theses. Instead, it leads us to them, and thus it is less that one decides to change one's life in the face of what an ur-poem discloses than that one finds oneself changed along the journey that ur-poetry initiates and ultimately is. Recall Simic's own testimony: "At times one comes across a poet who strikes one as being absolutely original. There's something genuinely different about him or her, a something that one has never quite encountered in all the poets one has read before. 'I will never look at the world in quite the same way,' one realizes at once, and that's what happens. From that day on, one feels deeply and fatefully changed by the experience of that reading" (Simic 1990c, 113). That's it. We realize it all at once. The cosmos is quite other than I had supposed. And thus I have written of ur-poetic conversions, of being turned around as a reigning sense of sense is displaced in favor of another until one realizes that things are not as one had assumed, even if only implicitly. Ur-poetic conversion is not unlike iron's transformation into steel, for in acquiring a new sense of sense, one becomes a new being, e.g., an orphan of silence instead of a created being.

In Chapter 7, I quoted Joseph Brodsky warning his readers that "an encounter with poetry in its pure form is pregnant with far-reaching consequences, that this volume is not where it will all end for you." I would close by repeating that warning and stressing that such a fate is unavoidable for those truly engaged by Simic's ur-poetry. In setting us within the folds of an underdetermined, unstable cosmos of singular characters, and in relinquishing figurative control over that cosmos, Simic's ur-poetry opens us to world without end. A brief poem, one cited earlier, makes this plain.

MY SECRET IDENTITY IS

> The room is empty,
> And the window is open
>
> (74)

My claim is that any burst of sense can lay claim to this "my," for in an underdetermined, polyphonic cosmos of co-presencing singularities, identities always lead elsewhere, namely, to those beings among whom one co-presences as well as on to History's next arrival. If so, then the fact that this poem closes without a period is significant, for it thereby draws itself within what Simic's ur-poetry leads us to realize: all that comes to presence is unfinished, open-ended, and that goes for ur-poems and their readers as well. Perhaps we should take to heart, therefore, the title of the book from which "My Secret Identity Is" is drawn, a book that closes with this poem, or rather, refuses to close—*The World Doesn't End.* Wherever one turns, an open window awaits, a window onto the white open dimension of presencing differentiated by, in, and as the arrival of the History of the underdetermined, co-presencing, singular characters with whom one dwells.

Bibliography

Abram, David. 1996. *The Spell of the Sensuous*. New York: Random House.
Adorno, Theodor. 1974. *Minima Moralia*. Translated by E. F. N. Jephcott. London: Verso Books.
———. 1991. *Notes to Literature*. Vol. 1. Translated by Sherry Weber Nicholson. New York: Columbia University Press.
———. 1992. *Notes to Literature*. Vol. 2. Translated by Sherry Weber Nicholson. New York: Columbia University Press.
———. 1997. *Aesthetic Theory*. Translated by Robert Hullot-Kentor. Minneapolis: University of Minnesota Press.
———. 2000. *Introduction to Sociology*. Translated by Edmund Jephcott and edited by Christoph Gödde. Stanford: Stanford University Press.
Akhmatova, Anna. 1992. *The Complete Poems of Anna Akhmatova*. Translated by Judith Hemschemeyer and edited by Roberta Reeder. Boston: Zephyr Press.
Allemann, Beda. 1954. *Hölderlin und Heidegger*. 2d ed. Zürich: Atlantis Verlag.
Ammons, A. R. 1993. *Garbage*. New York: W. W. Norton.
Arendt, Hannah. 1958. *The Origins of Totalitarianism*. Cleveland: World Publishing.
Aylesworth, Gary. 1988. "Heidegger and Hölderlin." *Philosophy Today* 32 (Summer): 143–55.
Ballinger, Jeff, and Claes Olsson. 1997. *Behind the Swoosh: The Struggle of Indonesians Making Nike Shoes*. Uppsala: Global Publications Foundation.
Baron, Frank. 1975. *The Visual Arts and Rilke's Poetry*. Lawrence: The University of Kansas, Department of Germanic Languages and Literatures.
Benjamin, Walter. 1968. *Illuminations*. Translated by Harry Zohn and edited by Hannah Arendt. New York: Schocken Books.
———. 1974–89. *Gesammelte Schriften in Sieben Bänden*. Frankfurt am Main: Suhrkamp Verlag.
———. 1996. *Selected Writings*. Vol. 1. Edited by Marcus Bullock and Michael W. Jennings. Cambridge: Harvard University Press.
Bernasconi, Robert. 1993. *Heidegger in Question: The Art of Existing*. Atlantic Highlands, N.J.: Humanities Press International.
Bigwood, Carol. 1993. *Earth Muse*. Philadelphia: Temple University Press.
Bishop, Elizabeth. 1984. *The Collected Prose*. New York: Farrar, Straus, Giroux.
Borges, J. L. 1998. *Collected Fictions*. Translated by Andrew Hurley. New York: Viking Penguin.

Bové, Paul. 1980. *Destructive Poetics.* New York: Columbia University Press.
Breton, André. 1969. *Manifestoes of Surrealism.* Translated by Richard Seaver and Helen R. Love. Ann Arbor: The University of Michigan Press.
Brodsky, Joseph. 1995. *On Grief and Reason.* New York: Farrar, Straus, Giroux.
Bruns, Gerald. 1974. *Modern Poetry and the Idea of Language.* New Haven: Yale University Press.
———. 1989. *Heidegger's Estrangements: Language, Truth, and Poetry in the Later Writings.* New Haven: Yale University Press.
Buddeberg, Else. 1953. *Heidegger und die Dichtung: Hölderlin, Rilke.* Stuttgart: J. B. Metzlersche Verlagsbuchhandlung and Carl Ernst Poeschel Verlag.
Callahan, Virginia Woods. 1967. *The Fathers of the Church.* Vol. 58. Washington, D.C.: The Catholic University of America Press.
Celan, Paul. 1983. *Gesammelte Werke in Fünf Bänden.* Frankfurt am Main: Suhrkamp Verlag.
Coleman, Simon, and John Elsner. 1995. *Pilgrimage.* Cambridge: Harvard University Press.
Dallmayr, Fred R. 1986. "Heidegger, Hölderlin, Politics." *Heidegger Studies* 2:81–95.
Derrida, Jacques. 1978. "The *Retrait* of Metaphor." *Enclitic* 2, no. 2:4–33.
———. 1982. *Margins of Philosophy.* Translated by Alan Bass. Chicago: The University of Chicago Press.
———. 1983. "Geschlecht: Sexual Difference, Ontological Difference." *Research in Phenomenology* 13:65–83.
Dewey, John. 1987. *The Later Works, 1925–1953.* Vol. 10, *Art as Experience.* Carbondale: Southern Illinois University Press.
Dickinson, Emily. 1955. *The Complete Poems of Emily Dickinson.* Boston: Little, Brown.
Fóti, Véronique. 1992. *Heidegger and the Poets: Poesis, Techne, Sophia.* Atlantic Highlands, N.J.: Humanities Press International.
Foucault, Michel. 1984. *The Foucault Reader.* Edited by Paul Rabinow. New York: Random House.
Frankfurter, David, ed. 1998. *Pilgrimage and Holy Space in Late Antiquity Egypt.* Leiden: Brill Publishers.
Fraser, Nancy. 1989. *Unruly Practices.* Minneapolis: University of Minnesota Press.
Friedman, Ralph. 1996. *Life of a Poet: Rainer Maria Rilke.* New York: Farrar, Straus, Giroux.
Froment-Meurice, Marc. 1998. *That Is to Say: Heidegger's Poetics.* Translated by Jan Plug. Stanford: Stanford University Press.
Frost, Robert. 1986. *Collected Poems.* Cutchogue, N.Y.: Buccaneer Books.
Fynsk, Christopher. 1989. "Noise at the Threshold." *Research in Phenomenology* 19:101–20.
———. 1993. *Heidegger: Thought and Historicity.* Expanded ed. Ithaca: Cornell University Press.
Gascoyne, David. 1982. *A Short Survey of Surrealism.* 2d ed. San Francisco: City Lights.
Gethman-Siefert, Annemarie. 1989. "Heidegger and Hölderlin: The Over-Usage of

Poets in an Impoverished Time." Translated by Richard Taft. *Research in Phenomenology* 19:59–88.

Ginsberg, Allen. 1959. *Howl*. San Francisco: City Lights.

Gioia, Dana. 1992. *Can Poetry Matter?* Saint Paul, Minn.: Graywolf Press.

Gómez-Peña, Guillermo. 1996. *The New World Border*. San Francisco: City Lights.

Grugan, Arthur A. 1989. "Heidegger Preparing to Read Hölderlin's *Germanien*." *Research in Phenomenology* 19:139–67.

Haar, Michel. 1993. *The Song of the Earth: Heidegger and the Grounds of the History of Being*. Translated by Reginald Lilly. Bloomington: Indiana University Press.

Habermas, Jürgen. 1983. *Philosophical-Political Profiles*. Translated by Frederick G. Lawrence. Cambridge: The MIT Press.

———. 1984. *The Theory of Communicative Action*. Vol. 1, *Reason and the Rationalization of Society*. Translated by Thomas McCarthy. Boston: Beacon Press.

———. 1987a. *The Theory of Communicative Action*. Vol. 2, *Lifeworld and System: A Critique of Functionalist Reason*. Translated by Thomas McCarthy. Boston: Beacon Press.

———. 1987b. *The Philosophical Discourse of Modernity: Twelve Lectures*. Translated by Frederick G. Lawrence. Cambridge: The MIT Press.

———. 1993. *Postmetaphysical Thinking: Philosophical Essays*. Translated by William Mark Hohengarten. Cambridge: The MIT Press.

Hart, Kevin. 1989. "Writing Things: Literary Property in Heidegger and Simic." *New Literary History* 21, no. 1:199–214.

Hegel, G. W. F. 1977. *Phenomenology of Spirit*. Translated by A. V. Miller. Oxford: Oxford University Press.

———. 1988. *Introduction to the Philosophy of History*. Translated by Leo Rauch. Indianapolis: Hackett Publishing.

Heidegger, Martin. 1954a. *Vortraege und Aufsaetze*. Pfullingen: Verlag Günther Neske.

———. 1954b. *Was Heisst Denken?* Tübingen: Max Niemeyer Verlag.

———. 1969. *Zur Sache des Denkens*. Tübingen: Max Niemeyer Verlag.

———. 1975. *Die Grundprobleme der Phänomenologie* [*The Basic Problems of Phenomenology*]. Frankfurt am Main: Vittorio Klostermann.

———. 1976. *Wegmarken*. Frankfurt am Main: Vittorio Klostermann.

———. 1977a. *Holzwege*. Frankfurt am Main: Vittorio Klostermann.

———. 1977b. *Sein und Zeit*. Frankfurt am Main: Vittorio Klostermann.

———. 1979a. *Heraklit*. Frankfurt am Main: Vittorio Klostermann.

———. 1979b. *Prolegomena zur Geschichte des Zeitbegriffs* [*Prolegomena to the History of the Concept of Time*]. Frankfurt am Main: Vittorio Klostermann.

———. 1980. *Hölderlins Hymnen »Germanien« und »Der Rhein«* [*Hölderlin's Hymns "Germania" and "The Rhine"*]. Frankfurt am Main: Vittorio Klostermann.

———. 1981. *Erläuterungen zu Hölderlins Dichtung* [*Elucidations of Hölderlin's Poetry*]. Frankfurt am Main: Vittorio Klostermann.

———. 1982a. *Hölderlins Hymne »Andenken«*. Frankfurt am Main: Vittorio Klostermann.

———. 1982b. *Parmenides*. Frankfurt am Main: Vittorio Klostermann.

———. 1984. *Hölderlins Hymne »Der Ister«*. Frankfurt am Main: Vittorio Klostermann.
———. 1985. *Unterwegs zur Sprache*. Pfullingen: Verlag Günther Neske.
———. 1989. *Beiträge zur Philosophie*. Frankfurt am Main: Vittorio Klostermann.
———. 1991. *The Principle of Reason*. Translated by Reginald Lilly. Bloomington: Indiana University Press.
———. 1993. *Basic Writings: Revised and Expanded Edition*. San Francisco: Harper San Francisco.
———. 1996a. *Being and Time*. Translated by Joan Stambaugh. Albany: State University of New York Press.
———. 1996b. *Hölderlin's Hymn "The Ister."* Translated by William McNeill and Julia Davis. Bloomington: Indiana University Press.
———. 1999. *Contributions to Philosophy*. Translated and with an introduction by Kenneth Maly and Parvis Emad. Bloomington: Indiana University Press.
Hirsch, Ed. 1999. *How to Read a Poem*. New York: Harcourt Brace.
Hirschfield, Jane. 2000. "Kingfishers Catching Fire: Seeing with Poetry's Eyes." *American Poetry Review* 29, no. 1:9–12.
Holland, Nancy. 1997. *Feminist Interpretations of Jacques Derrida*. University Park: The Pennsylvania State University Press.
Hollander, John. 1981. *Rhyme's Reason*. New Haven: Yale University Press.
Hongo, Garrett. 1988. *The River of Heaven*. New York: Alfred A. Knopf.
Horkheimer, Max. 1987. *Gesammelte Schriften Band 5: »Dialectic der Aufklärung« und Schriften 1940–1950*. Frankfurt am Main: Fischer Verlag.
Jackson, Richard. 1980. "Charles Simic and Mark Strand: The Presence of Absence." *Contemporary Literature* 21, no. 1:136–45.
Johnson, Denis. 1987. *The Veil*. New York: Alfred A. Knopf.
Kant, Immanuel. 1961. *Critique of Pure Reason*. Translated by Norman Kemp Smith. London: Macmillan.
Keats, John. 1990. *The Oxford Authors: John Keats*. Oxford: Oxford University Press.
Koch, Kenneth. 1998. "The Language of Poetry." *New York Review of Books*, May 14, 44–47.
Krell, David F. 1992. *Daimon Life*. Bloomington: Indiana University Press.
Kushner, Alexander. 1991. *Apollo in the Snow: Selected Poems*. Translated by Paul Graves and Carol Ueland with an introduction by Joseph Brodsky. New York: Farrar, Straus, Giroux.
Lacoue-Labarthe, Philippe, and Jean-Luc Nancy. 1997. *Retreating the Political*. London: Routledge.
Larkin, Philip. 1989. *Collected Poems*. New York: Farrar, Straus, Giroux.
Levine, Philip. 1981. *Don't Ask*. Ann Arbor: The University of Michigan Press.
Lyotard, Jean-François. 1984. *The Postmodern Condition: A Report on Knowledge*. Translated by Geoff Bennington and Brian Massumi. Minneapolis: University of Minnesota Press.
Lysaker, John T. 1993. "Heidegger After the Fall." *Research in Phenomenology* 23:201–11.

——. 1996. "The Shape of Selves to Come: Rorty and Self-Creation." *Philosophy and Social Criticism* 22:39–74.
——. 1998. "Binding the Beautiful: Art as Criticism in Adorno and Dewey." *Journal of Speculative Philosophy* 12, no. 4:233–44.
——. 1999a. "On What Is to Be Done with What Has Always Already Happened." *Studies in Practical Philosophy* 1, no. 1:86–113.
——. 1999b. "Lenin, Nancy, and the Politics of Total War." *Philosophy Today* 43:186–95.
——. 2000. "Heidegger's Absolute Music: What Are Poets for When the End of Metaphysics Is at Hand." *Research in Phenomenology* 30:180–210.
——. 2001. "White Dawns, Black Noons, Twilit Days: Charles Simic's Poems Before Poetry." *TriQuarterly* 110–111 (Fall): 525–80.
Lysaker, John T., and Michael Sullivan. 1992. "Between Impotence and Illusion: Adorno's Art of Theory and Practice." *New German Critique* 57:87–122.
Maly, Kenneth, and Parvis Emad. 1989. "Poetic Saying as Beckoning: The Opening of Hölderlin's *Germanien*." *Research in Phenomenology* 19:121–38.
Mandelstam, Nadezhda. 1970. *Hope Against Hope*. Translated by Max Hayward. New York: Atheneum Publishers.
Mandelstam, Osip. 1979. *The Complete Critical Prose and Letters*. Translated by Jane Gary Harris and Constance Link and edited by Jane Gary Harris. Ann Arbor, Mich.: Ardis.
——. 1991. *The Moscow Notebooks*. Translated by Richard McKane and Elizabeth McKane. Newcastle-upon-Tyne: Bloodaxe Books.
McCarthy, Thomas. 1991. *Ideals and Illusions*. Cambridge: The MIT Press.
McClatchy, J. D. 1981. "Figures in the Landscape." *Poetry* 138, no. 4:231–41.
Milosz, Czeslaw. 1983. *The Witness of Poetry*. Cambridge: Harvard University Press.
Milton, John. 1674. *Paradise Lost*.
Morinis, Alan. 1992. *Sacred Journeys: The Anthropology of Pilgrimage*. Westport, Conn.: Greenwood Press.
Muratori, Fred. 1984. Review of *White: New Version*, by Charles Simic. *Northwest Review* 22, no. 3:121–25.
Murray, Michael. 1980. "Heidegger's Hermeneutic Reading of Hölderlin: The Signs of Time." *The Eighteenth Century* 21, no. 1:41–66.
——. 1985. "The Conflict Between Poetry and Literature." *Philosophy and Literature* 9, no. 1:59–79.
Myers, Alan. 1988. *An Age Ago: A Selection of Nineteenth-Century Russian Poetry*. New York: Farrar, Straus, Giroux.
Nalewski, Horst. 1985. *Rainer Maria Rilke in seiner Zeit*. Leipzig: Insel Verlag.
Nancy, Jean-Luc. 1991. *The Inoperative Community*. Edited by Peter Connor. Minneapolis: University of Minnesota Press.
——. 1993a. *The Birth to Presence*. Translated by Brian Holmes and others. Stanford: Stanford University Press.
——. 1993b. *The Experience of Freedom*. Translated by Bridget McDonald. Stanford: Stanford University Press.
Nietzsche, Friedrich. 1966. *Beyond Good and Evil*. Translated by Walter Kaufman. New York: Random House.

Olds, Sharon. 1991. *The Gold Cell.* New York: Alfred A. Knopf.
Orlich, Ileana A. 1992. "The Poet on a Roll: Charles Simic's 'The Tomb of Stéphane Mallarmé.'" *The Centennial Review* 36, no. 2:413–28.
Pinsky, Robert. 1988. *Poetry and the World.* New York: The Ecco Press.
———. 1998. *The Sounds of Poetry.* New York: Farrar, Straus, Giroux.
Pöggeler, Otto. 1977. "Heideggers Begegnung mit Hölderlin." *Man and World* 10, no. 1:13–61.
Proffer, Carl. 1976. *Modern Russian Poets on Poetry.* Ann Arbor, Mich.: Ardis.
"A Pulitzer for—What?" 1990. *The New Criterion* 8, no. 10:2.
Reeder, Roberta. 1994. *Anna Akhmatova.* New York: St. Martin's Press.
Regan, Tom. 1980. "Animal Rights, Human Wrongs." *Environmental Ethics* 2, no. 2:99–120.
Rich, Adrienne. 1993. *What Is Found There.* New York: W. W. Norton.
Rilke, Rainer Maria. 1955–66. *Sämtliche Werke in Zwölf Bänden.* Frankfurt: Insel Verlag.
———. 1982. *The Selected Poetry of Rainer Maria Rilke.* Translated by Stephen Mitchell. New York: Random House.
———. 1985. *Sonnets to Orpheus.* Translated by Stephen Mitchell. New York: Random House.
Russell, John. 1998. "Anselm Kiefer: Works on Paper in the Metropolitan Museum of Art." *The New York Times,* December 17, sec. E, p. 1.
Sallis, John. 1987. *Deconstruction and Philosophy: The Texts of Jacques Derrida.* Chicago: The University of Chicago Press.
———. 1990. *Echoes After Heidegger.* Bloomington: Indiana University Press.
———. 1993. *Reading Heidegger: Commemorations.* Bloomington: Indiana University Press.
Schürmann, Reiner. 1987. *Heidegger on Being and Acting: From Principles to Anarchy.* Bloomington: Indiana University Press.
Scott, Charles. 1987. *The Language of Difference.* Atlantic Highlands, N.J.: Humanities Press International.
Simic, Charles. 1967. *What the Grass Says.* San Francisco: Kayak.
———. 1969. *Somewhere Among Us A Stone Is Taking Notes.* San Francisco: Kayak.
———. 1971. *Dismantling the Silence.* New York: Braziller.
———. 1972. *White.* New York: New Rivers Press Books.
———. 1974. *Return to a Place Lit by a Glass of Milk.* New York: Braziller.
———. 1977. *Charon's Cosmology.* New York: Braziller.
———. 1980a. *Classic Ballroom Dances.* New York: Braziller.
———. 1980b. *White: A New Version.* Durango, Colo.: Longbridge Rhodes.
———. 1982. *Austerities.* New York: Braziller.
———. 1984. *Weather Forecast for Utopia and Other Vicinities.* Barrytown, N.Y.: Station Hill.
———. 1985. *The Uncertain Certainty.* Ann Arbor: The University of Michigan Press.
———. 1986. *Unending Blues.* San Diego: Harcourt Brace.
———. 1989. *The World Doesn't End.* San Diego: Harcourt Brace.
———. 1990a. *The Book of Gods and Devils.* San Diego: Harcourt Brace.

———. 1990b. *Selected Poems, 1963–1983: Revised and Expanded.* New York: Braziller.
———. 1990c. *Wonderful Words, Silent Truth.* Ann Arbor: The University of Michigan Press.
———. 1992a. *Dime Store Alchemy: The Art of Joseph Cornell.* Hopewell, N.J.: The Ecco Press.
———. 1992b. *Hotel Insomnia.* San Diego: Harcourt Brace.
———. 1994a. *The Unemployed Fortune Teller.* Ann Arbor: The University of Michigan Press.
———. 1994b. *A Wedding in Hell.* New York: Harcourt Brace.
———. 1996. *Walking the Black Cat.* New York: Harcourt Brace.
———. 1997. *Orphan Factory.* Ann Arbor: The University of Michigan Press.
———. 1999. *Selected Early Poems.* New York: Braziller.
———. 2000. *A Fly in the Soup.* Ann Arbor: The University of Michigan Press.
———. 2001a. "The Thinking Man's Comedy." *The New York Review of Books,* May 31, 13–15.
———. 2001b. "That Elusive Something." *The New York Review of Books,* July 19, 13–15.
———. 2001c. *Night Picnic.* New York: Harcourt.
Singer, Peter. 1974. "All Animals Are Equal." *Philosophic Exchange* 1, no. 5:243–57.
Spanos, William V. 1993. *Heidegger and Criticism: Retrieving the Cultural Politics of Destruction.* Minneapolis: University of Minnesota Press.
Spinoza, Baruch. 1992. *Ethics.* Translated by Samuel Shinley and edited by Seymour Feldman. Indianapolis: Hackett Publishing.
Steinman, David B., and Sara Ruth Watson. 1941. *Bridges and Their Builders.* New York: G. P. Putnam's Sons.
Stevens, Wallace. 1971. *The Palm at the End of the Mind.* New York: Alfred A. Knopf.
Strand, Mark. 1990. *The Continuous Life.* New York: Alfred A. Knopf.
Strand, Mark, and Evan Boland. 2000. *The Making of a Poem.* New York: W. W. Norton.
Taylor, Paul. 1981. "The Ethics of Respect for Nature." *Environmental Ethics* 3, no. 3:197–218.
Trachtenberg, Alan. 1979. *Brooklyn Bridge: Fact and Symbol.* Chicago: The University of Chicago Press.
von Hermann, F. W. 1989. "The Flower in the Mouth: Hölderlin's Hint for Heidegger's Thinking of the Essence of Language." *Research in Phenomenology* 19:27–42.
Wagner, M. Monica. 1950. *The Fathers of the Church.* Vol. 9. New York: Fathers of the Church.
Walker, David. 1975. "Stone Soup." *Field,* no. 13 (Fall): 39–47.
Warminski, Andrzej. 1987. *Readings in Interpretation: Hölderlin, Hegel, Heidegger.* Minneapolis: University of Minnesota Press.
Weigl, Bruce. 1996. *Charles Simic: Essays on the Poetry.* Ann Arbor: The University of Michigan Press.

White, David A. 1978. *Heidegger and the Language of Poetry*. Lincoln: University of Nebraska Press.
Wiesel, Elie. 1978. *Four Hasidic Masters*. Notre Dame: Notre Dame University Press.
Wilde, Oscar. 1930. *Plays, Prose Writings, and Poems*. New York: Alfred A. Knopf.
Williams, Wes. 1998. *Pilgrimage and Narrative in the French Renaissance*. Oxford: Oxford University Press.
Williams, William Carlos. 1965. *The William Carlos Williams Reader*. New York: New Directions.
Wood, David. 1990. *Philosophy at the Limit*. London: Unwin Hyman.
Wood, Nancy. 2001. *Perspectives on Argument*. Upper Saddle River, N.J.: Prentice Hall.

Index

Abrams, David, 148 n. 11
Adorno, Theodor, 11, 15, 110, 123–24 n. 8, 127 n. 13, 190
Ahkmatova, Anna, 46 n. 1, 110, 114–15, 161 n. 4
allegory. *See also* representation; Simic, Charles
  Heidegger, 31–32, 32 n. 12
  history as, 184
  interruption, 193
  Simic, 118–23, 134, 136, 183–85, 204–5
  ur-poetry, 42, 117, 136, 186–87
Ammons, A. R. *See also* propositions; representation; ur-poetry
  Garbage, 58–63, 59 n. 12, 65–71, 73–75, 102
animism, 144–52, 155–56, 167, 179, 182–83
Arendt, Hannah, 188–89, 202
art. *See also* Benjamin, Walter; Simic, Charles
  life change, 1–7, 10, 17
  materiality, 8–9
  autofiguration, 29–31, 41–45, 50, 66–69, 77, 184

Basil of Caesura, 88 nn. 11, 12
Benjamin, Walter. *See also* Simic, Charles
  art, 15
  books, 3
  comedy, 200, 200 n. 9
  Judaism, 123 n. 7
  Theses on the Philosophy of History, 123, 167–69, 176
Bernasconi, Robert, 14–15, 153 n. 18
Berryman, John, 5
Bigwood, Carol, 148 n. 12
Blake, William, 7, 7 n. 2
Borges, Jorge Luis, 15, 72

Breton, André, 86–87 n. 9, 90 n. 14
Brodsky, Joseph, 27–28, 27 n. 9, 46 n. 1, 197, 209
Brooklyn Bridge, 177–78
Bruns, Gerald, 76 n. 21

causality, 139, 150, 152 n. 16, 155, 173, 179. *See also* singularity
Celan, Paul, 190–91, 190 n. 2, 197. *See also* Mandelstam, Osip
character, 142–52, 155–56, 167, 175–76, 179–80, 209–10
Coleman, Simon, 84 n. 7
contingency, 150–52, 167, 179, 209–10
conversion, 72–77, 149, 154–57, 170, 208–10
co-presencing, 150–51, 152 n. 16, 166–67, 175–76, 179, 208–10. *See also* dimension; Simic, Charles; synchronicity
critique, 193–94, 194–95 nn. 7–8, 196

Dallmayr, Fred, 14
Derrida, Jacques, 30–31, 114
Dewey, John, 5–6, 8, 10, 15
diachronicity. *See also* Simic, Charles
  concept of, 180
  Heidegger, 26 n. 6
  Simic, 112, 172–79, 209–10
Dickinson, Emily, 171 n. 9
dimension
  co-presencing, 167, 210
  difference, 54–58, 65, 68, 162, 180, 209
dwelling, 61, 65, 69, 75–76
  Heidegger, 54–58, 54 n. 10, 138
  presencing, 54–58, 60 n. 13, 63–69, 73 n. 20, 74–77
Dodd, Wayne, 197
dwelling
  appraisal of, 61, 63, 75–79

Heidegger, 51–58, 69, 76 n. 21
human, 197 n. 26, 131, 210
presencing, 69

Elsner, John, 84 n. 7
Emad, Parvis, 19 n. 3
empiricism, 107 n. 26
emptiness, 138–39, 150, 179, 191, 208–10
engagement, 4–5, 9, 207–8
epic, 21
essence
   Heidegger, 19–20, 37
   history, 19 n. 3, 20, 64, 104, 127 n. 13
   human being, 52
   language of, 64–66
   origins, 140 n. 5
   Ort, 18–19
exhortation. *See also* ur-poetry
   Heidegger, 64–66, 65 n. 15, 68–70
   Simic, 101, 119, 178, 186, 208
experience
   Heidegger, 11–12, 113 n. 3
   Simic, 105, 107 n. 26
   undergoing, as an, 174, 208
   ur-poetry, 136

fate. *See* history; Simic, Charles
form, 7–9, 24, 26, 59–61, 68
Fóti, Véronique
   Heidegger, 13, 13 nn. 5–6, 26 n. 37
   Rilke, 35, 40 n. 21
Foucault, Michel, 140
Fraser, Nancy, 194–95 n. 8
Frost, Robert, 47 n. 2
Fynsk, Christopher, 31–32, 32 n. 12

Gascoyne, David, 153 n. 18
Gethman-Siefert, Annemarie, 14
Ginsberg, Allen, 1–4, 8
Gioia, Dana, 48–49
Glass, Philip, 2–3
Gómez-Peña, Guillermo, 126 n. 12
Gregory of Nyssa, 88 n. 11
ground/consequent relation
   cosmos, 179
   expression, 42
   language of originary occurrence, 139
   presencing, 148, 162, 167, 208–10
   sense, 151
ground words, 35–38, 41–43, 68, 161
Grugan, Arthur, 30 n. 10

Haar, Michel, 35
Habermas, Jürgen, 53–54, 53–54 nn. 8–9
Hart, Kevin, 12 n. 4
Hegel, G. W. F., 11–12, 24 n. 5, 122 n. 6, 151 n. 15, 174, 174 n. 11
Heidegger, Martin. *See also* allegory; diachronicity; dimension; dwelling; essence; exhortation; experience; Fóti, Veronique; inception; metaphor; origination; *Ort*; Simic, Charles; subjectivity; synchronicity; ur-poetry
   being, 37, 55, 137 n. 1
   Being and Time, 26 n. 6
   "Building, Dwelling, Thinking," 51, 56–57
   Contributions to Philosophy, 11–13, 57 n. 11, 141 n. 6
   dialogue with poetry, 13–15, 17–18, 45
   "Essence of Language," 11
   heissen, 69
   Hölderlin: "Germania," 12 n. 3, 14 n. 7, 27, 32, 33 n. 13, 60; "The Ister," 28–29, 32, 47, 49–50, 72, 106; "Remembrance," 22, 28–29, 32, 33 n. 13, 106; ur-poetry, 34, 46–47, 52 n. 7
   "Hölderlin and the Essence of Poetry," 74–75
   "Language," 47 n. 2, 54, 65, 65 n. 16
   "Language in the Poem," 18–19, 32–33
   life change, 13, 44, 71, 73, 104, 208
   Nietzsche, 35 n. 14, 37, 113 n. 3
   "Origin of the Work of Art": art as created, 41 n. 23; clearing, the, 56–57, 60; equipment, 40 n. 22; life change, 71, 73, 208; origins, 140 n. 5; *Ort*, 39 n. 20; strife of earth and world, 116 n. 4; *Volk*, 14; work of art, 31–32, 113 n. 3
   "The Poem," 106
   ". . .poetically dwells the human . . . ," 55, 64–65
   poetic building, 56–58, 60, 69, 76
   poetic founding, 12–13, 44, 74
   Principle of Reason, 30
   Prolegomena to the History of the Concept of Time, 106
   "Question Concerning Technology," 139 n. 2
   reader, as, 18–19, 21–22, 26–34, 26 n. 6, 78
   Rilke, 34–43, 35–36 nn. 14–17, 113 n. 3
   "The Thing," 19
   "Time and Being," 141 n. 6

Trakl, 32, 47 n. 2
"What Are Poets For?," 34–43, 42–43 n. 24
Hirsch, Ed, 5, 191 n. 3
Hirschfield, Jane, 4
history. *See also* allegory; essence; presencing; sense; Simic, Charles; singularity; ur-poetry
　as discipline, 166–67, 173–74, 173 n. 10, 177–78
　fate, 113, 116, 162, 169–70, 199–200
　future, 90 n. 14, 159–62, 169–70, 175–76, 208–9
　language and thought, 19 n. 3, 119–34, 123–24 n. 8, 127 n. 14
　"Mother Tongue," 159–60, 162
　origination, 140–42, 164
　past, 90 n. 14, 171–79, 208–9
　poetry as, 160–62, 184–85
　presencing, 137, 208–10
　violence: death, 166, 169, 178; exploitation, 170–71; murder, 160–61; suffering, 118, 167, 185–86, 202; war, 108, 111–12, 168
Hölderlin, Friedrich. *See* Heidegger, Martin
Howard, Richard, 82 n. 4
Hongo, Garrett, 39–40
Hullot-Kentor, Robert, 123–24 n. 8
Husserl, Edmund. *See* Simic, Charles

inception
　Heidegger, 60
　origination, 158
　presencing, 60 n. 13, 158
　redundancy of, 158, 163
　Simic, 137, 141–44, 147, 151–54
intersubjectivity, 53–54, 129–33

Jackson, Richard, 12 n. 4
Jackson, Rick, 105
Johnson, Denis, 71

Kant, Immanuel, 107 n. 26, 143
Keats, John, 115
Koch, Kenneth, 82 n. 4

Larkin, Philip, 30, 66–67, 71. *See also* ur-poetry
Levine, Philip, 7 n. 2
Lyotard, Jean-François, 127 n. 14
lyric poetry, 21, 28, 111 n. 2, 131–32, 160 n. 2. *See also* Simic, Charles; subjectivity

Maly, Kenneth, 19 n. 3
Mandelstam, Nadezhda, 3
Mandelstam, Osip
　Celan, 190, 190 n. 2
　death of, 114
　life change, 3
　poetry's secret addressee, 131–32, 190–91, 190–91 nn. 2–3, 197
　Stalin, 46 n. 1, 131 n. 17, 189
　world culture, 27 n. 9
McClatchy, J. D., 153 n. 18
McCarthy, Tom, 194 n. 7
metaphor
　Heidegger, 21–22, 30–31, 30–32 nn. 11–12
　Simic, 84 n. 7
　ur-poetry, 42, 117, 183
method, 26, 34
Milton, John, 124 n. 9
Moore, Marianne, 49 n. 6
Morinis, Alan, 83 n. 6
Muratori, Fred, 82 n. 3

Nancy, Jean-Luc, 69 n. 17, 139 n. 3, 147 n. 10, 188, 192
narrative poetry, 21, 28, 160 n. 2
national socialism, 13–15, 54 n. 9, 189
necessity, 150–52, 167, 179, 191–92, 208–10
Nietzsche, Friedrich, 128 n. 15, 140, 145–46, 146 n. 8, 169. *See also* Heidegger, Martin
Nike, 170–71, 170 n. 7

Olds, Sharon, 20–21
ontic/ontological distinction, 163–64, 202
origination. *See also* history; inception
　everyday, the, 142–44
　extra-historical as, 140–41, 141 n. 6, 155, 179
　Heidegger, 60, 180
　inception, 158
　past, the, 173–74
　Simic, 138–43, 147, 150–51
　Sprung, 60 n. 13, 139, 141, 158 n. 1
　ur-poetry, 69
Ort. *See also* essence; Heidegger, Martin; exhortation
　contestation, 112
　Heidegger, 25–30, 30 n. 11
　Simic, 89, 96–97, 161
　ur-poetry, 63–64, 111 n. 2

Peirce, Charles Sanders, 52
Pinsky, Robert, 9, 48–49
Plumly, Stanley, 197
poetry. *See also* Heidegger, Martin; history; lyric poetry; Mandelstam, Osip; narrative poetry; Simic, Charles; ur-poetry
   confessional, 21, 21 n. 4, 28
   measure, as, 47, 56–58, 75–77, 127–28, 127 n. 14
   purpose of, 46–52
   vocation, 49–50
polyphony, 154, 157, 172, 176, 179, 209–10. *See also* ur-poetry
Pope, Alexander, 160 n. 3
possibility, 194–97, 203–4, 209–10
presencing. *See also* co-presencing; dimension; dwelling; ground/consequent relation; history; inception; sense
   being, 131
   beings, 61, 67–68, 75, 98
   event of, 70, 74
   history, 137, 208–10
   human being, 52–53
   metaphysics, 142
   presencing per se, 77, 104, 142, 163, 181
   subject/object distinction, 147–48, 157–58
   violence, 126–27, 169–70
   world of the, 15, 208–10
propositions
   Garbage, 60–61, 61–62 n. 14
   judgment, 152–53, 172–73
   Simic, 141, 183
   Stevens, Wallace, 24
   ur-poetry, 44, 68, 73 n. 20, 79, 136
psychology, 6–7, 27–28

Reagan, Ronald, 148
Regan, Tom, 149 n. 13
representation
   allegory, 31–21, 132
   American poetry, 10
   being, 38
   Garbage, 62
   human dwelling, 52
   Ort, 42–43
   Simic, 163–64
   subjectivity, 4, 96
   ur-poetry, 64–66, 75, 113, 161
   White, 99
Rich, Adrienne, 48–49, 49 n. 5

Rilke, Rainer Maria. *See also* Fóti, Veronique; Heidegger, Martin; ur-poetry
   "Archaic Torso of Apollo," 1, 26, 27 n. 9, 49 n. 5, 207
   Duino Elegies, 36, 36 n. 17, 121–23, 121 n. 5
   "Orpheus. Euridice. Hermes," 27
   poetic project of, 40 n. 21
   Sonnets to Orpheus, 36–37, 43 n. 24, 121, 121 n. 5
   ur-poetry, 66
Roosevelt, Franklin Delano, 177
Rorty, Richard, 15
Russell, John, 5

Sallis, John, 18, 65
Schmidt, Peter, 88 n. 10
Schürmann, Reiner, 137–43, 137 n. 1, 140 n. 4, 141 n. 6, 152
Scott, Charles, 91 n. 15
sense. *See also* ground/consequent relation; Simic, Charles
   being, 55
   birth of, 72, 102–4, 180–81
   cosmos, 10, 71
   defined, ix, 135
   history, 176, 201
   life change, ix, 209
   meaning versus, 61–62 n. 14
   presencing, 140 n. 4
   senses, the, 157, 208
   singularity, 155, 169, 179, 209–10
   time, 175
   ur-poetry, 73
Shoah, the, 123, 123–24 n. 8
silence, 91, 126–27, 164–65, 179, 209. *See also* Simic, Charles
Simic, Charles. *See also* allegory; diachronicity; exhortation; experience; inception; metaphor; origination; *Ort*; propositions; representation; synchronicity; ur-poetry
   being, 85, 85 n. 8, 105 n. 23, 136
   Benjamin, Walter, 169, 200 n. 9
   "Bestiary for the Fingers of My Right Hand," 145
   "Blindman's Bluff," 199–203
   "Butcher's Shop," 185–87
   "Crazy About Her Shrimp," 165–66, 166 n. 6

"Dead Letter Office," 95–96 n. 18
desire, 91, 165–66, 165 n. 5, 168–69, 204
"Emily's Theme," 171–77
"Empire of Dreams," 114–18, 120–21, 129, 133, 187–88, 191–92
"Figuring," 100 n. 19
God, 106 n. 25, 164, 201, 201 n. 10
Heidegger, 12, 12 n. 4, 78, 104, 105 n. 22
"History": absurdity, 198; art, 159–61, 161 n. 4; desire, 165–66; displacement, 175; everyday, the 159; poetry, 160–61; violence, 160, 162, 166–68, 185
humor: comedy, 200, 200 n. 9, 202; compassion, 199–201; cynicism, 199; disruption, 198–99; mourning, 201–2; ontological humor, 197–200
Husserl, Edmund, 105, 105 n. 22
individuality, 195–96
"Interlude," 181–83
"A Letter," 145–46
life change: banal, the, 205–6; beings, 208–9; co-presencing, 170–71; diachronicity, 177–79; infinite task as a, 153–55; politics, 192–94; sense of sense, 104–5, 14; singularity, 148, 153, 204, 209; suddenness of, 71–72, 209; world, the, 210
lyric poetry, 111 n. 2, 136, 187–88, 195–96, 205
"Mother Tongue," 119–33, 184–91
"Paradise Motel," 168–69
"Past Lives Therapy," 155
"Poem Without a Title," 110–18, 111 nn. 1–2, 116 n. 4, 120–21, 133, 195
poetry, 82 n. 3, 85
"The Road in the Clouds," 202–4
"Shadow Publishing Company," 165 n. 5
"Spoon," 144–46, 146–47 n. 9, 149, 157
"War," 126–27
White: allegory, 117–19, 184–85; asceticism, 82–95, 88 nn. 11–13; blindness, 81, 86, 112, 142; everyday, the, 82 n. 4, 88, 91–92, 99–102, 142; exile, 196; fate, 91–93, 99–100; gender, 80 n. 2, 82 n. 5; history, 126–27, 134, 175; infinity, 90 n. 14, 93, 142; origins, 81–84, 87–89, 93–105, 124–25 n. 10, 137–38; pilgrimage, 82–87, 83–84 nn. 6–7, 88 n. 12, 91–92, 95–96; riddles, 102, 102 n. 21, 129; senses, the, 86, 97–98, 102–3; silence, 117, 126–27, 134; subjectivity, 83–84, 88–89, 93, 96,
100, 105–6, 105 nn. 22–23; ventriloquism, 98–101
The World Doesn't End: dignity, 200; identity, 154–55, 210; poetry, 205–6; Pulitzer Prize, 125 n. 11; silence, 164; world, the, 152, 192
Singer, Peter, 149 n. 13
singularity. *See also* causality; sense; Simic, Charles
  atomism, contra, 146–47, 149, 154–55
  causality, 148, 151–53, 152 n. 16
  concept of, 149
  history, 167–68, 176
  individuality, contra, 196
  mortality, 94
  relations, 150
  uniqueness, 147–48, 153, 155–56, 209–10
social-construction, 20, 74–76, 142–44, 158, 167
Spinoza, Baruch, 150 n. 14, 202
Stevens, Wallace. *See also* propositions
  "Idea of Order at Key West," 8–9, 21
  "Reality is an Activity of the August Imagination," 22–26
  "Snow Man," 94, 94 n. 17
Strand, Mark, 12 n. 4
subjectivity. *See also* intersubjectivity; representation; Simic, Charles; ur-poetry
  action, 138
  body, the, 145, 155
  communicative subjectivity, 52–54
  epistemic subjectivity, 3–4, 52–53, 54 n. 10, 153
  Heidegger, 47, 106–7
  identity, 150
  language, 120–22
  lyric, 111 n. 2, 195
  metaphysics, 113 n. 3
  mind, 145–46, 146 n. 8
  poetic, 186–87, 190
  psychological, 6–7
  self-control, 112, 201
  Simic: autonomy, 83–84, 93, 100; consciousness, 105–6, 105 n. 22; epistemic subject, 96; unconsciousness, 105–6, 105 n. 23; self-mastery, 88–89
surrealism, 153 n. 18
symbol, 4, 21, 29–32, 117
synchronicity
  concept of, 181

co-presencing, 147–51
  Heidegger, 26 n. 6
  Simic, 112, 154, 172–77, 209–10

Taylor, Paul, 149 n. 13
totalitarianism, 187–94
Trachtenberg, Alan, 177
Trakl, Georg. *See* Heidegger, Martin
Tsvetayeva, Marina, 46, 51

ur-poetry. *See also* allegory; experience; Heidegger, Martin; metaphor; origination; *Ort*; propositions; representation; Rilke, Rainer Maria; sense
  annotation as, 78–80
  being, 46, 64, 75–77, 76 n. 21, 79, 196
  failure of, 113–17, 128–29, 131–33, 184, 195
  Garbage, 61
  Heidegger, 32–33, 76 n. 21
  journey as, 207–8
  language of originary occurrence: defined, 64–71; import of, 73–77, 79; Simic, 141, 163; subjectivity, 107
  life change, 44, 70–77, 73 n. 20, 149, 183, 194–97

manifestation, 41–44
metaphysics, 149
palimpsest, 43, 207
poem of poetry, 15, 32, 41–45, 77, 161, 207
political engagement, 204
repetition: history, 141, 161, 201; poetic figures, 39–45, 63, 110–12, 129, 181, 207–8; struggles, 113–17, 123–24, 128, 133–34; "To My Wife," 67; third repetition, 204–5, 207–8; traditional sayings, 38–45, 63, 110, 123, 128–29, 207–8
unsaid, as, 32–33, 43
ur-figures: exhortation, 68–70; figures of poetry as, 63, 77, 110; Heidegger, 41–44; life change, 77; mundane, as, 205–6; polyphonic, as, 187; Rilke, 41

Vendler, Helen, 107 n. 26

Walker, David, 108 n. 27
Warminski, Andrez, 13 n. 6, 70 n. 18
Wilde, Oscar, 50
Williams, W. C., 48, 48 n. 4, 51, 62
Williams, Wes, 84 n. 7
Wood, David, 30–31

www.ingramcontent.com/pod-product-compliance
Lightning Source LLC
Chambersburg PA
CBHW031549300426
44111CB00006BA/235